D1436002

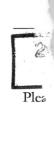

Plea

GARDENING
STEP BY STEP

THE ROYAL HORTICULTURAL SOCIETY

GARDENING
STEP BY STEP

Phil Clayton, Jenny Hendy,
Colin Crosbie, Jo Whittingham

LONDON, NEW YORK, MUNICH, MELBOURNE, DELHI

First published in Great Britain in 2009 by
Dorling Kindersley Ltd
Penguin Books Ltd
80 Strand
London WC2R 0RL

Reproduced by Colourscan, Singapore
Printed and bound by Toppan, China

To find out more about RHS membership, contact:
RHS Membership Department
PO Box 313, London SW1P 2PE
Telephone: 0845 062 1111
www.rhs.org.uk

Important notice
The author and the publishers can accept no liability for
any harm, damage, or illness arising from the use or
misuse of the plants described in this book.

Discover more at
www.dk.com

Contents

Planting a Small Garden

Easy-care Garden

Easy Pruning

Vegetables in a Small Garden

Plant Guide

Key to plant symbols

♖   Plants given the RHS Award of Garden Merit

Soil preference

🌢   Well-drained soil
🌢   Moist soil
◌   Wet soil

Preference for sun or shade

☀   Full sun
◐   Partial or dappled shade
☼   Full shade

Hardiness ratings

❅❅❅   Fully hardy plants

❅❅   Plants that survive outside in mild regions
       or sheltered sites

❅   Plants that need protection from frost
     over winter

❀   Tender plants that do not tolerate any
     degree of frost

Disguising boundaries

An exposed boundary, such as a fence or wall, can make a garden feel small and claustrophobic. Concealing boundaries with plants will radically improve the appearance of a garden, transforming it into an attractive space.

Pictures clockwise from top left

Back fence disguise In many gardens, the most obvious boundary is usually the back fence and, if visible, it immediately gives away the length of the garden. By creating a mixed border directly in front, using a range of plants that will grow as tall as, or taller than, the fence, you will succeed in blurring the edges of your plot. Make sure the border is a reasonable depth: a narrow strip in front of the fence, deep enough for only one plant, is likely to draw attention to the boundary rather than disguise it.

False perspective One of the most effective ways to disguise a boundary and also make a garden seem larger is by creating a false perspective. For example, in a garden that appears short, make the borders running down the sides of the garden taper outwards so that they are wider at their far end, making the garden appear longer. Another visual trick is to draw the eye away from the boundaries with a central, circular lawn or paved area, and surround it with dense planting. Evergreen shrubs will ensure that the effect lasts all year round.

Plant screen Dividing up the garden with various plant screens so that the entire garden is never completely visible from any one position will help make it feel larger and shift the emphasis away from the boundaries. Even a small plot can be divided up in this way using trellis or woven willow screens as supports for climbing plants; these also help to maximize growing space.

Courtyard enclosure Having a small garden does not mean that you should restrict yourself to small plants; in fact, doing so serves to underline a plot's limited size. Positioning a selection of quite large plants in front of fences or walls in generous-sized beds that have been pushed to the edges of the plot will help to maximize space in the centre of the garden, creating a courtyard. The plants will also help to hide fences and walls.

Using colour

The colour provided by flowers and foliage is particularly valuable in a garden. It can be used in a number of different ways, perhaps to evoke a particular mood or to give areas of the garden a theme or look.

Pictures clockwise from left

Rich colours If you spend a fair amount of time enjoying your garden from indoors, it makes sense to provide displays of rich colour that are easily visible from the house, perhaps in pots and containers on the terrace, or in beds and borders close to the windows. Harmonious colours that blend well together create a strong but restful feel; use softer, pastel hues further away from the house because they show up better at a distance than saturated colours.

Monochrome planting A garden or border composed of mostly white-flowering plants creates a cool, calming feel that is most striking at dusk, when the blooms glow in the fading light. Try using cream and pale yellow flowers, as well as very pale pink and blue ones, to prevent the effect from becoming stark and clinical. Silver-leaved and variegated plants will provide interest once the flowers have faded.

Hot hues Fiery colours, such as reds, oranges, and intense pinks, demand attention, but they should be used with care: they attract the eye away from softer shades and, if planted at the far end of the garden, may make the plot feel smaller. Often the simplest way to deal with hot-hued plants is to group them together and create a condensed and spectacular injection of colour. Alternatively, combine them with contrasting shades, such as rich blue or purple, to mitigate the effect.

Serene green It is important to remember that green is also a colour, and is the most commonplace in virtually every garden. There are many different shades of green but, generally, it has a restful effect, and gardens that are planted for foliage tend to be serene spaces. Set against other colours, though, green generally fades into the background, so use plants with variegated foliage or white or pastel-coloured flowers to shine out and provide additional interest.

Focal points

Gardens often benefit visually from a dramatic or arresting focal point, be it a statue, pot, or plant, which provides a point of reference within the design where the eye can rest.

Pictures clockwise from top left

Eye-catching trees In a garden that seeks to re-create the wild, focal points need to be natural objects, such as rocks or specimen plants. In this Mediterranean-style garden, the gnarled trunks and silvery foliage of a pair of old olive trees are as arresting as any classical sculpture.

Winding steps Even a utilitarian feature such as a flight of steps can provide a focal point, as long as it is well executed. Winding steps passing through lush foliage lead the eye on to brighter, more vibrant flowers and foliage, which then act as a visual full stop.

Dramatic containers Attractive pots and containers, planted or otherwise, are one of the simplest ways of creating a focal point. Used alone or in groups, they can be placed in a border, on a terrace, or at the end of a pathway, perhaps terminating a vista. Large, impressive pots are often best left empty; others can be enhanced with a dramatic plant, such as a *Dasylirion*.

Focus on colour Brightly coloured plants make small-scale focal points in beds and borders. The vivid flowers of bulbs, such as these orange tulips, provide short-term accents, lifting other planting and heightening interest.

Themed planting schemes

Some of the most successful gardens are developed around a particular theme or idea that helps to bind the planting and design together. Selecting plants that fit the overall concept help evoke the correct spirit and feel, which, in turn, lends a touch of authenticity to the garden.

Pictures clockwise from top left

Lush and subtropical There are many hardy and borderline hardy plants that can be used to create a subtropical-style garden. Generally, the lush feel is provided by foliage plants. Large specimens of hardy *Trachycarpus* palms, bamboos, phormiums, and tree ferns will provide structure; in summer, containers can be filled with tender plants such as begonias, cannas, *Lantana*, and gingers (*Hedychium*), which produce exotic flowers.

Classic Italian Italianate gardens tend to be rather formal, with plenty of topiary and clipped evergreens, such as box (*Buxus*). The layout is usually simple and the planting restrained, limited to a few favourites, such as acanthus, agapanthus, olives, slender conifers, jasmine, and herbs. Classical statuary plays an important role, often terminating a vista, and specimen plants in containers may feature, perhaps used along a terrace to introduce a sense of repetition and rhythm to the garden.

Meadow planting Informal and naturalistic, meadow planting uses a limited palette of different plants mixed randomly together in large groups. These schemes work well in large, open expanses and tend to be short-lived – many of the plants used are annuals, such as poppies (*Papaver*) and cornflowers (*Centaurea cyanus*). However, perennials can also feature, and the planting style scaled down to more modest-sized borders.

Moroccan oasis Water is a vital element for a Moroccan theme, and a wall fountain, perhaps with a blue-tiled surround, would make an ideal feature. Most of the planting should be in pots, with pelargoniums, date palms, agaves, and other succulents suitable choices, but avoid having too many plants. A few large foliage plants in darker corners, and climbers, such as *Trachelospermum*, scrambling up the walls would also fit in very well.

Themed planting schemes *continued*

Pictures clockwise from top left

Mediterranean style Gravel, terracotta pots, and a sunny site all help to create a Mediterranean feel. Avoid filling the garden with too much planting – the general scheme should not be too lush – and try a few formal elements, such as clipped box balls. Olive trees in pots can spend summer outside, while more permanent plants could include lavender (*Lavandula*), *Cistus*, and one or two exotics, such as *Yucca*.

Oriental calm Japanese-style gardens often feature a few manicured plants, such as Japanese maples (*Acer japonicum*), dwarf pines, bamboos, *Ophiopogon*, and *Ilex crenata,* set in a rock and gravel landscape. Strategically positioned bonsai specimens add a dramatic touch to the overall theme.

Cottage effects Borders overflowing with flowers are typical of cottage gardens. Old favourites include delphiniums, foxgloves (*Digitalis*), Shasta daisies (*Leucanthemum* x *superbum*), and lavender (*Lavandula*), with sweetly-scented roses and self-seeding annuals completing the informal look.

Modern mixes Architectural plants, such as tree ferns, phormiums and *Tetrapanax*, are the mainstays of highly designed contemporary gardens. Grasses and small-scale, naturalistic planting schemes are also popular, their soft foliage forms contrasting well with hard modern landscaping materials, such as concrete, glass, and steel.

Seasonal interest

Watching the way a garden changes its character with the seasons is part of the joy of gardening. To get the most from your plot, it should be designed and planted to provide interest for every day of the year. Each season has its own distinctive feel and appearance, and a well-designed garden will include plants that reflect this.

Spring (*top right*) As the days lengthen, the garden quickly wakes from its winter rest. Bulbs, such as daffodils and crocuses, produce showy flowers, while other herbaceous plants begin to emerge from the ground, and deciduous shrubs and trees produce fresh, verdant growth.

Summer (*right*) For many gardeners, this season represents the high point of the year. Most herbaceous plants reach their zenith, filling out borders and blooming for several months, while annuals flower and set seed. Leafy trees and shrubs provide structure, and tender plants flourish in the mild summer months.

Autumn (*bottom right*) This is arguably the most colourful and plentiful season. Late-flowering plants, such as asters and dahlias, blaze in borders, while many trees and shrubs produce vivid berries and fruits. The leaves of many deciduous plants also brighten up the garden with rich hues before falling. In the moist and still warm conditions, some bulbs, such as *Colchicum*, provide a welcome freshness.

Winter (*opposite page*) Once all the leaves have fallen, the shape and structure of the garden and its plants can be properly appreciated. This is a season of quiet, subtle beauty. Trees and shrubs, such as silver birch (*Betula pendula*) and *Cornus* with its red-coloured stems, evergreen plants, as well as the faded seedheads of herbaceous plants, provide interest. A few plants also produce delicate, often sweetly scented flowers. As cold weather sets in, frost and snow dust the plants, creating a magical feel.

Spring beds and borders

No season is more eagerly anticipated than spring. After the dark, cold days of winter, the garden bursts into life with verdant growth and colourful flowers, marking the start of a new gardening year. In late spring many gardens look their freshest, resplendent with the soft, glowing greens of young foliage.

Pictures clockwise from left

Colourful climbers Walls and fences can be clothed with a range of different climbers that will flower in spring. Wisteria, grown for its waterfalls of scented purple or white flowers, is perhaps the most well known. It is, however, a large plant and needs restrictive pruning to keep it within bounds. Alternatives include *Clematis montana* in white or pink, and *Akebia quinata* with purple blooms, although these climbers are also potentially large. More suited to a small garden are *Clematis alpina, C. macropetala*, and the early honeysuckle *Lonicera periclymenum* 'Belgica' with its deliciously scented flowers.

Vibrant bulbs and early perennials In beds and borders, herbaceous plants push through the soil, growing quickly in the damp, mild conditions. Many will flower early, especially those that enjoy woodland conditions, such as *Pulmonaria, Primula, Dicentra, Doronicum, Epimedium,* and *Anemone*. Some of these perennials can be grown successfully with spring bulbs, such as tulips and daffodils, injecting extra interest into plantings and helping to mask yellowing bulb foliage as the season progresses.

Carpets of spring flowers In less formal areas of the garden, where a more naturalistic display is desired, it is possible to plant and even naturalize some bulbs in grass. Snowdrops (*Galanthus*) and crocuses that flower in early spring can be interplanted with fritillaries, tulips, daffodils (*Narcissus*), and *Camassia* to create a display that will last until early summer. Areas under mature trees are ideal for this kind of treatment, but avoid mowing the grass until the bulb foliage has died away.

Summer beds and borders

Summer is the season of unrestrained colour, when most beds and borders are at their best. If well planted, the garden should provide a succession of flowers that lasts for months on end.

Pictures clockwise from top left

Mixing colours Planting a mix of herbaceous perennials and annuals is a quick and easy way to provide striking contrasts. Colour-themed plantings that use a restricted colour palette are effective at creating different moods. Contrasting colours evoke drama, while those that blend together produce a more relaxed feel.

Continuous colour Many perennials run out of steam as the summer progresses, especially in times of drought or extreme heat. Others, though, can be relied on to flower well into autumn, especially those that are natives of warmer climates, such as *Crocosmia* and *Rudbeckia*.

Calming foliage Without some order, too many bright flowers can become rather overpowering, especially in a small space. The mitigating effect of foliage can help create a calmer effect, softening bright colours. Silvery leaves, such as those of *Artemisia*, used with whites, creams, and pale pinks produce a cool feel; deep green foliage contrasts well with brightly coloured flowers.

Summer bulbs Summer-flowering bulbs, such as lilies, gladioli, and *Galtonia*, are often overlooked but, planted directly into borders or put in pots and plunged into the ground, they pack a powerful punch of colour.

Autumn beds and borders

As the days shorten, colour and interest in the garden come from new sources: the leaves of some plants acquire fiery tints, and fruits and seedheads replace many flowers. Some blooms are at their best during autumn, too.

Pictures clockwise from left

Deciduous trees Trees and shrubs, such as Japanese maples (*Acer japonicum*) and *Rhus*, produce autumnal tints that provide a spectacular backdrop to other plantings. The coloured leaves remain eye-catching once they have fallen, especially around the flowers of late-blooming perennials and bulbs, such as *Cyclamen*.

Structural seedheads Some summer-flowering perennials, such as *Echinops*, *Allium*, *Agapanthus,* and many grasses, produce attractive seedheads that last well into winter. They look particularly striking in the sloping autumn light, decorated with cobwebs or, later, frost.

Colourful fruits Many shrubs and trees produce handsome, long-lasting fruits at this time of year; certain roses, in particular, carry ruby hips, as long as they are not pruned in autumn. Consider leaving other plants unpruned, such as *Viburnum* and *Sorbus*, to help provide birds with food.

Perennial colour Some perennials, such as *Aster, Chrysanthemum, Cyclamen*, and *Saxifraga fortunei*, will produce vibrant flowers until the first hard frosts, and look wonderful in autumnal borders. They can also be useful in containers to inject colour into areas of the garden that are of little interest at this time of the year.

Winter beds and borders

Gardens are often neglected in winter once most showy flowers have faded, but with the right plants they can still be enchanting places at this time of year. Plants with winter interest often have special, rather subtle qualities, such as sweetly scented flowers, attractive stems, foliage, seedheads, berries, or structural shapes.

Pictures clockwise from top left

Winter flowers Hellebores, such as *Helleborus* x *hybridus*, are among the best winter-blooming plants. Flowering from midwinter to mid-spring, these clump-forming evergreen perennials are easily grown in light shade in any good soil, and form good ground cover when planted in drifts. Other perennials with winter interest worth seeking out include mauve-flowered *Iris unguicularis* and *Arum italicum* 'Marmoratum', with its white-veined leaves.

Transient beauty Frost and snow add an element of short-lived beauty to the garden in winter, often transforming it overnight. A light covering of snow or a hard frost can enhance structures, highlighting architectural features and plants, and briefly changing the whole feel of a garden.

Scented highlights Mahonias are among the finest evergreen shrubs for winter, with their spiny foliage and sweetly scented yellow blooms, followed by blue-tinged berries. They are also useful for their architectural form, which makes them an attractive backdrop for other plants such as *Euonymus*, with its colourful fruit.

Graceful grasses The seedheads of some grasses will survive well into winter, providing a touch of unexpected grace to plantings, especially when dusted with frost. Translucent, they allow views through to plants behind, such as the fruit-laden branches of a crab apple (*Malus*).

Scented shrubs Some shrubs flower in winter, such as witch hazel (*Hamamelis*) with its orange, yellow, or red, spider-like blooms. Other shrubs worth considering for their delicious scent include the honeysuckle *Lonicera* x *purpusii* and *Chimonanthus praecox*.

High and low maintenance

When planning a garden, be realistic about how much time you can afford to keep it looking at its best.

High maintenance

Gardens for plant lovers These gardens tend to be stocked with a wide range of choice plants, which will need their specific growing requirements matched in order to grow well. Careful placing of plants and constant manipulation of growing conditions by gardeners will keep these plots looking their best, and regular attention will be required to prevent plants outgrowing their space.

Dense planting Filling a garden with plants may reduce weeding, but competition for light and water causes problems. High-maintenance plants include tulips, which may need planting and lifting each year, annuals grown from seed, plants with specific watering, feeding, or pruning needs, and those prone to pests and diseases. A lawn also needs weekly mowing to keep it looking good.

High-maintenance planting suggestions

- *Aster* (some)
- *Astrantia*
- *Buxus* (if kept clipped)
- *Canna*
- *Clematis* (some)
- *Cornus sanguinea* 'Winter Beauty'
- *Dahlia*
- *Dicksonia antarctica*
- *Echinacea purpurea*
- *Erysimum*
- *Helenium*
- *Hosta*
- *Lavandula* (lavender)
- lilies
- *Melianthus major*
- roses (some)
- *Sambucus racemosa* 'Plumosa Aurea'
- tulips

Tulip bulbs should be planted in late autumn.

Hosta 'June', like all hostas, is loved by slugs.

Prune *Cornus sanguinea* in early spring.

Lilium regale bulbs should be planted in spring.

Low maintenance

Easy-care gardens These are a good choice for people with little spare time but who still want an attractive outdoor space. Lawns can be replaced by patios or decks, and the soil covered with a special membrane to cut down on weeding, and topped with bark or cobbles after planting. Irrigation systems can be installed, and plants chosen that do not need much attention.

Undemanding planting This can provide year-round interest and yet needs little attention. Large specimen plants provide immediate impact. Evergreen shrubs and trees are good because most need little pruning and do not drop leaves in autumn. Minimal use of herbaceous plants lessens end-of-season work, and using well-spaced larger plants reduces watering and trimming.

Low-maintenance planting suggestions

- *Acer*
- *Arbutus unedo*
- *Aucuba japonica*
- *Choisya ternata* Sundance
- *Cotoneaster horizontalis*

- *Fatsia japonica*
- *Hemerocallis* (day lily)
- *Ilex aquifolium* 'Silver Queen'
- *Jasminum nudiflorum*

- *Mahonia*
- *Nandina domestica*
- *Phormium*
- *Photinia* x *fraseri* 'Red Robin'

- *Phyllostachys nigra*
- *Stipa tenuissima*
- *Trachelospermum asiaticum*
- *Vinca* (periwinkle)

Ilex aquifolium 'Silver Queen' has beautiful evergreen foliage.

Stipa tenuissima is a trouble-free airy grass.

Hemerocallis 'Corky' is ablaze with golden blooms in summer.

Cotoneaster horizontalis has bright red autumn berries.

Choosing a planting style

When planting up your garden, if you decide to follow a particular style, first ensure that it is practical and fits your lifestyle.

What do you want?

Find inspiration for your plot by visiting other gardens, and looking at books, magazines, and television shows. If you long for a tropical garden with exotic plants, such as palms and other architectural specimens, you can achieve it with the use of containers on a sun-drenched terrace, even in the UK.

What do you need?

If entertaining outdoors is important to you, a large patio with a dining/barbecue area will be useful, while a lawn is a good idea if children are likely to play in the garden in summer. Your lifestyle may dictate that you have a low-maintenance garden with plants that are easy to care for, but look good all year round. Consider, also, how much privacy you need.

Examine the visual appeal of your chosen scheme. Will you include plants with impact to create impressive planting schemes? Or would you prefer a themed garden with an exotic feel, or simply an oasis of tranquillity. When selecting plants, make sure you choose those that will suit the style of garden you have in mind.

Keeping it neat

A wonderful garden filled with unusual plants and flowers is all very well, but it may require a great deal of time to keep it in tip-top condition. When planting and designing a garden, decide how much time you can spare to look after it. Some planting styles require less effort to keep them looking good than others. A formal garden with a central lawn, for example, looks tidy once mown, but it may be better to reduce the area of grass or replace it with gravel or decking, if free time is limited. Planting in formal schemes tends to be confined to geometric-shaped beds or borders. Designs can be either high-maintenance, with a mix of perennials, annuals, and shrubs, or low-maintenance, with easy-care shrub borders.

A natural approach

For many people, choosing a naturalistic planting style, using drifts of perennials or a large number of native plants, creates a garden that feels at one with nature. With this approach, you may also decide to avoid using chemicals on your plants, and adopt organic growing methods. Encourage birds, insects, and other wildlife into your garden, to enrich your gardening experience, and create curved or sinuous borders for your informal planting designs.

Planting style ideas

Setting a particular style for your planting and layout helps to create a feeling of cohesion, and makes selecting plants and garden objects much easier. The main hurdle is making a choice and sticking to it.

Oriental

An authentic Japanese garden is difficult to create, and requires discipline and subject knowledge. It is possible to use elements from the style, however, to create a distinctive oriental feel. Minimalist lines, the use of certain plants, rocks, raked gravel or slate chippings, and focal points, such as stone lanterns, prove effective. Colours are restrained, derived mostly from foliage; showy flowers are seldom used.

Planting suggestions
- *Acer japonicum* (Japanese maple)
- *Camellia sasanqua*
- *Ophiopogon* 'Nigrescens'
- *Phyllostachys nigra*
- *Pinus mugo* 'Ophir'

Maintenance tips Keep raked gravel weed- and leaf-free: the garden should appear immaculate.

Knot gardens and Parterres

Knot gardens are generally small scale and feature low, clipped hedges, usually box (*Buxus*) but sometimes *Santolina* or lavender (*Lavandula*), set out in simple patterns. Between the hedges are blocks of colour, normally from bedding plants or coloured gravel. Parterres are more ambitious in scale and design, but they also use low hedges with colourful flowers and often topiary. Both styles of garden are highly formal, labour intensive, and best seen from above.

Planting suggestions
- bedding plants, eg, dahlias, cosmos
- *Buxus sempervirens* (box)
- culinary herbs
- *Santolina chamaecyparissus*
- *Taxus baccata* (yew)

Maintenance tips Clip the hedges 2–3 times a year to keep them neat.

Modernist

The overall feel of most modernist gardens is one of simplicity and restraint, with planting often taking second place to hard landscaping, giving a minimalist feel. Plants are carefully selected and sited, with architectural specimen plants providing instant impact. The palette of plants is usually limited, with a restricted colour theme, and maximum use is made of form and texture. Broad sweeps of perennials and grasses, often planted in a naturalistic way, provide summer colour.

Planting suggestions
- *Acer japonicum* (Japanese maple)
- *Dicksonia antarctica*
- *Fatsia japonica*
- *Phyllostachys nigra*
- *Stipa tenuissima*
- topiary shapes, box (*Buxus*), yew (*Taxus*)
- *Verbena bonariensis*

Maintenance tips Modernist gardens tend to be naturally low maintenance, but ensure plants are well watered, especially when they are establishing, and top up mulches of gravel or aggregates, as required.

Maple foliage provides vibrant colour in an oriental-themed garden.

A well-tended knot garden makes a fine garden feature, even without flowers.

Clipped box balls in a sea of lavender give this garden a modern twist.

Tropical

For sheer floral drama, few gardening styles can match a tropical border. These displays of exotic-looking plants, usually a mix of hardy and tender plants grown for both foliage and flowers, provide great interest in both summer and autumn. Planting is informal, with plants massed together in profusion; huge bold leaves and vibrantly coloured flowers predominate, while the displays improve as the season progresses. This style is labour-intensive and displays usually last only until the first frosts.

Planting suggestions
- *Canna*
- dahlias
- *Hedychium gardnerianum*
- *Melianthus major*
- *Musa basjoo* (banana)
- *Phoenix canariensis*
- *Phormium tenax*
- *Ricinus communis*

Maintenance tips Plant out a tropical border after the last frosts have passed. Feed and water well for rapid, lush growth. Ensure you protect tender plants well from winter cold.

Cottage

A traditional cottage garden represents many people's idea of the ultimate garden. Planting tends to be informal, but contained within a simple, formal layout, which is usually little more than a network of paths. Flowering herbaceous perennials predominate, and these gardens are usually at their best in early summer. Later on, roses and clematis provide plenty of colour, and in winter, well-chosen shrubs lend the garden structure once the flowers have faded. Colours are often soft and muted, giving a relaxed feel.

Planting suggestions
- *Astrantia*
- delphiniums
- *Dianthus* (pinks)
- *Digitalis purpurea* (foxglove)
- geraniums
- *Philadelphus*
- *Ribes* (flowering currant)
- roses

Maintenance tips Regular top-ups of garden compost in spring will keep perennials growing well. Remember to divide clumps of herbaceous plants every 2–3 years for healthy growth.

Contemporary

The contemporary garden is usually thought of as an extension of the home, a so-called "outdoor room" that often includes dining and seating areas. This modern and practical garden style often features expanses of hard standing or wooden decking, ideal for massed displays of brightly coloured yet colour-themed container plants in the summer. Beds tend to be filled with easy-care, usually evergreen plants, to provide year-round interest, and are often planted through a weed-suppressing membrane, topped with mulch to minimize aftercare.

Planting suggestions
- *Acer japonicum* (Japanese maple)
- *Astelia nervosa*
- *Aucuba japonica* (spotted laurel)
- *Photinia* 'Red Robin'
- *Choisya ternata*
- *Clematis armandii*
- *Pittosporum tenuifolium* 'Tom Thumb'

Maintenance tips Ensure plants are well watered while establishing. Keep mulches topped up, and plant containers when frost has passed.

Spectacular flowers and foliage provide high-impact summer displays.

Borders overflowing with flowers are typical of the cottage-garden style.

Wooden decking is used to give this garden a contemporary feel.

The effects of aspect

The direction in which your garden faces affects the amount of sunlight it receives, while altitude influences temperatures. Take both factors into account when choosing your plants.

Which way does your garden face? Simply observing how much sun your garden receives gives an idea of its orientation. To work it out accurately, use a compass. Stand with your back to your house wall – the reading from here shows the direction your garden faces. South-facing gardens get the most sun; north-facing sites the least.

Sunny and shady sites Some gardens are sunnier than others as a result of their aspect and other factors, such as shade-casting buildings, but in all sites, the amount of direct sun and the sun's position in the garden change as the day progresses. A south-facing garden will have sun all day; north-facing much less, perhaps none in winter.

Sunny gardens are usually more desirable, but shade does have its advantages. These gardens are cooler, have a more humid microclimate, and are less prone to drought. There are many wonderful shade-loving plants that will not tolerate direct sun, while in a sunny garden, slightly tender plants from Mediterranean regions, for example, flourish. The key is to work with what you have.

Morning: areas that are in sun now may be in shade by the afternoon.

Midday: the sun is overhead, so the garden receives maximum sunlight.

Evening: as the sun sets, the glancing light casts soft shadows.

Beware frost pockets Frost occurs when temperatures fall below freezing. Spring frosts can be particularly lethal in the garden, especially where many near-tender plants are grown. Even on a local scale, some sites will be more vulnerable than others, usually in areas where pockets of freezing air develop. Cold air is heavy, and sinks to the lowest point. If it cannot escape, it collects, forming a "frost pocket". Here, frosts will be harder and linger longer, and you may get a frost when other areas remain above freezing. Gardens in valleys or in a hollow often suffer badly. Hedges or walls may create or worsen the effect, preventing cold air from flowing down the hillside. Thinning a hedge, using trellis instead of a solid barrier, or leaving a gate open on cold nights may help.

Creating microclimates Even within a single garden, you may notice great differences in the growing conditions. A border by a sunny wall or fence will be far warmer and drier than one in the shade, perhaps beneath a tree, which is likely to be more humid with a more even temperature range. A low-lying area will remain wetter than a border at the top of a slope, and some parts of the garden may be sheltered, others exposed. Gardeners can capitalize on these differences; even in small areas, they allow you to grow a wider range of plants. A sunny spot can be enhanced with a raised bed to improve drainage for tender plants; low-lying areas could be turned into a bog garden for moisture-loving plants. You can make a windy area more sheltered with a permeable barrier, such as a trellis.

Seasonal impact The direction your garden faces gives it particular properties throughout the year. A north-facing garden, or border in front of a north-facing fence, will receive little sun in winter, remaining cold and damp, but temperatures will be more constant than in a south-facing area that is warmed after a sunny winter day, only to be chilled at night. Plants exposed to constant chill also start into growth later, but are affected less by late frosts. While potentially dank in winter, a north-facing area offers a cool retreat in summer, and lush, moisture-loving woodland plants will thrive there. Spring bulbs take advantage of the sun spots under bare deciduous trees, areas that receive little light in summer. Sunny patios are ideal for tender plants, but may get too hot and dry in summer for some plants.

Understanding soils

Before you decide what to plant in your garden, take a look at the soil. The acidity or alkalinity of the soil and its composition determine what will grow, and an understanding of its properties helps you to keep plants in good health.

Types of soil

Soils comprise two elements: a mineral portion (tiny particles of weathered rock, larger gravels, and stones) and an organic (dead plant and animal remains, and living organisms). The most important part of the soil is found in the top 30cm (12in). Below this lies less fertile subsoil.

Soil particle size, the amount of organic matter, and available water determine soil characteristics. The smallest soil particles will form clay, those a little larger create silts, and even bigger particles form sandy soils. Soils with a mix of different particle sizes are known as loams.

The descriptions below will help determine your soil type:

Chalk soil Soils that are pale and contain chunks of white limestone (usually the underlying rock) and often flint, are chalk soils. They are free-draining and fertile, often rather thin, and almost always alkaline.

Peat soil Distinctively dark, peat soils are rich in organic matter that helps them retain soil moisture. Peat forms where wet, acid conditions stop plant and animal remains decomposing fully. These soils are usually acidic.

Clay soil Composed of more than 25 per cent moisture-retaining clay particles, clay is heavy to dig and may be waterlogged in winter (it dries out in summer). Organic matter is easily trapped, resulting in good fertility.

Silty soil With particles not as fine as those of a clay soil, silts are also fairly moisture-retentive and fertile. They tend to be dark in colour, which is the result of the accumulated organic matter that they often contain.

Sandy soil Sandy soils are easy to spot, being light and free-draining. They are composed of relatively large individual soil particles that allow water to drain quickly.

Testing the soil's acidity or alkalinity

Use a soil-testing kit to assess the acidity or alkalinity (pH) of your soil – the results will indicate what plants will grow well. Carry out several tests across the garden, using soil from just below the surface. Soil pH is measured on a scale of 1–14. Above neutral (7) is alkaline, below is acidic; pH 6.5 is usually considered the optimum.

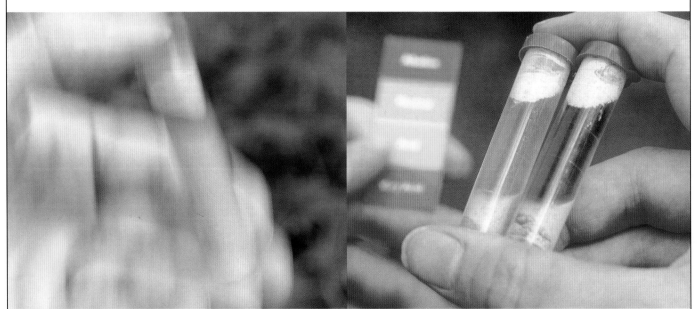

Following the kit's instructions, add garden soil and water to the test tube provided and shake the contents well.

Compare results from around the garden with the chart provided: a red/yellow colour shows an acid soil; dark green an alkaline one.

Testing sandy soil

To determine whether your garden has a sandy soil, and thus one that may need regular irrigation and boosting with organic matter, carry out a simple test to examine the texture of the soil. Take your sample from just below the soil surface and repeat at intervals across the garden to ensure an even overall result.

Rub a small amount of soil between your fingers. If the soil has a gritty, granular feel, it is likely to contain a high proportion of sand.

Try to squeeze the soil into a ball – the grains of a sandy soil will not stick together but if it is loamy, the shape may hold a little.

Testing clay soil

To check if you have clay soil, and thus one that may become waterlogged in winter and be more difficult to dig than other soil types, remove small samples of soil from different spots around the garden from just below the soil surface. Clay soil will feel quite sticky and heavy when shaped in the hand.

Try to mould the soil in your hands – the particles of a clay soil will hold together well and change shape when pressed.

Heavy clay can even be rolled into a thin cylinder; it will often appear smooth and shiny.

Making the most of your soil

Different types of soil have differing characteristics, some aiding cultivation of certain plants, others providing a challenge to gardeners. Various techniques can be used to improve the soil to maximize its potential.

Sandy soil

Advantages Sandy soil is free-draining, which prevents plants from becoming waterlogged in winter and aids the survival of species sensitive to wet conditions. It is easy and light to dig all year round, and warms up quickly in the spring.

Disadvantages In dry conditions, plants will often require extra irrigation, and moisture-loving species will be unreliable in these soils. Sandy soils have a tendency to be poor, so you will need to apply plenty of plant food and organic matter.

Improving sandy soil Dig in large amounts of organic matter each year to help improve the soil's ability to hold water and nutrients. Mulches such as gravel help to keep in moisture. Digging in clay may also be useful.

Plants for sandy soils

- *Acacia dealbata*
- *Calluna vulgaris* 'Silver Knight'
- *Catananche caerulea*
- *Cistus* x *hybridus*
- *Convolvulus cneorum*
- *Cotoneaster horizontalis*
- *Erysimum* 'Bowles' Mauve'
- *Euphorbia characias*
- *Euphorbia rigida*
- *Grevillea* 'Canberra Gem'
- *Helianthemum* 'Rhodanthe Carneum' ('Wisley Pink')
- *Helleborus argutifolius*
- *Iris unguicularis*
- *Melianthus major*
- *Olea europaea* (olive)
- *Pittosporum tobira*
- *Romneya coulteri*
- *Rosmarinus officinalis* (rosemary)
- *Solanum crispum* 'Glasnevin'
- *Verbena bonariensis*

Abutilon x suntense   *Allium hollandicum* 'Purple Sensation'   *Artemisia alba* 'Canescens'

Bupleurum fruticosum   *Lavandula stoechas*   *Perovskia* 'Blue Spire'

Clay soil

Advantages Clay soils are usually highly fertile and many plants thrive in them. They also retain water well. The more clay soil is worked, the better it is for planting, as the soil gradually becomes more crumbly and drainage improves. Avoid working the soil when it is wet and easily compacted.

Disadvantages Despite its high fertility, a clay soil has a number of problems that can be hard to tackle. In winter it may become waterlogged and impossible to dig. Attempts to work the soil in this state usually create compaction where the soil particles are compressed, resulting in yet further waterlogging. In summer, the opposite problem occurs; clay bakes hard and even simple digging can be impossible. Even when soils are manageable they are heavy, breaking into large clods, and they are slow to warm up in spring.

Improving clay soil The key to success is often simply perseverance. By adding organic matter to the soil, you will eventually improve its structure, making it more crumbly and easier to work. In small areas, perhaps in a raised bed, dig in horticultural grit. Avoid walking on the garden when it is waterlogged and do not dig the soil when wet. Try to carry out most planting in spring or autumn when the soil is more manageable. In areas where waterlogging is severe, you may need to install drains.

Plants for clay soils

- *Alchemilla mollis*
- *Arum italicum* subsp. *italicum* 'Marmoratum'
- *Aruncus dioicus*
- *Aucuba japonica* (spotted laurel)
- *Berberis darwinii*
- *Buxus sempervirens* (box)
- *Campanula glomerata*
- *Carex elata*
- *Cornus sanguinea* 'Winter Beauty'
- *Digitalis purpurea* (foxglove)
- *Geranium*
- *Hemerocallis* (day lily)
- *Hosta*
- *Hydrangea macrophylla* 'Lanarth White'
- *Iris laevigata*
- *Jasminum nudiflorum*
- *Leycesteria formosa*
- *Mahonia x media* 'Buckland'
- *Viburnum tinus* 'Eve Price'

Anemone x *hybrida* 'Honorine Jobert'   *Euphorbia characias*   *Iris sibirica* 'Perry's Blue'

Malus 'John Downie'   *Primula pulverulenta*   *Sambucus racemosa* 'Plumosa Aurea'

Making the most of your soil *continued*

Alkaline soil

Advantages An alkaline soil enables you to grow a wide range of plants; many vegetables (such as members of the cabbage family) will not grow as well in acidic soil. Ornamentals, such as clematis, are said to grow better in an alkaline soil, and the finest rose gardens tend to be in alkaline areas. These soils suit earthworms; some pests and diseases, such as club root, are less of a problem.

Disadvantages There are certain plants that simply will not grow in alkaline conditions and, unfortunately they are often among the most desirable. Rhododendrons, camellias, *Pieris*, some magnolias, and other woodland plants, such as *Uvularia* and *Trillium*, need the cool, moist, acid soil associated with their native habitats. These plants are known as "calcifuge" or lime-hating. Some acid-loving plants may survive on alkaline soils but will look sick, with yellowing leaves (chlorosis). Alkaline soils tend to be deficient in manganese, boron, and phosphorus, all of which are important for healthy plant growth.

Improving alkaline soil You cannot, as such, improve alkaline soil, since a high pH can be both good and bad. Gardeners are best advised to grow what suits their particular soil. Many acid-loving plants can be grown in containers, or in a raised bed filled with ericaceous (acid) compost. Where the soil pH is neutral or just alkaline, years of adding organic matter may lower the pH enough for some smaller acid-loving plants.

Plants for alkaline soils

- *Aquilegia* McKana Group
- *Aster* 'Coombe Fishacre'
- *Buddleja davidii* 'Dartmoor'
- *Buxus sempervirens*
- *Choisya ternata* Sundance
- *Clematis*
- *Cotoneaster horizontalis*

- *Erica carnea* 'Foxhollow'
- *Erysimum* 'Bowles Mauve'
- *Hebe*
- *Hibiscus syriacus* 'Oiseau Bleu'
- *Iris unguicularis*
- *Lavandula stoechas*
- *Mahonia* x *media* 'Buckland'

- *Nepeta* x *faassenii*
- *Phormium* 'Yellow Wave'
- *Primula vulgaris*
- *Pulsatilla vulgaris*
- roses
- *Salvia officinalis* 'Purpurascens'
- *Sedum* 'Herbstfreude'

Alchemilla mollis   *Campanula glomerata*   *Clematis cirrhosa*

Cotinus coggygria 'Royal Purple'   *Jasminum nudiflorum*   *Lonicera* (honeysuckle)

Acid soil

Advantages Some of the most spectacular garden plants, including rhododendrons, *Meconopsis*, and *Desfontainia*, will grow well only on acidic soil. Other species, such as *Hamamelis*, may survive on alkaline soil but simply perform better on acid. Few garden plants will not tolerate a mildly acid soil, although a very low pH will limit your choice. Acid soils are often associated with woodland conditions and tend to be cool and moist.

Disadvantages Acid soil, though usually rich in organic matter, can be quite poor, especially if it is also sandy. To improve it, dig in plenty of well-rotted manure each year. Very peaty soils can, conversely, be waterlogged and require draining. These are often the most acid of

all and you may need to add lime to them for a range of plants to thrive. Most fruit and veg do not like strongly acid soil and other plants simply will not grow – these are known as "calcicoles" or lime-loving. Acid soils are often deficient in phosphorus and may have too much manganese and aluminium for healthy plant growth.

Improving acid soils If your soil is strongly acidic, you may need to increase the pH to broaden the range of plants you can grow. Adding spent mushroom compost is an excellent way of doing this. Powdered lime is an alternative. However, most gardeners usually feel that a mildly acidic soil is desirable, and simply grow plants that enjoy their conditions.

Plants for acid soils

- *Astilboides tabularis*
- *Betula* (birch)
- *Camellia*
- *Cercis canadensis* 'Forest Pansy'
- *Cornus canadensis*
- *Corydalis flexuosa*
- *Daphne bholua* 'Jacqueline Postill'

- *Desfontainea spinosa*
- *Digitalis purpurea* (foxglove)
- *Hedychium densiflorum*
- *Leucothoe fontanesiana* 'Rainbow'
- *Meconopsis*
- *Photinia* x *fraseri* 'Red Robin'

- *Pieris*
- *Primula pulverulenta*
- *Rhododendron*
- *Romneya coulteri*
- *Skimmia* x *confusa* 'Kew Green'
- *Stewartia monadelpha*
- *Uvularia grandiflora*

Acer palmatum　　　*Calluna vulgaris* 'Silver Knight'　　　*Carex elata* 'Aurea'

Cornus kousa var. *chinensis*　　　*Grevillea* 'Canberra Gem'　　　*Hydrangea quercifolia*

Making a border

Flower and shrub borders provide colour, scent, and seasonal interest, making them an essential part of the garden. Follow these basic steps when planning and preparing your borders to ensure their success through the year.

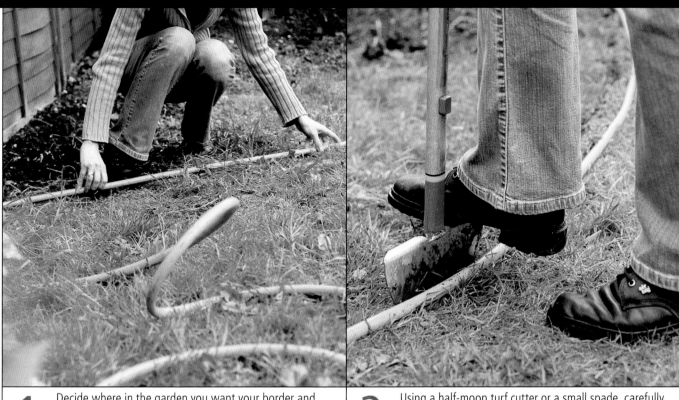

1 Decide where in the garden you want your border and mark out its shape. For a curved edge, use a garden hose. Make sure the border is not too narrow and that its shape fits well within the overall layout of the garden.

2 Using a half-moon turf cutter or a small spade, carefully slice through the grass, following the contours of the hose. Make sure the cuts join up properly and push the full depth of the cutter into the ground.

3 With a spade, begin stripping off the turf. Cut it into manageable-sized squares from above, then slide the blade of the spade under the roots of the grass. Try to avoid removing an excessively deep layer of soil.

4 Stack the turves in a spare corner of the garden, grass-side down. The soil in these turves is nutrient-rich and should be reused. After several months, the grass will die off and the pile can be cut up, sieved, and dug into the borders.

Making a border *continued*

5 Dig over the exposed soil with a fork, pushing the tines down to their full depth. Remove old roots, large stones, and debris that you unearth, and break up large clods of soil. Work the soil until it has a crumbly texture.

6 With a spade, spread about 5cm (2in) of organic matter, such as well-rotted farmyard manure or garden compost, over the surface of the border. Turn the compost into the soil, and mix it in evenly.

7 If the soil is heavy or poorly drained, spread an 8cm (3in) layer of coarse grit or gravel over it, and dig this into the top 15cm (6in) of soil with a spade. This will help open up drainage channels through the soil in the root zone.

8 Using a soil rake, remove any remaining stones, roots, or debris that may have worked their way up to the surface. Then, with the flat back of the rake, carefully level off any mounds and hollows.

Tip for success

To stop soil spilling out onto the lawn, consider adding edging to the front of the border before planting. Use a spirit level to make sure the edging is level.

9 Set out the plants, still in their pots, on the ground, adjusting their positions until you are happy. Pay attention to their eventual size, flower and foliage colour, and season of interest to achieve your desired effect.

Finishing touches

To help set off planting and add a touch of "polish" to the garden, small additions, such as edgings and mulches, can make a big impact.

Soft lawn edging

It is surprising how much difference a well-edged lawn makes to the overall look of a garden. Where borders meet grass, trim with edging shears after mowing to maintain the shape of the lawn. Edging irons are also useful for reshaping when required. Plants that spill from borders onto the lawn may add a touch of informality, but will damage the lawn in the long run.

Choosing a hard edge

Borders that meet with hard landscaping materials require less maintenance than soft edging. Sprawling plants are best grown next to hard surfaces where the border's shape can be maintained more easily. Use paving for formal or informal situations, and areas where grass struggles to grow, such as in shade or next to narrow paths.

Brick edging Laid as a path or in a single row between a border and lawn, or along gravel paths, bricks create a traditional feel. They also blend well with planting.

Paved edging Where paving meets a border, attractive informal effects can be achieved. Allow plants, such as lavender, to billow out from flower beds, softening the hard layout.

Wood edging If you have border soil to retain, wood edging is an easy-to-install option. Partially conceal with planting to help it blend in, and apply wood preservative to prevent rotting.

The benefits of mulching

Mulches help to conserve soil moisture, reduce weeding, provide a decorative element, and some add organic matter to soil, improving its fertility and promoting plant growth. A mulch is simply a layer of material spread over the soil surface, and different situations and planting require different types. Avoid applying them too thickly – about 3cm (1¼in) is ideal – or over the crowns of plants. Mulches are usually applied in early spring.

Organic matter Garden compost or well-rotted manure is an ideal mulch because it aids plant growth, improves the soil and helps retain moisture. It needs re-applying every year.

Cocoa shells Lightweight and easy to apply, cocoa shells break down, enriching the soil. They are, however, easily disturbed by wind, animals, or birds, and can look unsightly.

Gravel Long-lasting and inexpensive, gravel preserves moisture in summer and keeps damp away from sensitive plants, such as alpines, in the winter. It is heavy to apply.

Decorative mulches Coloured glass chippings, crushed seashells, and other decorative mulches are ideal for pots and containers. They will reduce weeds and conserve moisture.

Weed membranes Laid beneath mulches before planting, porous membranes drastically reduce weeds. Adding plants after a membrane has been laid can be tricky, though.

Bark chips Lightweight, organic, and weed-suppressing, bark chips are a popular mulch, but as they slowly break down, they may remove valuable nitrogen from the soil.

Making your own compost

Making compost from your kitchen and garden waste is a sustainable and environmentally friendly way of recycling. Applied as a mulch, compost helps to improve the fertility and moisture-retaining qualities of your soil.

Types of composter The basic way of making compost is to pile it into a heap, but this can be unsightly, and better compost is often achieved more quickly using a composter. The simplest structures are bays, usually made of corrugated plastic or metal, in which waste is piled. Wooden compost bins are easier on the eye, and can be built at home from scrap wood; otherwise you can buy ready-made bins, often with slatted sides or vents for air circulation. Effective and inexpensive, lightweight plastic compost bins (*right*) are also a popular choice.

Filling your bin Almost any vegetable matter can be added to a compost bin and the more diverse the range of materials, the better the compost. It is also important to keep woody and nitrogen-rich leafy materials in proportion: you should try to include about twice as much woody material (twigs, paper) as nitrogen rich-material (grass, kitchen scraps). Mix grass cuttings with woodier clippings or even shredded paper, because a thick layer of grass will inhibit important air movement. Chop bigger cuttings into small pieces and avoid adding weeds with seeds, or persistent perennial weeds. Place a layer of coarser twigs in the bottom of the bin and then add the material in layers. Spread a little farmyard manure between layers to help speed up the composting process.

Leafy material adds nitrogen and moisture:
- Grass clippings and weeds
- Kitchen vegetable waste
- Fallen leaves
- Herbaceous plant clippings
- Sappy hedge trimmings
- Windfall fruit
- Old bedding plant material

Woody, carbon-rich material improves airflow:
- Woody plant clippings and twigs
- Shredded paper
- Scraps of cardboard
- Untreated wood shavings
- Stems of herbaceous plants
- Bark mulch

Layer woody and leafy material in your compost heap.

Speeding up composting Nitrogen-rich manure contains micro-organisms that promote composting, so add it to your heap to help the material break down more quickly. Alternatively, you can buy special compost additives. Turning the heap also improves air circulation, speeds up rotting, and ensures that all the material is composted.

Tip for success

Too much wet, green, nitrogen-rich material, such as grass clippings, will quickly turn the compost heap sour and smelly. Mix it with coarser woody matter in layers, and aim to turn the heap regularly.

Planting a perennial

Perennials are plants that grow from year to year, and many are long-lived. But for these plants to perform well as they mature, they must be planted and established with care.

1 Place the plant in its pot on the ground in a position that suits its growing needs and not too close to other plants. The soil in the pot should be thoroughly soaked before planting to help give the plant a good start.

2 With a spade, dig a hole wider and deeper than the size of the plant's container. Add organic matter, such as garden compost, to the base of the hole and dig it in well. Pour some water into the hole before planting.

3 Remove the plant carefully from its pot. If the roots tightly encircle the root ball, the plant is pot-bound and the roots need to be teased out gently. Place the plant in the hole, slightly deeper in the ground than when it was in its pot.

4 Backfill in around the root ball, firming the soil as you go and ensuring the plant stands straight in its hole. Avoid mounding the soil around the stems; the plant should be in the centre of a shallow depression. Water well.

Planting a tree

Planting a tree may seem a simple task, but these plants are long-lived and should be planted well and given the appropriate aftercare if they are to fulfil their potential in years to come.

1 Soak the root ball of the tree in its container before planting. This will compensate for any water loss from the roots during the planting process and ensure that the tree settles into its position well.

2 With a spade, dig a planting hole about three times as wide as the diameter of the pot and 30cm (12in) deep (most root activity takes place in the top layer of soil). Lightly fork the base and sides of the hole.

3 Check the hole is the correct depth by putting the pot in the hole and placing a cane across the top – it should rest on both sides of the hole and on the top of the root ball. You may need to add or remove soil in the hole.

4 Gently remove the root ball from its pot – the pot should slide off easily, leaving the root ball intact. Carefully tease out some of the larger encircling roots, to help the tree root into the surrounding ground more successfully.

Planting a tree *continued*

5 Stand the tree in its final position. Drive a stout stake into the ground close to the tree trunk and at a 45° angle over the root ball, to avoid damaging the roots. Make sure that the stake faces into the prevailing wind.

6 Backfill the hole with soil, working it in around the roots. Unless the soil is poor or sandy, do not add organic matter because this seems to prevent the roots spreading out in search of nutrients. Firm the soil in gently.

7 Tie the tree quite loosely to the stake with a tree tie, about 45cm (18in) from the ground, to allow the stem to flex in the wind. Check the tie regularly and loosen it as the tree girth expands, to prevent damage to the bark.

8 Water the tree well after planting and during dry periods for the first couple of seasons. Add a mulch of well-rotted garden compost, about 8cm (3in) deep, around the tree. Keep the mulch about 15cm (6in) away from the trunk.

9   Over the next two to three years, use sharp secateurs to remove any damaged wood or branches that spoil the tree's shape, such as crossing, rubbing branches. Do not leave stumps, cutting fairly close to the main stem.

Planting a shrub

Shrubs form the backbone of a planting scheme, providing important structure as well as flower and foliage effects. Before planting, check the plant label for the shrub's preferred site and soil, since moving it at a later date will be difficult.

Tip for success

Once planted, apply a top-dressing of fertilizer above the roots in spring. Later watering or rain will wash it down.

1 Soak the plant thoroughly in its pot. With a spade, dig a large hole, approximately two to three times the diameter of the pot. Remove any old roots and large stones, and break up the soil in the base of the hole with a fork.

2 To check the hole is the correct depth, place a cane across the top; it should rest on both sides of the hole and on the top of the root ball. Position the plant with its best side facing the direction from which it will be viewed.

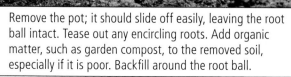

3 Remove the pot; it should slide off easily, leaving the root ball intact. Tease out any encircling roots. Add organic matter, such as garden compost, to the removed soil, especially if it is poor. Backfill around the root ball.

4 Firm the earth down gently. The plant should sit at the centre of a shallow depression, which will assist watering. Spread a mulch of organic matter around the plant, keeping it away from the stems. Water the plant well.

Planting a climber

Climbing plants are particularly useful in small gardens because they add height without too much bulk, maximizing the use of limited space. They are also a quick and effective way of covering dull fences and garden structures.

Tip for success

A system of vine eyes threaded with wire along a fence is perhaps the simplest and least visible way of providing support for climbers. The system is easy to attach and allows plants to grow to their full potential.

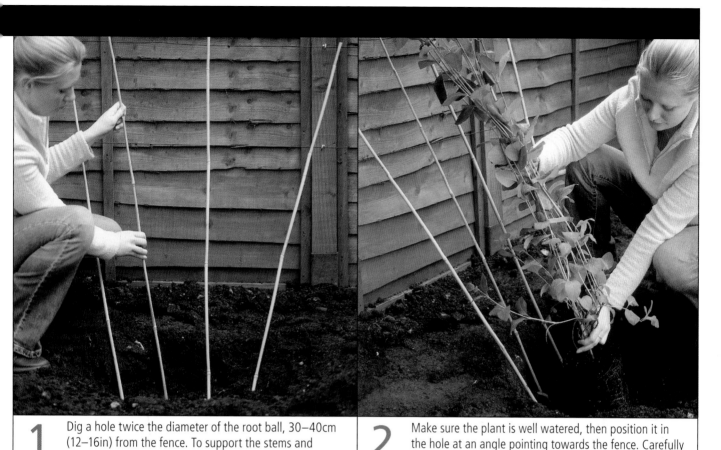

1 Dig a hole twice the diameter of the root ball, 30–40cm (12–16in) from the fence. To support the stems and achieve good initial coverage, construct a fan from canes pushed into the soil and angled towards the fence.

2 Make sure the plant is well watered, then position it in the hole at an angle pointing towards the fence. Carefully remove the pot and any supporting stakes. Separate multiple stems growing from the base of the plant.

3 Backfill the hole with the removed soil mixed with some organic matter, such as garden compost. Firm the soil gently as you go. The plant should be at the centre of a shallow depression, to aid watering and establishment.

4 Select the stems to be trained up the canes, tying in one to two stems per cane with gardener's twine. Spread a mulch of bark chips or organic matter over the soil to keep in the moisture and suppress weeds.

Sowing annuals outside

Many hardy annuals, such as California poppies (*Eschscholzia*), are best sown *in situ* outside, avoiding the root disturbance that occurs when seedlings are removed from their pots. Plants grow quickly to give fine summer displays.

Tip for success

The fine soil of a seedbed is attractive to cats, and young seedlings may be disturbed by birds. To avoid these problems, protect the area with twiggy sticks pushed into the ground.

1 Select an open area without any competing plants for sowing the seeds. Lightly fork over the soil, breaking up large clods, and then remove large stones, weeds, and debris with a rake. Work the soil into a fine, level tilth.

2 Make drills (shallow depressions to sow seed into) in the soil by pushing a pole or bamboo cane into the soil surface. Drills make it easier to identify seedlings; weed seedlings are unlikely to emerge in straight lines.

3 Place the seeds into the palm of your hand, and aim to pour the seed gently from a crease as you pass your hand along the drill. Do not sow the seed too thickly. Larger seeds can be placed in the drill with your fingertips.

4 Lightly cover the drills with fine soil and water well using a can with a fine rose to avoid disturbing the seeds. Keep the seedbed moist and remove any weeds. When the seedlings emerge, carefully thin out close-growing plants.

Sowing hardy annuals

While many hardy annuals can be sown outside *in situ*, it is often safer and more rewarding to plant seeds in pots under cover, either in a cold frame, greenhouse, or on a sunny windowsill.

Tip for success

Always label your seeds using a waterproof pen. Include the name of the plant and the date of sowing.

1   Fill a clean or new 9cm (3½in) pot with a good-quality seed-sowing compost, leaving a 2–3cm (¾–1¼in) gap beneath the rim of the pot. Firm the compost gently to create an even surface for the seeds.

2   Using a watering can with a fine rose spray, dampen the compost, being careful not to disturb it by splashing too much. Alternatively, stand the pots in a tray of water until the surface is moist, then remove.

3   Sow the seed evenly. Large seeds are easy to position, but fine seeds should be spread from the palm of the hand. Some seeds need to be covered by a fine layer of compost or vermiculite; follow the instructions on the seed packet.

4   When the seeds have germinated and produced a few sets of leaves, harden them off by placing the pots outside during the day for a few weeks. Then you can plant them out in the garden.

Sun-baked gravel garden

In a sunny corner, a gravel garden offers the chance to grow an interesting range of plants: herbs with aromatic leaves, plants with silvery foliage, alpines, and some grasses are good choices. These plants enjoy growing through gravel because it keeps excessive moisture away from their stems, yet helps to keep the roots cool and moist. Gravel also warms up quickly during the day and retains warmth at night.

Border basics

Size 3x2m (10x6ft)

Suits Herbs, low-growing plants, annuals, bulbs, grey-leaved plants

Soil Well-drained, poor soils

Site Open and sunny, not too exposed

Shopping list

- 2 x *Parahebe perfoliata*
- 1 x *Helictotrichon sempervirens*
- 1 x *Thymus pulegioides* 'Bertram Anderson'
- 1 x *Santolina chamaecyparissus*
- 1 x *Aurinia saxatilis* 'Variegata'
- 1 x *Rosmarinus officinalis* Prostratus Group

Planting and aftercare

Dig over the site, removing large stones, rubbish, and weeds; spot-treat perennial weeds like bindweed, because they will be hard to remove once gravel is spread. Add organic matter, such as well-rotted garden compost, to the soil, and dig in plenty of gravel to at least a spade's depth to help provide good drainage.

Place any feature rocks or driftwood as focal points. Position plants with plenty of space between each one. Add grit to the planting holes and place plants slightly proud of the soil surface. As you spread the gravel, work some into the crowns of plants. Water well. Once settled, the plants will need watering only in the driest periods.

Parahebe perfoliata
❄❄ ◊ ☼ ♆

Helictotrichon sempervirens
❄❄❄ ◊ ☼ ♆

Thymus pulegioides 'Bertram Anderson' ❄❄❄ ◊ ☼ ♆

Santolina chamaecyparissus
❄❄ ◊ ☼ ♆

Aurinia saxatilis 'Variegata'
❄❄❄ ◊ ☼

Rosmarinus officinalis Prostratus Group ❄❄ ◊ ☼

Cottage garden medley

This ever-popular, typically English style of planting uses mainly herbaceous flowering plants in a relaxed, informal way. The flowers are usually pale pastel colours with a few brighter hues added as highlights. Traditional cottage garden favourites include delphiniums, foxgloves (*Digitalis*), verbascums, penstemons, as well as woody plants, such as roses and lavender (*Lavandula*). Although not low maintenance, such planting schemes are certainly beautiful in summer, when the plants all bloom together in profusion.

Border basics

Size 2x1.5m (6x5ft)

Suits A mixture of herbaceous perennials

Soil Well drained

Site Sunny with some shelter from wind

Shopping list

- 3 x *Delphinium grandiflorum* 'Summer Blues'
- 3 x *Verbascum* x *hybridum* 'Snow Maiden'
- 3 x *Delphinium* 'New Zealand Hybrids'
- 3 x *Geum* 'Blazing Sunset'
- 3 x *Penstemon digitalis* 'Husker Red'
- 3 x *Digitalis purpurea*

Planting and aftercare

Prepare the border before planting, adding well-rotted farmyard manure. Ensure drainage is good; if not, add some gravel. Planting in spring is best for perennials. Three of each plant will guarantee a decent show of flowers in the first year, and odd numbers of plants look best in informal plantings. Plant in small drifts, with taller plants positioned towards the back, but do not be too rigid about this – the effect should appear relaxed. The delphiniums, in particular, may need staking with canes or pea-sticks. In autumn after flowering or the following spring, cut down old foliage, and mulch with manure.

Delphinium grandiflorum 'Summer Blues' ✽✽✽ ⬤ ☼

Verbascum x *hybridum* 'Snow Maiden' ✽✽✽ ◇ ☼

Delphinium New Zealand Hybrids ✽✽✽ ⬤ ☼

Geum 'Blazing Sunset' ✽✽✽ ⬤ ◇ ☼

Penstemon digitalis 'Husker Red' ✽✽ ⬤ ◇ ☼

Foliage effects

Raised beds are easy to maintain and can be constructed almost anywhere. For a contemporary look, planting should be colourful and stylish, and provide year-round interest. Pick plants that complement each other in a range of colours and textures – here, much of the interest is provided by foliage.

Bed basics

Size 1x1m (3x3ft)

Suits A range of non-vigorous plants with similar requirements

Soil Moist but well drained

Site Sunny, and sheltered from strong, drying winds

Shopping list

- 1 x *Euphorbia amygdaloides* 'Purpurea'
- 1 x *Sedum spectabile*
- 1 x *Carex comans* 'Frosted Curls' or *Molinia caerulea* subsp. *caerulea* 'Variegata'
- 3 x *Ophiopogon planiscapus* 'Nigrescens'
- 1 x *Heuchera* 'Plum Pudding'

Planting and aftercare

Any raised bed must have adequate drainage holes; without them the plants will rot. A layer of crocks or polystyrene at the base will help water to run away freely. In a small bed, use a soil-based compost mixed with some organic matter, such as well-rotted manure; a large bed should be filled with good-quality topsoil with some well-rotted garden compost worked into it. Leave the bed for a few days to let the soil settle. Position shorter plants, such as the *Ophiopogon*, at the edges, and taller plants, like the *Euphorbia*, in the centre of the bed. Water well. Make sure that the compost never dries out, weed the bed regularly, and cut down any faded herbaceous growth, such as the *Sedum* flowerheads, in autumn or spring.

Euphorbia amygdaloides 'Purpurea'
❄❄❄ ◐ ☼

Sedum spectabile
❄❄❄ ◐ ☼ ♕

Carex comans 'Frosted Curls'
❄❄ ◐ ◇ ☼

Ophiopogon planiscapus 'Nigrescens'
❄❄❄ ◐ ◇ ☼ ♕

Heuchera 'Plum Pudding'
❄❄❄ ◐ ◇ ☼

Alternative plant idea

Molinia caerulea subsp. *caerulea* 'Variegata' ❄❄❄ ◐ ◇ ☼ ♕

Tree and shrub combination

Trees and shrubs can be used to create exciting combinations for beds and borders. They also tend to require less maintenance than herbaceous plants, and retain structure and sometimes foliage over winter. Include a range of growth habits and sizes, foliage colour and texture, plants with attractive flowers and others with winter interest, all of which will thrive in the given conditions.

Border basics

Size 3x2.5m (10x8ft)

Suits Wide range of shrubs and small trees; compact selections are best

Soil Acidic, free-draining, moisture-retentive soil

Site Sunny and sheltered

Shopping list

- 1 x *Aucuba japonica* 'Picturata'
- 1 x *Cotinus* 'Grace'
- 1 x *Phormium tenax* 'Atropurpureum'
- 1 x *Grevillea juniperina*
- 1 x *Magnolia grandiflora* 'Goliath'
- 1 x *Pittosporum tobira* 'Nanum'

Planting and aftercare

Dig the soil thoroughly, adding plenty of rotted garden compost. Space plants out well because they will be difficult to move when larger. The biggest plant is likely to be the magnolia, so put it at the back of the border. The evergreen gold-splashed foliage of the *Aucuba* is a focal point, so position the plant centrally. Its rounded form contrasts well with the spiky *Phormium*. The lower-growing *Pittosporum* and *Grevillea* (which needs acid soil) can be placed at the front. The *Cotinus* balances the composition, its purple leaves matching those of the *Phormium*. Make sure all are well watered and firmed in at planting. Some pruning, especially of the *Grevillea* and *Cotinus*, may be required later on, to stop them outgrowing their positions.

Aucuba japonica 'Picturata'
❋❋❋ ◐ ◌ ☼

Cotinus 'Grace'
❋❋❋ ◐ ◌ ☼

Phormium tenax 'Atropurpureum'
❋❋ ◐ ◌ ☼

Grevillea juniperina
❋❋ ◌ ☼

Magnolia grandiflora 'Goliath'
❋❋❋ ◐ ◌ ☼

Pittosporum tobira 'Nanum'
❋❋ ◌ ☼

Spring hot spot

Vibrant, fiery colours are not solely for late summer; there are various perennials and bulbs that provide similar hues in late spring, although the effect is different. The reds, oranges, and yellows of plants such as tulips, the first lupins, *Doronicum*, and *Euphorbia* can be combined with verdant new growth to create a glowing display.

These hot colour combinations contrast with the whites, blues, and cool yellows found in abundance elsewhere at this time, making a dazzling display.

Border basics

Size 2x2m (6x6ft)

Suits Early-flowering perennials, bulbs (especially tulips), perennials with attractive young foliage

Soil Any fertile and moist soil

Site Sheltered with some direct sun

Shopping list

- 20 x *Tulipa* 'Ballerina'
- 20 x tulips of contrasting shape
- 5 x *Polygonatum* x *hybridum*
- 5 x *Euphorbia griffithii* 'Fireglow'
- 5 x *Foeniculum vulgare* 'Purpureum' (just visible)

Planting and aftercare

Prepare the border by adding plenty of organic matter, such as garden compost, to the soil. Position the perennials first, with the tallest plant, Solomon's seal (*Polygonatum*), towards the back. Interplant the *Euphorbia* with the bronze fennel (*Foeniculum*), leaving reasonable spaces in between to allow planting pockets for the tulips. Plant the bulbs at three times their depth, in eight groups of five. Avoid mixing the tulip cultivars because this will dilute the effect.

The *Euphorbia*, in particular, will suffer if the soil becomes too dry. Watch out for sawfly larvae on the Solomon's seal.

Tulipa 'Ballerina'
❋❋❋ ◊ ◊ ☼ ♈

Polygonatum x hybridum
❋❋❋ ◊ ☼ ♈

Tulipa (pinky-red)
❋❋❋ ◊ ◊ ☼

Euphorbia griffithii 'Fireglow'
❋❋❋ ◊ ☼

Lush leaves for shade

In a shaded courtyard or corner of a terrace, a modern planting scheme in a raised bed can create a dramatic, rather exotic, effect. Many foliage plants grow well in some shade, and a mix of evergreen shrubs and herbaceous plants provides year-round interest. A tall bamboo (*Phyllostachys*) will catch the breeze, adding a dynamic element to the planting, while a few variegated plants, such as hostas, help lift the planting out of the shadows, as will painting the backdrop and raised walls a pale colour.

Border basics

Size 2.5x1.5m (8x5ft)

Suits Lush foliage plants

Soil Fertile and moisture-retentive

Site Sheltered, semi-shaded corner

Shopping list

- 2 x *Hosta* 'Francee'
- 1 x *Hebe salicifolia*
- 3 x *Fatsia japonica*
- 1 x *Phyllostachys nigra*
- 1 x *Miscanthus sinensis* 'Variegatus'
- 3 x *Ophiopogon planiscapus* 'Nigrescens'
- 2 x *Hedera helix* (ivies)

Planting and aftercare

Make sure the bed has enough drainage holes to prevent waterlogging. Choose a good quality topsoil and add well-rotted manure to it before planting. Position taller plants at the back (the bamboo will look best in the corner). The hostas, *Ophiopogon*, and ivies should go at the front. Contrast the hand-shaped foliage of the *Fatsia* with the white-edged blades of the *Miscanthus*. Spread white or grey pebbles as a mulch over the soil, and water the plants in well, ensuring they do not go short of water while establishing. Aftercare is easy: cut down old herbaceous growth in late autumn or spring, and watch out for slugs.

Hosta 'Francee'
❄❄❄ ◐ ○ ☼ ♔

Hebe salicifolia
❄❄ ◐ ○ ☼

Fatsia japonica
❄❄ ◐ ○ ☼ ☼ ♔

Phyllostachys nigra
❄❄❄ ◐ ○ ☼ ☼ ♔

Miscanthus sinensis 'Variegatus'
❄❄❄ ◐ ○ ☼ ♔

Ophiopogon planiscapus 'Nigrescens'
❄❄❄ ◐ ○ ☼ ♔

Formal front garden

Small front gardens lend themselves to formal planting. Traditionally, these designs feature a low perimeter wall of clipped box (*Buxus*) hedges in a simple shape, such as a square, filled with a mixture of brightly coloured foliage and flowering plants, some tender, others perennials. There is often a central "dot plant," such as a *Cordyline*, to serve as a focal point. Any bare soil is then mulched with a layer of gravel. This helps to reduce weeding and keeps the garden looking smart.

Border basics

Size 1.5x1.5m (5x5 ft)

Suits Box hedges, bright tender perennials, colourful hardy plants

Soil Ideally, fertile, well drained, and not too dry

Site Small, formal situation, preferably with some sun

Shopping list

- 5 x *Pelargonium* (red)
- 3 x *Deschampsia flexuosa* 'Tatra Gold'
- 2 x *Phormium* 'Tom Thumb'
- 1 x *Penstemon digitalis* 'Husker Red'
- *Buxus sempervirens* (enough to make a border)
- 3 x *Spiraea japonica* 'White Gold'

Planting and aftercare

Dig over the site, removing any weeds, and add well-rotted organic matter, such as manure. Firm and level the soil with a rake. Plant the box plants first, about 15–20 cm (6–8 in) apart, to form the framework of your design. Then arrange the remaining plants in bands of colour. The border will need regular upkeep to keep it looking immaculate. Deadhead the pelargonium throughout the season; in early summer, trim the box and, if required, the spiraea. In spring, replace the tender pelargoniums and reduce the flowering stems of the penstemons.

Pelargonium (red)
❀ ◐ ◊ ☼

Deschampsia flexuosa 'Tatra Gold'
❆❆❆ ◐ ☼

Phormium 'Tom Thumb'
❆❆ ◐ ◊ ☼

Penstemon digitalis 'Husker Red'
❆❆ ◐ ◊ ☼

Buxus sempervirens
❆❆❆ ◐ ◊ ☼ ☼

Spiraea japonica 'White Gold'
❆❆❆ ◐ ◊ ☼

Mediterranean moods

Choose the sunniest spot in the garden, away from cold winds, and select plants reminiscent of Mediterranean holidays: irises, grasses, euphorbias, and evergreen shrubs, such as olearia. Add herbs, like rosemary or sage, and bright-flowered bulbs, such as alliums. Terracotta pots planted with more tender species, such as succulent agaves, will help reinforce the Mediterranean feel.

Border basics

Size 3x3m (10x10ft)

Suits Grasses, neat evergreen shrubs, irises, bulbs, herbs, succulents, semi-tender plants

Soil Any free-draining

Site Sunny and sheltered, ideally by a wall

Shopping list

- 3 x *Iris* 'Jane Phillips'
- 1 x *Olearia* x *haastii*
- 3 x *Euphorbia characias* subsp. *wulfenii*
- 5 x *Allium hollandicum* 'Purple Sensation'
- 1 x *Anemanthele lessoniana* (*Stipa arundinacea*)
- 1 x *Bergenia cordifolia*
- 2 x *Ballota pseudodictamnus*

Planting and aftercare

Dig over the soil, removing any stones and weeds, and add plenty of organic matter, such as manure. If the site is not well drained, dig in gravel. Set taller plants at the back of the border, at least 30cm (12in) from the base of the wall. Plant shrubs and perennials first; bulbs are best planted in drifts around the key plants later. The iris rhizomes should be near the soil surface, so that they are partially exposed. Mulch with gravel and water well.

Remove the flowering stems of irises after the blooms have faded. In spring, cut out the previous year's flowering stems of euphorbias as close to the base as possible, avoiding the toxic sap.

Iris 'Jane Phillips'
❋❋❋ ◊ ☼ ♔

Olearia x *haastii*
❋❋❋ ◊ ☼

horbia characias subsp. *wulfenii*
❋ ◊ ☼ ♈

Allium hollandicum 'Purple
Sensation' ❋❋❋ ◊ ☼ ♈

Anemanthele lessoniana
❋❋ ◊ ☼

Mixed herb tapestry

Well-planted herb borders should delight the senses: not only are they attractive to look at, but the aroma of foliage and flowers provides an extra element of interest, and some herbs can also be used to flavour food. Many have variegated or silver leaves, so they are still attractive when out of flower. Try also to include some evergreen herbs, such as lavender (*Lavandula*) or rosemary (*Rosmarinus*).

Border basics

Size 2x2m (6x6ft)

Suits Culinary herbs, such as thyme, oregano, marjoram, sage, chives, rosemary, and also those with more medicinal properties, such as lavender and feverfew

Soil Any well-drained, fairly poor soil

Site An open site in sun, but not too exposed to cold

Shopping list

- 10 x *Origanum vulgare* 'Polyphant'
- 5 x *Lavandula angustifolia* 'Twickel Purple' or *Salvia officinalis* 'Icterina'
- 10 x *Thymus doerfleri* 'Doone Valley'
- 10 x *Thymus x citriodorus*
- 10 x *Origanum vulgare* 'Aureum'

Planting and aftercare

Try adopting a formal pattern with the plants, as in the style of a simple knot garden. The plants can be positioned in rows or bands, where they will knit together well. The lavender is the tallest plant and should go at the back, or in the centre if the bed is circular; the variegated sage *Salvia officinalis* 'Icterina' could be used as a culinary alternative. Next, plant contrasting bands of the smaller herbs.

A gravel mulch placed over the soil after planting helps to suppress weeds and keeps winter wet away from the crowns of the plants.

Origanum vulgare 'Polyphant'
❋❋❋ ◊ ☼

Lavandula angustifolia 'Twickel Purple' ❋❋❋ ◊ ☼

Thymus doerfleri 'Doone Valley'
❋❋❋ ◊ ☼

Thymus x citriodorus
❋❋❋ ◊ ☼

Origanum vulgare 'Aureum'
❋❋❋ ◊ ☼ ♈

Alternative plant idea

Salvia officinalis 'Icterina'
❋❋ ◊ ☼ ♈

Autumn elegance

A border designed for a fine autumn scheme can make a great addition to the garden. After the dazzling displays of summer, this is a forgotten season in many gardens, and yet there are many plants that are at their best at this time. Certain grasses and various other late performing perennials, such as *Sedum*, *Aster*, *Salvia*, *Kniphofia*, and *Verbena*, can be combined with the seedheads of plants that flowered in summer, perhaps set against the vivid autumnal hues of deciduous shrubs and trees.

Border basics

Size 3x3m (10x10ft)

Suits Late-flowering perennials, grasses, and plants with ornamental seedheads or berries

Soil Any well-drained, fertile soil

Site An open site in sun, not too exposed

Shopping list

- 3 x *Stipa gigantea*
- 7 x *Verbena bonariensis*
- 7 x *Sedum* 'Herbstfreude'
- 5 x *Calamagrostis brachytricha*
- 3 x *Perovskia* 'Blue Spire'

Planting and aftercare

For this scheme, it is better to plant in sweeps rather than groups for a more flowing effect. The *Stipa* is the tallest plant, so place towards the back. In front, plant the dainty *Perovskia* and upright *Calamagrostis*. This grass flowers earlier in the season, but in autumn the seedheads are an attractive rich brown. Allow the grass to mingle with the *Sedum*, best planted towards the front in a broad sweep, providing contrast and intense colour. Dot the slender *Verbena* throughout because its transparent form provides no visual barrier.

Retain the seedheads of these plants for as long as possible, cutting down in spring before new growth begins.

Stipa gigantea
❄❄❄ ◊ ◌ ☼ ♆

Verbena bonariensis
❄❄ ◊ ☼ ♆

Sedum 'Herbstfreude'
❄❄❄ ◊ ☼ ♆

Calamagrostis brachytricha
❄❄❄ ◊ ◌ ☼

Winter blaze

Although winter is the season of snow and ice, there is still plenty to see in the garden if you include plants that provide seemingly unseasonal colour. The stems of some deciduous shrubs, such as *Cornus* and *Salix*, are brightly hued, and the foliage of many conifers intensifies in colour as low temperatures bite. A few plants produce showy flowers during this season, in particular winter heathers (*Erica*), but also bulbs such as snowdrops (*Galanthus*) and winter aconites (*Aconitum*).

Border basics

Size 3x3m (10x10ft)

Suits A range of winter interest plants

Soil Reasonably well drained and not too dry

Site Somewhere open that catches the winter sun

Shopping list

- 1 x *Chamaecyparis lawsoniana* 'Elwoodii'
- 9 x *Erica* x *darleyensis* 'Archie Graham'
- 5 x *Cornus sanguinea* 'Winter Beauty'
- 1 x *Pinus sylvestris* Aurea Group
- 7 x white *Erica carnea*

Planting and aftercare

Position the *Chamaecyparis* towards the back of the border – it will serve as a fine foil for the brighter colours. The golden pine (*Pinus*) should also be towards the back, in front of the *Chamaecyparis*. Plant the *Cornus* in a drift, mostly in the middle of the border, edging towards the front. Underplant with the heathers, creating seams of colour. Do not intermingle the colours.

The best stem colour from the *Cornus* is found on young growth, so after a couple of years, cut out one-third of old stems from each plant annually in spring. Trim the winter heathers with shears after they have flowered.

Chamaecyparis lawsoniana 'Elwoodii' ❄❄❄ ◐ ◊ ☼ ♈

Erica x darleyensis 'Archie Graham' ❄❄❄ ◐ ◊ ☼

Cornus sanguinea 'Winter Beauty' ❄❄❄ ◐ ☼

Pinus sylvestris Aurea Group ❄❄❄ ◐ ◊ ☼ ♈

Choosing a container

When selecting pots and containers from the wide range available at garden centres, there are some key factors to take into account before you buy. As well as choosing a style, shape, and colour that suits your garden design, also consider the material from which the container is made, since each has its pros and cons.

Clay pots

Clay pots may be glazed or unglazed, coloured or patterned, light or dark in colour. Orange terracotta brings a taste of the Mediterranean to the garden.

Advantages They are attractive to look at, and can make a long-lasting addition to the garden, often improving with age and wear. There is a clay pot for most situations, and they can represent good value for money.

Disadvantages Many clay pots are not fully frost-proof and are prone to winter damage. They are also best avoided in exposed sites because they are easily broken. Fired clay is a porous material, so plants can dry out quickly, especially in summer, and moving these containers can be hard work since they are often heavy.

Metal containers

Containers made of metal may seem like a contemporary idea, but in fact some of the most desirable antique pots are lead, and suitable for a range of situations. Modern metal containers tend to be made of steel or galvanized aluminium and are simply styled, unlike lead planters, which feature more elaborate, classical designs.

Advantages By nature, metal containers are long-lasting, and can be heavy (especially lead ones), which makes them good for open sites. They can also be very stylish.

Disadvantages Metal containers can be expensive, particularly those made of lead; these are also exceptionally heavy. They also usually look out of place in an informal garden and may not suit some plants.

Wooden containers

Wood is a good material for a planter; it is soft and easily shaped, weathers well if treated with preservative, and suits a range of situations. It is also hard wearing and can tolerate rough treatment.

Advantages Although fairly lightweight and therefore easily moved, wooden containers are strong and durable. They are also most attractive and a good choice for situations where large planters are required.

Disadvantages Good-quality wooden containers can be quite expensive, especially those suited to more formal sites. They also need regular treatment with preservative to keep them looking good. Ensure they are made from sustainably harvested timber.

Stone containers

Pots and containers made of stone make beautiful ornamental planters. Granite containers can be used to give a Japanese feel, while old stone sinks suit alpines and other small plants.

Advantages Stone containers are very heavy, so not easily stolen or blown over, and long-lasting. Stone also looks good and gives a feel of permanency, especially once it has become colonized with mosses and lichens.

Disadvantages Genuine stone containers are very expensive, antique ones especially so, and you may feel that a concrete alternative is better value. The weight of stone must also be considered when transporting the pot and manoeuvring it into place in the garden.

Synthetic pots

Plastic has long been used as a material for pots and it may be disguised to look like clay, wood, or stone, although not always very convincingly. Increasingly, resins and other new materials are being used instead of plastic.

Advantages Synthetic pots are generally lightweight and easy to handle and transport. They tend to be tougher and more durable (and frost-resistant) than clay, and are far cheaper than stone or lead alternatives.

Disadvantages Synthetic pots lack the charm of traditional materials: an authentic stone, lead, or even clay planter feels more characterful than one made of plastic. Synthetic pots do not age well and may have a short life span. Being light, they are easily blown over.

Plant up a colourful container

One of the simplest ways of injecting seasonal interest into your garden is to plant up a few pots. Follow these easy guidelines to help ensure that your displays are attractive and long-lasting.

1 Before you plant the container, add water-retaining crystals to the compost. These swell up once moist, and provide plants with an extra reservoir of water, which helps to ensure plants do not suffer during dry spells.

2 Arrange your selected plants in their original pots in the container to see how they look – this way, adjustments can be easily made. When you are satisfied, remove the plants from their pots and plant up the container.

3 Fill around the plants with compost when they are in their final positions, and ensure you leave a 5cm (2in) gap between the top of the soil and the rim of the container, to allow for easy watering and a gravel mulch.

4 Spread a 2cm (¾in) deep gravel mulch over the top of the compost to help to conserve moisture in summer, deter weeds, and prevent unsightly compost splash when watering. It also makes an attractive finish to the planting.

Spring selection

Few plants are a more welcome sight than spring-flowering bulbs, and most are easy to grow and care for. These versatile plants are wonderful for pots and windowboxes or for planting out in the garden, and they can be treated as permanent planting or simply discarded after flowering. A good selection should provide colour over a long period, from the first snowdrops in late winter to the last tulips in early summer. Try planting the same types of bulbs together in pots and grouping them, or mix them.

Container basics

Size Approx. 15cm (6in) diameter terracotta pots

Suits Potted flowering bulbs

Soil Free-draining

Site Sunny, not too exposed

Shopping list

- 6 x *Hyacinthus orientalis* 'Ostara'
- 12 x *Narcissus* 'Sweetness'
- 10 x *Iris winogradowii*
- 12 x *Iris reticulata*
- 6 x *Iris* 'Katharine Hodgkin' or *Muscari armeniacum*

Planting and aftercare

Many spring bulbs are bought as bare dry bulbs in autumn, before they have come into active growth. It is important to choose firm, healthy bulbs and to plant them as soon as possible. Observe the correct planting depth for each kind of bulb, using free-draining multi-purpose compost with plenty of crocks in the base of each pot. Keep the pots somewhere sheltered. As the bulbs begin to grow, water more freely.

Once the flowers have faded, either discard the bulbs or allow the foliage to yellow and wither. Bulbs may then be lifted, dried, and replanted in pots, or put in the garden in autumn.

Hyacinthus orientalis 'Ostara'
❄❄❄ ◊◊ ☼ ♗

Narcissus 'Sweetness'
❄❄❄ ◊◊ ☼ ♗

Iris winogradowii
❄❄❄ ◊◊ ☼ ♗

Iris reticulata
❄❄❄ ◊◊ ☼ ♗

Iris 'Katharine Hodgkin'
❄❄❄ ◊◊ ☼ ♗

Alternative plant

Muscari armeniacum
❄❄❄ ◊◊ ☼ ♗

Sizzling tropics

A themed planting of subtropical species in a large pot will look dramatic and exotic until the first frosts. Choose a mix of bold foliage and flowers, and try to use a limited palette of "hot colours" to tie in with the terracotta pot. Arrange the larger plants towards the centre and back. The scheme will look most effective against a neutral background, where the textures and colours of the plants can be more easily appreciated.

Container basics

Size Approx. 60x60cm (24x24in) square terracotta pot or a similar-sized round one

Suits Subtropical plants with bold flowers and foliage

Compost Good-quality, multi-purpose

Site A sheltered, sunny position

Shopping list

- 1 x *Canna* 'Musifolia'
- 3 x *Begonia fuchsioides*
- 3 x *Crocosmia* x *crocosmiiflora* 'Star of the East'
- 1 x *Pelargonium tomentosum*
- 1 x *Isoplexis canariensis*
- 2 x *Canna* (orange hybrid)

Planting and aftercare

Arrange the plants carefully in their pots before planting them to see how they will look in their final positions. The scented foliage of the pelargonium is best used spilling over the pot's edge. Place plenty of crocks in the base of the container before pouring in the compost. After planting, water well and keep in a glasshouse or cool, light area indoors before placing the pot outside once any danger of frost has passed. Feed the plants regularly during the summer and make sure the compost is kept moist. Deadhead the canna as the blooms fade to encourage further flowers. In autumn, before the first frosts, bring the pot under cover.

Canna 'Musifolia'

Begonia fuchsioides

Crocosmia x *crocosmiiflora*

Pelargonium tomentosum

Isoplexis canariensis

Canna (orange hybrid)

Colour clash

For a dramatic and eye-catching container display, well-considered colour clashes can produce the best results, although the careful use of texture and form is even more important in such schemes. Here, yellow variegated foliage contrasts harmoniously with the dark glazed pot, while the rich red mini petunias (*Calibrachoa*) clash. Touches of red in the linear foliage of the grass *Hakonechloa*, though, help to tie the planting together. The gently arching growth of the grass is complemented by the trailing periwinkle (*Vinca*), which mingles well with the petunias that spill over the sides of the pot.

Container basics

Size Approx. 40cm (16in) diameter glazed pot

Suits A mix of bedding plants and garden perennials

Compost Good-quality, multi-purpose

Site A sheltered, sunny position

Shopping list

- 2 x *Hakonechloa macra* 'Aureola'
- 4 x *Calibrachoa* Million Bells Cherry
- 4 x *Calibrachoa* Million Bells Red
- 4 x *Vinca minor* 'Illumination'

Planting and aftercare

Place a good layer of crocks in the base of the pot for drainage, and add the compost. Position the grass centrally and then plant the *Vinca* and mini petunias around the outside. The petunias are frost-tender but they will flower for a long season in a sunny position, provided they are kept well fed and watered. In a more shaded spot, the petunias can be substituted by a red busy Lizzie (*Impatiens*) or a bedding begonia. After the frosts have browned the bedding, surviving plants can be planted out in the garden, or kept in the pot and used again the following year.

Hakonechloa macra 'Aureola'
❋❋❋ ◊ ☼ ☼ ☀ ☆

Calibrachoa Million Bells Cherry
✿ ◊ ☼

Calibrachoa Million Bells Red
✿ ◊ ☼

Vinca minor 'Illumination'
❋❋❋ ◊ ◊ ☼ ☼ ☀

Fire and ice

A striking combination of silvery-blue foliage and flame-red flowers gives this autumn interest container great appeal. The flower-power is provided by bedding cyclamen, which often prove surprisingly hardy in a sheltered situation, and should flower well from autumn until the first really hard frosts. White crocuses could continue the show in spring. Bright silver *Senecio*, tufts of the blue grass *Festuca glauca*, and an upright juniper complete the display. A matching pair of these planted pots would look particularly striking on either side of a doorway.

Container basics

Size Approx. 40cm (16in) diameter terracotta pot

Suits Evergreens and winter bedding plants

Compost Good-quality multi-purpose

Site A sheltered spot in semi-shade

Shopping list

- 1 x *Juniperus chinensis* 'Stricta'
- 2 x *Festuca glauca* 'Elijah Blue'
- 5 x *Senecio cineraria*
- 3 x *Cyclamen hederifolium*

Planting and aftercare

Place a layer of crocks in the pot and three-quarters fill with compost. Plant the juniper centrally towards the back of the pot and use the grasses to help soften the edges. The cyclamen and *Senecio* can be mingled at the front. (If you are including crocuses, plant them now; they will appear in spring, replacing any cyclamen killed by sustained hard frost.) Top up the pot with compost, water well, and place in a sheltered spot in good light. Keep the compost moist but not wet, and deadhead the cyclamen flowers as they fade to prolong the display. In late spring, the hardy plants can be planted out in the garden, or transferred to a larger container.

Juniperus chinensis 'Stricta'
❋❋❋ ◗ ◌ ☼ ☽

Senecio cineraria
❋ ◗ ◌ ☼ ♔

Cyclamen hederifolium
❋ ◌ ◗ ☼ ♔

Festuca glauca 'Elijah Blue'
❋❋❋ ◗ ◌ ☼ ☽

Winter perfume

This attractive display provides colourful winter cheer and a delicious spicy scent, which comes from the *Sarcococca confusa*, a neat evergreen shrub with little white blooms. While not particularly showy, they scent the air for several weeks. Flower and foliage colour is provided by winter pansies (*Viola*), a variegated standard *Euonymus*, and ivy (*Hedera*) to soften the rim of the barrel. You could also add primroses (*Primula vulgaris*), which flower into spring.

Container basics

Size Approx. 60cm (24in) diameter wooden half-barrel

Suits Winter bedding and evergreen shrubs

Compost Multi-purpose with added John Innes compost

Site A sunny, sheltered spot by a doorway

Shopping list

- 5 x *Hedera helix* 'Glacier'
- 5 x yellow winter pansies
- 5 x pale yellow winter pansies or 3 x double yellow primroses
- 3 x *Sarcococca confusa*
- 1 x *Euonymus fortunei* Blondy (standard-trained)

Planting and aftercare

Place crocks at the bottom of the barrel and three-quarters fill with compost. Arrange the plants with the *Euonymus* in the middle, underplanted with the *Sarcococca*, the ivies over the edges of the barrel, and the pansies and primroses in between. Fill in around the plants with compost. Water well and keep moist. Position the container where the perfume of the *Sarcococca* will be enjoyed. Remove faded blooms as the season progresses, and any plain green shoots on the *Euonymus*. In summer, replace the bedding with summer flowers, such as busy Lizzies or begonias.

Hedera helix 'Glacier'
❄❄❄ ◑ ◊ ☀ ♈

Yellow winter pansies
❄❄❄ ◑ ◊ ☀

Pale yellow winter pansies
❄❄❄ ◑ ◊ ☀

Sarcococca confusa
❄❄❄ ◑ ◊ ☀ ◑ ♈

Euonymus fortunei Blondy
❄❄❄ ◑ ◊ ☀ ◑ ♈

Alternative plant idea

Primula vulgaris 'Double Sulphur'
❄❄❄ ◑ ◑

Design ideas for easy-care gardens

There are a great many reasons why you may want to make your garden easier and less time-consuming to maintain.

Happily, there are numerous strategies and solutions that can be employed without sacrificing aesthetics.

Pictures clockwise from left

Outdoor gallery The planting of a garden can be quite sparse if each specimen is chosen and sited with care, rather like an arrangement of sculptures. With a simple, uncluttered backdrop, this approach creates an opportunity to really appreciate the form and texture of the plants in your collection. Gravel laid over a weed-suppressing membrane provides a foil for the plants, and to keep the design interesting, aggregates can be enlivened with decorative paving, or cobbles and boulders. In this garden, large rocks anchor the planting and treated timbers, laid like stepping-stones, direct the eye to a circular mosaic feature with a striking contemporary container providing a focus in the centre. Alternatively, you could use a self-contained water feature, such as a bubbling millstone.

Dining room Decking brings a room-like quality and can be used to create a stylish outdoor dining area. This is especially valuable where space indoors is at a premium, for example in a ground-floor flat or small house. To create a visually exciting design that requires very little upkeep, make sure the backdrop and planting around the deck are as simple as possible. A few bold colour highlights and night-time illumination will add designer sparkle.

Simple division Larger gardens designed for minimum maintenance are often best divided into a series of compartments. These can be partially screened from one another, or left open to enjoy the sense of space. To give each section its own character, and to add interest, try using contrasting landscape materials – on flat surfaces you can introduce changes in level, such as a raised deck or beds, or a sunken seating area. With a limited planting palette, it is important to be creative with flooring detail, and to include plenty of evergreens, such as the grasses (*Stipa tenuissima*) and sedges (*Carex*) used here.

Design ideas for easy-care gardens *continued*

Pictures clockwise from top left

Paved patio Small, enclosed spaces are perfect for paving – a low-maintenance, relatively weed-free alternative to grass. By planting in raised beds, narrow borders and pots, you can maintain a range of plants that would satisfy even the keenest gardener. Spend time designing your garden, building in practical requirements as well as incorporating different textures and patterns to create interest. Here, cobbles and a ceramic water feature provide a focus, with hostas and bamboo adding an oriental note.

Mediterranean garden This swirling rendered wall, painted a dusty terracotta, suggests a garden built in a sunny climate. Slender Italian cypress, an old oil jar, and ironwork furniture strengthen the Mediterranean flavour. The wall is the right height to act as impromptu seating and, adding to the ambience, the air is filled with perfume from the white lilies, pink roses and aromatic herbs.

Space for children Although children enjoy playing on lawns, other surfaces are more versatile. Little ones will enjoy a sandpit (covered when not in use), and varying the flooring materials and incorporating changes in level create opportunities for play. A splinter-free deck suits bare feet and the level surface is ideal for a variety of toys and activities. Choose robust plants, such as the phormium, grasses and bamboos in this child-friendly garden.

Raised beds As well as providing easy-reach planting spaces, raised beds are design features in their own right. They also offer casual seating and welcome changes in level in otherwise flat, featureless spaces. This bed, with its curved dry-stone walling effect, provides ideal, sharply-drained conditions for a wide range of hardy alpines.

Formal design

An ordered or symmetrical garden, with a combination of simple geometric shapes, inspires a feeling of calm. The style is adaptable, and it is easy to create stunning vistas and dramatic focal points.

Pictures clockwise from top left

Creating a focus The elements of this charming little garden are simple and unfussy yet, because of the strong central axis guiding the eye down the narrow pathway, the effect is quite theatrical. Tall *Verbena bonariensis* are neatly enclosed by clipped, dwarf box hedging, which, being evergreen, provides a strong architectural framework, even in the depths of winter. A traditional brick path opens out into a circular paving feature with a large Greek pot at its centre, but this could be replaced by a pebble mosaic or an eye-catching piece of sculpture.

Elegant dining Although most often associated with grand period properties, a formal touch, utilizing symmetry, works in a variety of situations and can make a previously ordinary space look stunning. Here, French windows open out onto a raised deck used for dining. Elevated views of the garden are framed by tall, stylish containers filled with lavender, and a grapevine-covered pergola. The formality continues with matching steps, clipped box edging and twin potted marguerites.

Contemporary twist There's no reason why you can't take elements of Renaissance period gardens and use them to add style to a contemporary space. Here tall perennials (*Miscanthus* and *Rudbeckia*) are contained by low evergreen hedging – just like a modern-day parterre – and clipped topiary in matching terracotta pots makes a smart statement. A rill or narrow canal set into the deck would also work well.

Mirror image This study in symmetry and minimalism has created a garden that is extremely easy to maintain. Simply planted, the design succeeds by clever stage setting. The onlooker's eye is drawn to the water curtain sculpture by a line of cube-shaped box topiaries running along the central axis. Meanwhile, the two formal white containers, matching raised beds planted with bamboo, and the arching tree branches frame the view perfectly. Keep the surfaces immaculate to avoid visual distractions.

Contemporary creations

Modern minimalism has much to offer busy garden owners. Simple layouts, easily maintained hard landscaping, and colour and interest that don't rely solely on planting are useful elements often exploited by contemporary designers.

Pictures clockwise from far left

Colour impact Use bold shades, like purple or red, to enhance contemporary designs and create exciting backdrops. Here, architectural foliage plants, including phormium and eucalyptus, are all the more striking against the painted fence. A rendered wall could also act as a modern minimalist canvas, if painted with masonry paint.

Sculptural focus The gleaming white spiral of this art installation stands out dramatically against the dark uncluttered backdrop and restrained planting scheme. Alternative sculptural elements, such as a large container or fountain, could be used to create a focal point strong enough to carry the simple design.

Restrained planting While gardens often rely on colourful flowers and foliage for interest, you can still create an attractive outdoor space using a limited planting palette. This ground plan is well defined, and strengthened by innovative flooring and dividing walls. Only a few of the rectangular compartments contain plants – many are filled with water and bridged by decking walkways.

Novel materials You can achieve contemporary effects using a variety of hi-tech materials. Consider perspex panels, or polished and galvanized metal sheeting for facing walls and edging beds, and metal grids for flooring. Here, corrugated metal contains a grass-filled border.

Simple composition Taking inspiration from Zen gardens, this simple but effective scheme, with a background of white stone chippings and black trellis, features a single phormium surrounded by carefully selected rocks and a black glazed sphere.

Havens for wildlife

Low-maintenance gardens can be surprisingly wildlife friendly. Many easy-care plants attract bees and butterflies, and shrubs and trees with ornamental fruits offer a feast for birds.

Pictures clockwise from top left

Watering hole Providing a safe vantage point to drink and bathe, a birdbath can become a hive of activity for birds; site conveniently, as you'll need to top it up regularly. To avoid problems with cats, plant around the base with low ground cover. Here blue fescues (*Festuca*), houseleeks (*Sempervivum*) and sedums are used. A shallow-sided pebble pool would also attract amphibians and dragonflies.

Carefree meadow One way to reduce the need for regular mowing in a large garden, whilst increasing wildlife potential, is by converting sections of formal lawn into wildflower meadows. On poor, sandy soils you can establish a meadow using wildflower plugs and bulbs suitable for naturalizing. More reliable results are achieved by removing turf with a turf-cutting machine and then re-sowing with a perennial wildflower mix.

Insect attractors Beneficial hoverflies seek out single-flowered, hardy summer annuals, such as *Eschscholzia* and *Limnanthes*, and bees love blue flowers like this Californian bluebell (*Phacelia campanularia*). *Verbena bonariensis* and *Buddleja davidii* are magnets for bees and butterflies. For the first insects of the season, plant sunny gravel or raised beds with spring alpines – alyssum, arabis, aubrietia, heathers, grape hyacinth (*Muscari*) and crocus.

Bird cover Large evergreen and deciduous shrubs, dense hedges, and trees are vital for birds. They not only need safe nesting and night-time roosting sites, but also places to shelter during bad weather and to escape air-borne predators. Without cover nearby, birds are nervous about entering a garden, even one with feeders.

Berry banquet Provide a wide range of fruiting and berrying plants, with some ripening in late summer and others ready for harvest well into winter. This long-lasting buffet will cater for local birds as well as visiting migrants. Low ground-cover plants such as *Cotoneaster salicifolius* 'Gnom' (*illustrated*), wall shrubs like pyracantha, roses with large colourful hips, and small ornamental trees, such as rowans (*Sorbus*) and crab apples (*Malus*), are ideal.

Courtyard gardens

Textures and colours are viewed close up in these intimate spaces, so choose materials and plants for maximum effect. Also include some shade and water, as well as lighting for evenings outside.

Pictures clockwise from top left

Big, bold pots Some outdoor spaces are completely paved, but you can grow almost any plant in a container – provided it is big enough – including small trees, elegant bamboos and grasses, a wide range of shrubs and climbers, as well as perennials, bulbs, and ferns. This pot contains *Nandina domestica*, purple cordyline, heuchera, and trailing ivy. Evergreens help the garden to look good all year round, and courtyards often have a sheltered microclimate, allowing more tender species to be grown. Install automatic irrigation to make light work of watering.

Tranquil oasis This striking, contemporary walled garden has a Moorish feel. The lush planting, inspired by a rich purple and cerise colour palette, features a glowing *Cercis canadensis* 'Forest Pansy' in the corner, and a large formal pool with "floating" stepping-stones. The pergola-covered, paved terrace juts out over the surface, taking you right to the water's edge.

Hot property Courtyards can feel gloomy if surrounded by high walls, but you can lift the atmosphere and create more light by applying colour (on taller walls just paint to a line above the ground floor windows). Here, a vibrant orange has been used on a curved wall, contrasting with beds of Mediterranean herbs, perennials and grasses. Where shade is a problem, whitewashed walls may appear to be the answer, but these need frequent touching up and white can seem harsh in a cool climate; instead, try light pink, pale green, a watery blue, or pearly grey. Also consider wall-mounted mirrors or reflective metal panels, murals and *trompe l'oeil* (illusory 3D effects) or, for a period look, decorative trellis panels.

Garden café Courtyards can be transformed into an extra room for your house or flat, and an *al fresco* dining room or outdoor kitchen can be used in fine weather at any time of year. Raise or sink the dining area to give it definition, and construct screens with giant pots or raised beds filled with architectural evergreens, like the cordyline and clipped box balls in this stylish garden.

New-wave planting

This impressionistic style of gardening, sometimes known as prairie planting, uses harmonious combinations of herbaceous perennials and ornamental grasses to create naturalistic and long-lasting displays.

Pictures clockwise from top left

Planting philosophy Choose easy-care perennials that don't need deadheading, staking, or frequent division. Plants that have everlasting flowers or sculptural seedheads in autumn and winter are particularly useful; most grasses, even deciduous types, retain foliage and diaphanous seedheads through winter. For the prairie look, plant swathes of single cultivars and punctuate with isolated clusters. Soften the effect of heavier flower and foliage forms by using airy flower stems and billowing grasses, and vary the height of plants to create interesting undulations. Here, crimson astrantia rise above a ribbon of erigeron interspersed by tussocks of *Stipa tenuissima*.

Stylized nature Planted *en masse*, colour-restricted displays of flowering perennials and grasses produce a stylized, contemporary version of a meadow. Here raised beds lift the planting to create a feeling of enclosure around this outdoor dining area. An elegant mixture of tall miscanthus grasses and *Verbena bonariensis* opens up to reveal blocks of lavender on the opposite side.

Lingering effects From midsummer onwards, *Rudbeckia fulgida*, as well as plants like the heleniums and achilleas seen growing here, put on a long-lasting show. Interspersed with hardy grasses – such as calamagrostis, miscanthus, panicum and stipa – they knit together seamlessly, covering the ground and preventing weed growth. Many of the grasses also flower in late summer, adding to the display, and the foliage fades to biscuit or develops red and purple hues as autumn approaches. It is only necessary to cut back hard when growth begins again in spring.

Grassy retreat The planting in this gravel garden is relaxed and informal – the seating area is completely cocooned by billowing grasses, and narrow pathways wind lazily through the subtle planting. Although there are few coloured blooms, this garden will change throughout the year and will look magical with a dusting of frost.

Benefits of a low-maintenance garden

With adjustments to your existing plot, or strategic planning when building from scratch, you can enjoy a beautiful garden even if you have little time or energy to look after it. Most high-maintenance plants and schemes have low-maintenance alternatives, and many routine jobs can be omitted altogether.

Who needs a low-maintenance garden?

We simply do not have as much time as we used to, and yet the garden is increasingly seen as a sanctuary and an antidote to modern living. Whether you are pursuing a career, working odd shifts, spending hours commuting, or looking after a young family, you will need to find a way to manage your garden more easily.

New gardeners may lack confidence in their abilities and want to start simply, and some homeowners are not particularly interested in the practical side of gardening, yet still appreciate and desire an attractive outdoor space. Older gardeners may find they no longer have the physical strength and energy to cultivate in the way they used to or, adopting a more carefree lifestyle, might be too busy travelling to garden regularly! And, if you are one of the increasing number of buy-to-let landlords, you may only be able to visit your properties a few times a year.

Creative design and planting will ensure that ultra easy-care gardens like this urban plot are attractive, practical, and never boring.

With easy-care gardening strategies in place, you can cut down on regular or seasonal chores like raking leaves and lawn maintenance.

How much time do you have?

When designing your garden, first think about how often you will have time to maintain it.

Weekends If you have a few hours at the weekend, you may only have time to mow the lawn, do a little deadheading and tidying, and perhaps some hand-weeding, hoeing or hedge-trimming. Drought-tolerant shrubs and flowers in pots will tolerate weekly watering.

Once a month Lawns are not a good idea if you can only tackle gardening tasks once a month. Instead, replace them with paving, decking, or gravel. Reduce deadheading and pruning with a selection of easy-care plants, and install an automatic watering system.

A few times a year Gardening only once in a while restricts your options, so choose a combination of low-maintenance plants and hard landscaping. You can then limit jobs to tidying borders, cutting back old growth on perennials in late winter, and occasionally pruning overgrown trees and shrubs

Time-saving tips

Watering Select drought-tolerant specimens, and plant in autumn or spring to cut down the need to water whilst the roots are establishing. Fit pots with automatic irrigation.

Feeding Mulch with manure in late winter to keep the soil fertile. Once or twice a year, feed flowering plants, including those in containers, using a slow-release fertilizer.

Deadheading Choose plants with ornamental seedheads and avoid any that need deadheading to keep them blooming. Tidy ground-cover perennials and lavenders with shears.

Weeding Cover the ground with a weed-suppressing fabric camouflaged with gravel. Spray weeds with systemic weedkiller to kill the roots. Avoid soil disturbance and self-seeding plants.

Mowing Choose an easy-care grass seed mix. Reduce the lawn size and buy an efficient mower. Install a brick mowing strip next to borders and walls to cut out the need for edging.

Pruning Choose evergreens, as they rarely need pruning, and plants that only need one cut a year, such as *Buddleja davidii*. Avoid over-vigorous shrubs and allow plants room to grow.

Low- and high-maintenance ingredients

Choose the plants and materials in your garden carefully to minimize the workload.

Easy-care gardens

Paved or decked surfaces are easy to keep tidy and weed free, and surrounding your plants with hard landscaping, or growing them in raised beds, keeps them within bounds; you can also carry out most jobs, whatever the weather. Although there is an excellent selection of low-maintenance flowering shrubs and perennials, choosing specimens for their architectural qualities, foliage colour, and texture, rather than for their blooms, will ensure that the planting is interesting all year round.

Hardy bulbs Dwarf and low-growing hardy bulbs, like crocus, scillas and small daffodils, offer a maintenance-free spring show. For summer, plant alliums and low-growing lilies that do not need staking. Dying down gracefully, these bulbs are left in the ground to come up year after year.

Drought busters Plants like these houseleeks do not need watering at all. If you live in a dry region, or the garden has a hot, sunny aspect and free-draining soil, focus on drought-tolerant plants, such as succulents or silver-leaved varieties. Avoid pots or consider installing automatic irrigation.

Plant-free features Bringing colour into the garden with painted walls or trellis reduces the need for bright bedding displays. Decorative paving elements, such as pebble mosaics, add textural interest, while sculpture and stylish outdoor furniture provide maintenance-free highlights.

Labour-intensive gardens

Manicured lawns require a lot of upkeep: mowing and edging, weeding and feeding, moss-killing, scarifying to remove dead material, aerating to improve drainage, and sweeping up leaves in autumn. Of course, a roughly maintained family lawn, or one where daisies and other attractive "weeds" are allowed to grow, needs much less attention. Traditional borders full of blooms, and backed by flower-festooned walls and fences, look spectacular in summer, but it is difficult to keep on top of deadheading, staking, weeding, and watering, not to mention tying climbers and wall shrubs onto their supports. Self-seeding can also become a time-consuming problem.

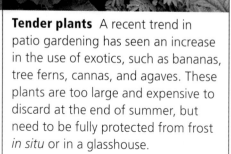

Pots If you plant tender bedding plants, annual flowers, and bulbs in containers, you are committing yourself to time-consuming tidying as well as daily watering during hot weather, and regular feeding to keep plants healthy. At the end of each season, displays have to be replanted.

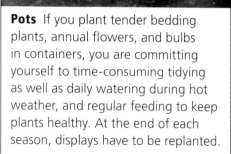

Fast-growing hedge One of the most challenging tasks is keeping on top of quick-growing plants, like privet and tall conifers. Several cuts a year are required to maintain a neat profile and control height and spread, and removing the clippings can also be laborious.

Tender plants A recent trend in patio gardening has seen an increase in the use of exotics, such as bananas, tree ferns, cannas, and agaves. These plants are too large and expensive to discard at the end of summer, but need to be fully protected from frost *in situ* or in a glasshouse.

Assessing your site

Look critically at your garden before carrying out any major changes. Weigh up the pros and cons of features before removing them, and remember that mature, established plants may need less maintenance than new ones.

Which way does your garden face? Work out where the sun rises (east) and sets (west). East-facing aspects are sunny in the morning – winter and spring-flowering shrubs are vulnerable to frost here. West-facing walls and fences have sun in the afternoon and evening – ideal for relaxing after work. Areas in sun for much of the day are south facing, and shady, cool spots opposite have a northern aspect.

What do you need?

Make a list of the various activities and areas planned for your garden, including places for growing plants, supporting wildlife, relaxing, cooking and dining *al fresco*. Bear in mind factors like sun and shade, drainage, shelter from wind, and proximity to water and electricity outlets. Don't forget practicalities like drying laundry, easy access to waste or recycling bins and compost heaps, as well as planning in storage space for garden tools and furniture.

Guinea pigs and rabbits like to graze and run on grass; lawns also benefit songbirds.

Make children's gardens versatile, and easy to adapt when they tire of play equipment.

Areas for outdoor entertaining might include a barbecue, a sunken fire pit, or a gazebo.

Understanding climate

You can live in an area that suffers from early and late frosts or that's battered by winds, while enjoying milder conditions in your garden. South- and west-facing gardens are suntraps; walls and paving absorb daytime heat and radiate it back at night, keeping surrounding areas frost-free. Trees and hedges act as buffers against wind but, conversely, buildings can cause damaging turbulence. Such local variations are known as microclimates.

As sunny walls radiate heat, tender plants like this ceanothus can thrive in frosty regions.

Hedges and shrub borders slow the wind and provide shelter for plants and people.

Cold air pools at the bottom of slopes and plants here are more vulnerable to frosts.

Boundaries and garden dividers

The style and fabric of the elements you choose to enclose or separate parts of your plot have a major impact on the overall effect of the garden. Boundary materials frequently act as a foil, but can also make a bold statement.

Wooden fence Choose the highest quality fencing that you can afford for long-lasting results. Pressure-treated posts are easier to replace and last longer if fitted into metal sockets rather than directly into concrete.

Trellis A decorative screening material with panels in various styles, a trellis may also include shaped pieces for special features. Letting in more light but offering less privacy than solid panelling, it is best for internal divisions.

Willow or hazel hurdles These hand-woven panels are perfect for cottage-style gardens. For a contemporary look, fix to aluminium posts or set into a solid timber frame. Panels last for about eight years.

Rendered wall Breezeblock walls are quicker and cheaper to build than brick and, when rendered, can be painted in a range of colours to create a smart and stylish finish. Rendering is often used for contemporary designs.

Brick wall Garden walls are decorative and practical, and frostproof bricks are available in a range of styles to match adjacent buildings. Antique or reclaimed bricks create the illusion of age and are ideal for period gardens.

Green dividers

Fences and walls provide opportunities to grow a wide variety of climbers and wall shrubs, and the plants help to camouflage boundary imperfections. Also, living screens of tall ornamental grasses, bamboos, shrubs and trees offer exciting alternatives to formal hedging.

Bamboo screen Some bamboos make beautiful evergreen screens, which suit both oriental-style and contemporary plots. Non-invasive, clump-forming cultivars of *Phyllostachys* and *Fargesia* are ideal, their upright canes often developing attractive tints and banding. Plant a row in moisture-retentive ground, allowing them room to spread sideways. To control the width of the screen, remove unwanted bamboo shoots at ground level in late spring. Periodically thin out some mature canes, and remove leafy growth from the lower half of the screen.

Climbers There are only a few climbers that are self-clinging and do not require wires or trellis. These include *Hydrangea anomala* subsp. *petiolaris* (*above*) and ivy. Be sure to choose the right plant for the site and soil type – some prefer cool shade, whilst others bloom best on a sunny wall. Also consider the plant's ultimate height and vigour, to avoid problems in the future.

Yew hedge When clipped formally, this dark evergreen forms a dense wall or plain backcloth for borders. Relatively slow growing, it can eventually be trained into arches and other pieces of green architecture. Yew is long-lived and regenerates from old wood if pruned hard. Although shade tolerant, hedges are best cut wide at the base and narrow at the top, so that light falls evenly on the foliage.

Tree and shrub divide Ideal for protecting windswept gardens, a boundary of trees and shrubs makes a particularly effective shelterbelt. Mix different shapes, textures and colours, including flowering and berrying types, for maximum interest, and prune to control size.

Living willow screen On heavy clay soil, willow stems pushed into the ground will root easily. Setting these hardwood cuttings at an angle forms the beginning of a diamond lattice. Simply hook the willow stems under and over one another to the desired height, and then weave the excess at right angles to secure the upper edge of the screen. Trim the stems as necessary.

Fedge This is a cross between a fence and a hedge, and is an ingenious way to camouflage ugly chainlink fencing. It is best to use a plain green ivy for rapid cover and to produce a slim, dense, hedge-like structure. Plant pots of young, vigorous ivies at the base of the screen, and weave the shoots in and out as they grow. Once the fence is covered, trim the ivy using hand shears.

Selecting landscape materials

The natural or man-made products you choose, and the patterns and designs you employ, make a big difference to the overall look of the garden. Other considerations include the cost of materials, ease of laying or installation, and long-term durability.

Granite setts These hard-wearing cubes of granite are ideal for driveways and areas in heavy use, and can be arranged to make very attractive circular, curving or interlocking paving patterns as well as the straightforward grid design illustrated. Made of natural stone, these paving blocks suit period properties and country residences, but they can also be used in a variety of situations to add textural interest to areas paved with slabs. Granite setts are expensive but concrete substitutes are available.

Using contractors When hiring someone to carry out hard landscaping work, be prepared to show them a scale drawing or at least mark out the areas to be paved or decked to avoid confusion. Get a number of quotes and, especially if the contractor hasn't been personally recommended, ask to see examples of their work so that you can do your own quality check. After considering your ideas, contractors may help you select suitable materials and provide paving samples; also discuss clearing and preparing the ground, waste removal, drainage requirements, electricity cables, and paving patterns and designs. Once you are happy with a quote, draw up a formal agreement for the contractor to sign, stating exactly what you expect them to do for the price, with start and end dates.

Natural stone Ethically sourced sandstone, limestone, and granite paving reveals subtle colours when wet and does not chip or fade, but it tends to be thicker, heavier and less uniform, and is more expensive than concrete reproductions. Consider hiring an experienced paving contractor.

Concrete paving There is a wide range of concrete paving available, from plain, contemporary designs to textured stone reproductions and modular paving sets. Quality varies, and some styles are thicker and more hardwearing with better resistance to chipping or fading in sunlight.

Woodstone A convincing substitute for wooden sleepers, the concrete is imprinted with the texture of weathered, reclaimed wood and suits country or cottage garden situations. It can also be used for steps, stepping stones in gravel, and to construct low raised flower beds.

Timber decking Decking is warm underfoot and dries rapidly after rain. Do not use in shady areas as it quickly develops slippery algae. Off-the-shelf kits are available from do-it-yourself stores but hire a specialist for larger, more complex areas. Western red cedar is naturally rot-resistant.

Turf New gardens are often laid with turf prior to implementing a design. A well-maintained lawn makes an attractive foil for borders and contrasts well with hard landscaping. Lawns are important for many birds and provide a safe play surface for children. Install a mowing edge.

Bricks Frostproof bricks, engineering bricks, setts, and pavers, can be laid in a wide variety of patterns, such as curving shapes and circular designs; they also add texture to areas paved with slabs. Bricks come in different shades and styles, including antique effects that suit older properties.

Cobbles Pebbles and cobbles of different colours and grades can be used with other materials, such as slate shards and tile fragments, to create paving mosaics like the circular feature above. Simple designs are not difficult to make, as the pebbles are bedded into a dry mortar.

Gravel This versatile and inexpensive material comes in many different grades and colours, allowing it to blend with other landscape materials. Laid over a permeable membrane, it's an easy way to create pathways and patios. Contain gravel to separate it from soil using slightly raised edgings.

Decorative aggregates Slate chippings (*above*) are one of several stone aggregates now available for garden landscapes. More dramatic or contemporary effects can be created with coloured stone chippings and glass chippings. Lay as for gravel, over a permeable membrane.

Designing with different materials

Hard surfaces act as a framework around which plants can grow and mature. The chosen material, and the style in which it is laid, can enhance the design of your outdoor space.

Decking jetty This substantial wooden platform hangs over the pool below, allowing close access to the water. The clean lines and restrained planting combine to create an open expanse of warm wood and tranquil water.

Basketweave bricks This garden is paved in a traditional design that suits older properties and has cottage garden appeal. The weathered terracotta colouring and intricately textured surface of the bricks gives an aged quality.

Sleek slabs Smooth, simple concrete pavers laid in a uniform row or geometric grid create a contemporary feel. This minimalist style of paving helps to emphasize the planting as well as architectural and design features.

Vintage stone Reclaimed stone from architectural salvage merchants gives a garden a feeling of permanence. The worn and weathered surface of the stone adds character, which is perfect for this formal pool terrace edged in box.

Zen gravel garden Gravel is used here to emulate a dry Zen garden or *karesansui*. The rugged boulders and simple evergreen plantings represent islands in a sea or lake, reflecting traditional Japanese designs.

Spring mix

This woodland carpet could be recreated under the dappled shade of deciduous trees or large shrubs. The planting reaches its peak in early spring when the snowdrops open and the bronze-pink fronds of the maidenhair fern (*Adiantum*) unfurl. The marbled arum foliage makes a lovely foil for various forms of hellebore that flower through winter; select these in bloom as catalogue descriptions can be misleading. The coloured petals are long lasting and the nodding flowers of the *H. orientalis* subsp. *guttatus* have speckled throats.

Border basics

Size 1.5m x 1.5m (5 x 5ft)
Suits Shade-loving woodland plants that flower in late winter or early spring
Soil Moist, with a deep organic mulch
Site Under trees or north-facing border

Shopping list

- 7 x *Adiantum venustum*
- 9 x *Arum italicum* subsp. *italicum* 'Marmoratum'
- 5 x *Helleborus* x *hybridus* cultivar
- 5 x *Helleborus orientalis* subsp. *guttatus*
- 50–100 x *Galanthus nivalis*

Planting and aftercare

Work in plenty of well-rotted manure, garden compost or leafmould to improve clay soils or make sandy or free-draining ground more moisture retentive. Plant the border in autumn or in mild spells during winter and early spring. Pot-grown snowdrops, or those lifted and replanted in clumps just after flowering, often establish better than dry bulbs planted in early autumn. Mulch with chipped bark or cocoa shells to retain moisture and suppress weeds. Remove old leaves from the hellebores when the flowers start to open so that they don't mar the display. Also snip off dead or damaged leaves from the maidenhair fern when the new fronds unfurl.

Arum italicum subsp. *italicum* 'Marmoratum' ❄❄❄ ◐ ☼ ♔

Helleborus orientalis subsp. *guttatus* ❄❄❄ ◐ ☼

Helleborus x *hybridus* cultivar ❄❄❄ ◐ ☼

Galanthus nivalis ❄❄❄ ◌◐ ☼ ♔

Adiantum venustum ❄❄❄ ◐ ☼ ♔

Sparkling summer bed

This silver and pink colour scheme is perfect for a sunny hot spot. Dotted through the planting, metallic-leaved astelia, commonly called silver spear, adds a distinctly Mediterranean feel. The compact form of the evergreen *Artemisia schmidtiana* appears like a shimmering river running through the border, with blue-leaved fescues on one side and pink-flowered thrift or sea pink on the other. The thrift (*Armeria*) blooms from late spring into early summer from wiry green tussocks. At the rear, the cut-leaved artemisia adds height and texture.

Border basics

Size 1.8 x 1.5m (6 x 5ft)
Suits Drought-tolerant grasses, alpines and perennials
Soil Sharply drained
Site Hot, sunny and sheltered

Shopping list

- 3 x *Astelia chathamica*
- 3 x *Artemisia ludoviciana* 'Valerie Finnis'
- 7 x *Artemisia schmidtiana* 'Nana'
- 7 x *Festuca glauca* 'Blauglut'
- 9 x *Armeria maritima* 'Splendens'

Planting and aftercare

Prepare heavier ground by digging in plenty of grit to improve drainage. This scheme is best planted in late spring when the weather has become warmer and drier. Plants like the slightly tender astelia will have a chance to establish before winter and the grasses and silvery artemisias should be in active growth. To maintain the display, cut back dead heads on the thrift and, at the end of the season, the dead stems of the broad-leaved artemisia. Wrap the astelia with horticultural fleece if a cold snap is forecast, and mulch with bark to protect the roots. In spring, tidy the grasses by combing the dead leaves out of the tussocks with your fingers. Lightly trim the evergreen artemisia with shears.

Astelia chathamica
❄❄ ◊ ☼ ♛

Artemisia ludoviciana 'Valerie Finnis'
❄❄❄ ◊ ☼ ♛

Artemisia schmidtiana 'Nana'
❄❄❄ ◊ ☼ ♛

Festuca glauca 'Blauglut'
❄❄❄ ◊ ☼

Armeria maritima 'Splendens'
❄❄❄ ◊ ☼

Elegant autumn border

This sparkling arrangement starts blooming in midsummer. First in flower is the pearly everlasting (*Anaphalis*) with clusters of papery ball-shaped heads, which remain attractive for many weeks, over grey-green felted leaves. Mingled in, the vibrant aster 'Veilchenkönigin' is a Michaelmas daisy with compact growth and good disease resistance. At the back, Russian sage (*Perovskia*) makes a delicate but long-lasting foil (try globe thistle, *Echinops*, as an alternative) and clumps of stipa add structure and movement.

Border basics

Size 1.8 x 1.4m (6 x 4ft)
Suits Late summer- and autumn-flowering perennials and grasses
Soil Well-drained, neutral to alkaline
Site Open, full sun

Shopping list

- 3 x *Stipa calamagrostis*
- 5 x *Aster amellus* 'Veilchenkönigin' syn. Violet Queen
- 5 x *Perovskia atriplicifolia* 'Blue Spire' or 5 x *Echinops ritro*
- 7 x *Anaphalis triplinervis*

Planting and aftercare

The plants in this scheme enjoy fertile, well-drained soil so remedy any drainage problems before planting in spring, and dig in organic matter if the soil is poor and dry. After soaking the pots, lay the plants out in long overlapping drifts. This arrangement suits relatively narrow borders because it creates the illusion of depth. Intermingle the asters and pearl everlasting where the two drifts meet to give a more naturalistic feel. Mulch to retain moisture, keep down weeds and help plants establish through the summer months. In midwinter, cut down old flower stems of foreground plantings if they look untidy, but delay cutting back the grass and Russian sage until spring.

Stipa calamagrostis
❄❄❄ ◊ ☀

Aster amellus 'Veilchenkönigin'
❄❄❄ ◊ ☀ ♈

ovskia atriplicifolia 'Blue Spire'
❋❋ ◊ ☀ ▽

Anaphalis triplinervis
❋❋❋ ◊ ☀ ◑ ▽

Alternative plant idea

Echinops ritro
❋❋❋ ◊ ☀ ▽

Winter colour

The flame-coloured willow (*Salix*) sets this sunny border alight. It thrives on heavy soils, including waterlogged clays. Hard pruning in spring helps control its vigour, but in a small garden consider using the dogwood (*Cornus sanguinea* 'Midwinter Fire') instead. The ghostly white-stemmed rubus has dainty divided leaves in summer – a subtle contrast with the diaphanous stipa. On heavier soils, consider substituting this grass with the coppery pheasant's tail (*Anemanthele lessoniana*). In winter, the tawny red sedum flowers dry out, forming stiff, long-lasting maroon heads.

Border basics

Size 1.8 x 1.8m (6 x 6ft)
Suits Deciduous shrubs, grasses and late-flowering perennials
Soil Fertile, well-drained, not too dry
Site Full sun

Shopping list

- 1 x *Salix alba* var. *vitellina* 'Britzensis'
- 1 x *Rubus thibetanus*
- 7 x *Sedum* 'Herbstfreude'
- 9–11 x *Stipa tenuissima*

Planting and aftercare

For best results, plant in spring to allow plants to establish before putting on a show through the winter. Cut the white-stemmed rubus and willow back hard the following spring to encourage plenty of new stems, which colour up better than the old. Also cut back the grass foliage as you see new growth appearing, and clear away old sedum stems. Every three years lift and split the sedum clumps in spring to keep them strong and stop them from collapsing during late summer. Apply a granular, slow-release fertilizer annually in spring and/or well-rotted manure at pruning time. Consider adding tall *Verbena bonariensis* for extra colour in the "quiet" summer phase of this display.

Salix alba var. *vitellina* 'Britzensis'
❄❄❄ ◌ ◆ ☼ ♔

Rubus thibetanus
❄❄❄ ◌ ☼ ♔

Sedum 'Herbstfreude'
❄❄❄ ◌ ◆ ☼ ♔

Stipa tenuissima
❄❄❄ ◌ ☼

Cool foliage collection

In spring, the lungwort (*Pulmonaria*) puts on a pretty display of white blooms, and the silver spotted leaves that follow are just as attractive. The cream-variegated elder (*Sambucus*) brightens this shady spot, and clumps of dwarf box (*Buxus*), along with the cherry red stems of variegated dogwood (*Cornus*), maintain structure in winter. Tall flag iris makes a bold vertical statement and, though normally grown in water, its vigour is controlled in drier soil. Silver curry plants (*Helichrysum*) thrive in a patch of sunlight.

Border basics

Size 1.8 x 4m (6 x 12ft)
Suits Shade-tolerant shrubs and perennials grown for foliage contrast
Soil Fertile, moisture retentive
Site Cool, lightly shaded

Shopping list

- 1 x *Cornus alba* 'Elegantissima'
- 1 x *Sambucus nigra* 'Marginata'
- 3 x *Helichrysum italicum*
- 3 x *Iris pseudacorus* var. *bastardii*
- 7 x *Pulmonaria saccharata* 'Sissinghurst White'
- 3 x *Buxus sempervirens* 'Suffruticosa'

Planting and aftercare

Most plants here would thrive on clay-rich soils. Improve dry soil by working in plenty of well-rotted manure. The curry plant requires sharply drained ground, so dig in plenty of grit before planting or swap with pearl everlasting (*Anaphalis triplinervis*) as this tolerates clay and shade. Siberian iris (*Iris sibirica*) could also replace the flag iris. Mulch with bark after planting. Clip the box to shape in early summer. In early spring, prune the elder back to a low framework and, once established, remove a third of the oldest stems of the dogwood. Prune the curry plant in spring to keep it bushy and, if mildew attacks the pulmonaria, cut back, feed and water to aid healthy regrowth.

Cornus alba 'Elegantissima'
❄❄❄ ◊ ☼ ◑ ♉

Sambucus nigra 'Marginata'
❄❄❄ ◊ ☼ ◑

Helichrysum italicum
❄❄❄ ◊ ☼ ♉

Iris pseudacorus var. *bastardii*
❄❄❄ ◊ ◕ ☼ ◑

Pulmonaria saccharata 'Sissinghurst White' ❄❄❄ ◊ ☼ ◕ ♉

Buxus sempervirens 'Suffruticosa'
❄❄❄ ◊ ◕ ☼ ♉

Architectural designs

All these plants have such a sculptural profile that the overall effect is very dramatic. The yellow-stemmed bamboo (*Phyllostachys*) makes an effective screen and, building a subtropical theme, two bold variegated yuccas dominate the foreground. Giant feather grass (*Stipa gigantea*) carries shimmering seedheads well into autumn, its vertical form contrasting with the spreading tussocks of the New Zealand sedge (*Carex comans*). This bronze evergreen's colour and form work beautifully with the broad, thick, textured foliage of the blue-leaved hosta and spiky black ophiopogon.

Border basics

Size 2.5 x 2.5m (8 x 8ft)
Suits Sculptural evergreens, bamboos, and grass-like plants
Soil Well-drained to moisture retentive
Site Sunny

Shopping list

- 1 x *Stipa gigantea*
- 1 x *Phyllostachys aureosulcata* f. *aureocaulis*
- 2 x *Yucca filamentosa* 'Bright Edge'
- 3 x *Hosta sieboldiana* var. *elegans*
- 5 x *Ophiopogon planiscapus* 'Nigrescens'
- 3 x *Carex comans* bronze-leaved

Planting and aftercare

Prepare individual planting holes. The stipa, yucca, and ophiopogon thrive in sharply drained soil, so on heavier soils work in plenty of grit. The sedges, hostas and bamboo meanwhile enjoy moisture-retentive conditions. Improve dry, sandy ground by digging in well-rotted manure. Mulch with bark. The hosta has good slug resistance but watch for damage to new leaves. In spring, cut the sedge back hard, as the regrowth is more colourful, and trim back the old flower stems of the stipa. Cut a few older bamboo canes at the base to maintain an open habit.

Stipa gigantea
❄❄❄ ◌ ☼ ♛

Phyllostachys aureosulcata
f. *aureocaulis* ❄❄❄ ◌ ☼ ☽ ♛

Yucca filamentosa 'Bright Edge'
❄❄❄ ◌ ☼ ♛

Hosta sieboldiana var. *elegans*
❄❄❄ ◌ ☽ ♛

Ophiopogon planiscapus 'Nigrescens'
❄❄❄ ◌ ☼ ☽ ♛

Carex comans bronze-leaved
❄❄❄ ◌ ☼ ☽

Easy perennials

With the right plants you can sit back and enjoy fabulous flowering displays all summer long for next to no effort. This recipe combines colourful blooms and handsome foliage set off against the dark backdrop of a yew hedge. Relatively new on the scene, the blue geranium 'Nimbus' blooms from late spring to midsummer and is furnished with intricately cut foliage. Pincushion-flowered knautia takes over from mid- to late summer accompanied by tall spikes of the ornamental sage, 'Ostfriesland'. The silvery felted lamb's ears (*Stachys*) and hair-like stipa make a textural foil.

Border basics

Size 1.5 x 1.8m (5 x 6ft)
Suits Easy-care perennials and grasses
Soil Fertile, moist but well-drained
Site Sunny

Shopping list

- 3 x *Geranium* 'Nimbus'
- 5 x *Knautia macedonica*
- 5 x *Salvia nemorosa* 'Ostfriesland'
- 3 x *Stachys byzantina* 'Silver Carpet'
- 5 x *Stipa tenuissima*
- *Taxus baccata* (hedge)

Planting and aftercare

Cut the yew hedge towards the end of summer; leave a gap between the hedge and the border for access. Improve poor, dry soil with well-rotted manure, garden compost, or spent mushroom compost. This arrangement is best planted in spring or early autumn. Mulch with bark to control weeds. The following spring, cut plants back to new growth arising from the base – none of them should require staking, but pushing a few twiggy sticks in around the geranium in spring will help to stop plants sprawling too far. Deadhead the knautia as often as you can to prolong flowering. Cutting back geranium foliage after flowering encourages compact, new leafy growth.

Geranium 'Nimbus'
❄❄❄ ◌ ◍ ☼ ◐ ♈

Knautia macedonica
❄❄❄ ◌ ☼

Salvia nemorosa 'Ostfriesland'
❄❄❄ ◌ ☼ ♈

Stachys byzantina 'Silver Carpet'
❄❄❄ ◌ ☼

Stipa tenuissima
❄❄❄ ◌ ☼

Taxus baccata
❄❄❄ ◌ ☼ ◑ ♈

Contemporary prairie

This example of new wave or prairie-style planting is stylish and easy to care for. The ornamental sage, yellow foxglove and verbena attract bees and butterflies and, if you leave this "meadow" to die down naturally, it will provide a valuable habitat for beneficial insects, small mammals, and birds. Flowering begins with the foxglove (*Digitalis*) and the violet-purple sage ('Mainacht' or 'May Night') in early summer, and reaches a peak in midsummer when the verbena joins the display. Giant feather grass (*Stipa*) throws up tall wands of glistening seedheads which, along with the verbena, last well into autumn. You could consider maiden grass (*Miscanthus sinensis* 'Gracillimus') as a tall, narrow-leaved alternative to the stipa.

Border basics

Size 2.5 x 2.5m (8 x 8ft)
Suits Grasses, natural-looking perennials
Soil Fertile, well-drained but not dry
Site Sunny, open

Shopping list

- 5 x *Stipa gigantea* or *Miscanthus sinensis* 'Gracillimus'
- 9 x *Verbena bonariensis*
- 7 x *Salvia* x *sylvestris* 'Mainacht'
- 7 x *Digitalis lutea*

Planting and aftercare

Plant in early autumn or mid- to late spring, improving dry or poor soils by adding well-rotted manure or garden compost. Lay out the plants in large overlapping blocks or swathes and use the tall, "see-through" verbena at intervals between shorter plants to create a more dynamic and naturalistic arrangement. All of the plants can be left to die down naturally at the end of the season, as the old flower stems and seedheads remain attractive well into the winter. Trim back in spring but leave the evergreen grass tussocks.

Stipa gigantea
❄❄❄ ◊ ☼ ☖

Verbena bonariensis
❄❄ ◊ ☼ ☖

Digitalis lutea
❄❄❄ ◊ ◊ ☼ ☼

Salvia x *sylvestris* 'Mainacht'
❄❄❄ ◊ ☼ ☖

Alternative plant idea

Miscanthus sinensis 'Gracillimus'
❄❄❄ ◊ ☼ ☼

Aromatic herb border

Many traditional herb-garden plants have potential for use in low-maintenance schemes, as they are mostly evergreen and drought-resistant. Here, aromatic lavender and common thyme blend with a cream-flowered cotton lavender (*Santolina*) and giant, silver-leaved cardoon (*Cynara*). Wispy bronze sedges weave through the planting, linking the various elements. The resulting slate-mulched bed has a muted, contemporary feel and would work well in full sun, adjacent to an open expanse of paving or decking. Add cream *Crocus chrysanthus* at the front for spring colour.

Border basics

Size　1.8 x 1.5m (6 x 5ft)
Suits　Drought-tolerant herbs, perennials and sedges
Soil　Reasonably fertile, sharply drained
Site　Sunny, sheltered from wind

Shopping list

- 3 x *Santolina pinnata* subsp. *neapolitana* 'Edward Bowles'
- 5 x *Thymus vulgaris*
- 1 x *Cynara cardunculus*
- 5 x *Lavandula* 'Fathead'
- 7 x *Carex flagellifera*

Planting and aftercare

Plant between spring and early summer, to give the herbs a chance to establish before winter. Improve the drainage of clay soils by digging in grit or gravel. Soak plants, remove pots, and set out to make a pleasing arrangement. For weed-free gardening, plant through membrane and mulch with slate chippings or gravel. Clip over the lavender after flowering in late summer and, in autumn, tidy the faded leaves and woody flower stalk of the cardoon. The following spring, cut the cotton lavender back to a low framework, and lightly trim the thymes. Trimming the sedges close to the base in spring encourages colourful regrowth.

Santolina pinnata subsp. *neapolitana* 'Edward Bowles' ❋❋❋ ◊ ☼

Thymus vulgaris ❋❋❋ ◊ ☼

cardunculus
◌ ☼ ▽

Lavandula 'Fathead'
✱✱✱ ◌ ☼

Carex flagellifera
✱✱✱ ◌ ◗ ☼ ◑

Chic foliage collection

The key to creating a contemporary look is to limit your scheme to a single subject or just a handful of texturally interesting plants. Here the pink-leaved phormium adds height and vibrancy, its strap-like foliage contrasting strongly with the bold, rounded leaves of the bergenia. Flowering in spring, *Bergenia* 'Red Beauty' gives early season interest and is followed by the simple white blooms of the convolvulus. An evergreen with leaves like strips of metal, the elegant convolvulus mirrors the silver container and complements the other plants, especially the "black" ophiopogon.

Container basics

Size Galvanized metal container, approx. 40cm (16in) in diameter
Suits Architectural evergreen shrubs and perennials
Soil Loam-based, free-draining potting mix
Site Sunny, sheltered from hard frosts

Shopping list

- 1 x *Bergenia* 'Red Beauty'
- 1 x *Ophiopogon planiscapus* 'Nigrescens'
- 1 x *Convolvulus cneorum*
- 1 x *Phormium* 'Jester'

Planting and aftercare

Metal containers heat and cool rapidly, potentially damaging roots, so insulate with a layer of bubble plastic or use a plastic pot as a liner, filling the gap with horticultural fleece. Cover the drainage holes with crocks and pour in 5cm (2in) of gravel. Half fill with a good quality soil-based potting mix, adding slow-release fertilizer at the recommended rate. Arrange the plants to find the best fit, then plunge each pot into a bucket of water, drain, and plant. Fill any gaps with more soil and water thoroughly. Water regularly, remove faded bergenia flowers, and renew fertilizer granules annually.

Bergenia 'Red Beauty'
❄❄❄ ◊ ◐ ☀ ☀

Convolvulus cneorum
❄❄ ◊ ☀ ▽

Ophiopogon planiscapus 'Nigrescens'
❄❄❄ ◊ ◐ ☀ ☀ ▽

Phormium 'Jester'
❄❄ ◊ ☀

Cottage garden in a container

Plain or decorated, terracotta tends to fit in well with older period properties and traditional types of garden, such as formal or cottage style. When buying, check that the pots are guaranteed frostproof and have no visible cracks or chips; a bell-like ring when struck indicates that the pot is sound. Being porous, clay is ideal for herbs, alpines, succulents, and drought-tolerant plants; if you want to use other plants, and still cut down on watering, it is best to line the pots with plastic.

Container basics

Size Terracotta pot, approx. 38cm (15in) in diameter
Suits Mediterranean-style perennials, herbs, and succulents
Soil Loam-based, free-draining potting mix
Site Sunny for most of the day

Shopping list

- 1 x *Lavandula angustifolia* 'Hidcote'
- 2 x *Scabiosa* 'Pink Mist' or *Osteospermum* 'White Pim'
- 1 x *Sedum* 'Ruby Glow'
- 2 x *Diascia* 'Sunchimes Lilac'

Planting and aftercare

Soak the pot until the sides have turned a darker shade, indicating saturation, as this reduces the amount of moisture absorbed from the soil by the clay. Otherwise, line with black plastic, making sure that the drainage holes are uncovered. Protect the holes with fine mesh, flat stones or broken crocks, and add a layer of gravel for drainage. Half fill with loam-based compost mixed with a slow-release fertilizer. After soaking the plants, arrange them to create a pleasing display. Carefully fill around the rootballs, and finish at a final compost level 5cm (2in) below the rim to allow for watering. Regularly deadhead the scabious and diascia, and shear the lavender after flowering.

Diascia 'Sunchimes Lilac'
❉❉ ◊ ◗ ☀

Lavandula angustifolia 'Hidcote'
❉❉❉ ◊ ☀ ♈

Scabiosa 'Pink Mist'
❉❉❉ ◊ ☀

Alternative plant idea

Sedum 'Ruby Glow'
❉❉❉ ◊ ☀ ♈

Osteospermum 'White Pim'
❉❉❉ ◊ ☀ ♈

Tidying your garden

A well-planned, easy-care garden can be spruced up in no time, especially if lawns have been replaced by low-maintenance surfaces, and borders contain plenty of evergreens and non-flowering plants that don't need deadheading.

Garden facelift

During the growing season, weekly jobs, like mowing, deadheading, and sweeping, make a big difference to the look of the garden. Other tasks, such as hedge trimming and patio cleaning, as well as painting or refinishing various surfaces, may only be necessary once or twice a year. This "spring-cleaning", however, is vital in easy-care gardens, where much more emphasis is placed on hard landscaping features. Shabby, mismatched fencing panels, peeling wall paint, faded decking, and paving slabs covered with algae catch the eye and mar your overall enjoyment. Provided you have appropriate tools (some can be hired) you should be able to take care of such problem areas with ease.

Vacuum outside These handy but noisy tools allow debris, litter, and autumn leaves to be collected from paving and lawns, as well as from gravel and pebble surfaces, where it is difficult to use a brush.

Better mowing Maintain your own machine, or have it serviced regularly, to achieve the most efficient performance. Consider investing in a larger, more powerful mower if yours is too small for tackling the size of your lawn.

Keeping hedges trim Electric or petrol-powered hedge trimmers are so much faster and less wearing to use than hand shears. To avoid raking up the debris, lay a groundsheet down to catch the trimmings.

Lift off dirt The strong jet of water produced by a pressure washer will lift grime and algae from paving, leaving a finish that looks like new. Check on a hidden corner first to make sure the surface won't be damaged.

Instant makeover Rolls of bamboo, willow, and heather screening can be used to cover mismatched fencing panels or ugly chain link for an instant and economical facelift. Attach with wire or plastic ties, or a heavy-duty staple gun.

Easy cover-up Repainting a wall freshens it up nicely, and applying a new colour can add a designer touch to a patio or courtyard. After rubbing down the surface thoroughly, apply a quality exterior paint with a roller for ease.

Protect your timber Decking, fencing, trellis, and other wooden structures benefit from an application of all-weather paints, stains and preservatives. Many companies offer specialist tools for speedy and efficient application.

Informal pruning

Most gardeners love the appearance of a naturalistic, seemingly unpruned garden, brimming with flowers and foliage.

Although the look can be achieved with the minimal amount of work, to create this informal style takes a little practice.

Picture clockwise from left

Wild and free The scene of roses growing in the garden of an old-fashioned country cottage typifies the naturalistic look but, despite appearances, regular pruning has achieved this effect. Long, leggy growths that spoil the shape of the rambler on the wall are cut back into the main body of the plant as soon as they are seen. In autumn or early spring, the plant is given a gentle overall trim to keep its shape. A hard pruning is needed every three to five years.

Beautiful berries Firethorns (*Pyracantha*) make excellent informal, burglar-proof boundary hedges, their thorny stems keeping unwanted visitors at bay. These shrubs come into their own in autumn when covered in berries, and are pruned lightly in spring. Take care not to cut back too much, or you risk losing the berries.

Natural border The success of this scheme is no accident; clever plant selection and a careful pruning regime ensure its natural appeal. If left completely unpruned, one or two plants would become dominant and take over. The silver-leaved *Santolina* and golden sage are lightly trimmed annually, while the *Hypericum* 'Hidcote' is pruned every two or three years to maintain its shape. When in full bloom, the border looks like it has never been pruned.

Colour and texture A good planting combination and the correct plant spacing ensures that this border of *Ceanothus* 'Puget Blue', Mexican orange blossom (*Choisya* 'Aztec Pearl'), and shrubby honeysuckle (*Lonicera nitida* 'Baggesen's Gold') needs only minimal pruning. If vigorous plants had been chosen or this selection had been placed too close together, the border would need much more work. The stems of the *Ceanothus* are shortened annually after flowering and the sideshoots of the *Choisya* and shrubby honeysuckle are removed every two or three years to keep them balanced.

Pruning for a formal look

Trees and shrubs can be pruned and trained into many different shapes, and used to great effect in formal designs. Use them as focal points, to create views or backdrops, and to introduce shape and structure into the garden.

Pictures clockwise from top left

Pleached effects Trees such as limes (*Tilia*) or hornbeams (*Carpinus*) can be trained into a structure that resembles a formal hedge on top of a series of straight trunks. This is achieved by training the branches horizontally so that they touch those of the next tree, which is trained in a similar fashion. Each year, the shoots that grow from these branches are pruned hard back to the main branch, resulting in a hedge with a distinctive structure. Use pleached trees to create high hedged effects or as a screen for a formal garden.

Plant patterns A parterre is made from hedges laid out in formal patterns and flowerbeds. The hedges can be of different heights and widths, and the designs intricate or simple. Plants used for a parterre must have a dense growing habit and be tolerant of close clipping, such as box (*Buxus*) or yew (*Taxus*).

Rose cladding Roses have been pruned and trained to cover the wooden supports that frame the view of the formal garden beyond. Mass plantings of hybrid tea and floribunda roses also add to the formal design.

Elegant head This beautiful shrub, *Viburnum rhytidophyllum,* has been pruned to create a stunning focal point. The lowest side stems have been removed, and the top allowed to form a branched head, which appears to float on its elegant "legs". This style of pruning can be practised on many different plants but works best with evergreen shrubs.

Leafy canopy To create this leafy roof structure, several *Sorbus aria* have been trained so that the upper branches arch over to meet in the middle. No branches must be allowed to grow from the trunks, as this would spoil the effect, and those used to form the roof are pruned annually so the structure doesn't lose its shape. This eye-catching canopy takes many years to create.

Pruning to create space

Plants are often pruned to keep them in check, but some delightful effects can be achieved with more imaginative techniques, like clearing lower stems of trees and shrubs to create elegant shapes and extra planting space beneath them.

Pictures from left to right

Training standard bays Lollipop shapes are very useful in a garden's design, as they create interest and structure. Plants that are pruned to create a bare trunk are called "standards". This technique is an excellent way of confining the size of large shrubs, and creating space underneath for a bed of shade-loving plants.

Tiny tree-like wisterias If left unpruned wisterias are large climbers, but it is possible to restrain them with careful pruning. Fruit trees can be trained and pruned in a similar way to fit restricted spaces.

Long-legged birches The most beautiful feature of a silver birch (*Betula*) is its gleaming white stem. To show the trunks off to the best effect, remove the lower branches. This opens up planting spaces beneath, which are perfect for shade-lovers, such as these *Rodgersia*. This pruning technique can be used for any tree or shrub with attractive bark.

Pruning to encourage flowering

Pruning plants correctly can increase the number of flowering shoots produced by the plant, giving you more flowers.

Knowing when and where to prune can make the difference between a poor show and a mass of colour and scent.

Pictures clockwise from left

Purple rain A curtain of scented flowers in late spring, *Wisteria sinensis* needs to be carefully trained and spur pruned each year in late winter to encourage flower bud formation. *Wisteria* grows very vigorously, so in midsummer shorten the current season's growth by at least half, which also helps encourage the formation of flower buds.

Snowy summer show During early summer *Philadelphus* 'Belle Etoile' is covered with large white scented flowers on arching branches. *Philadelphus* produces flowers on stems that formed the previous summer, so after it has flowered, remove about one-third of the oldest flowering stems, pruning them almost to ground level. Do this annually to help contain the overall size and shape of the plant and encourage plenty of new growth, which will be the flowering stems of the future.

Rose heaven Training a climbing rose, such as this *Rosa* 'Climbing Mrs Sam McGredy', over supports shows off the blooms to their best effect. In late winter or early spring, remove approximately one-third of the oldest stems close to ground level. On the remaining older stems, spur prune all the sideshoots and last year's flowering stems back to two or three healthy buds from the main stem. Flowering growths will be produced from all these spurs during the summer. At the same time, tie in strong new growths that formed the previous year, which need this support when they produce flowers.

Less is more *Clematis montana* is a vigorous plant, often grown over buildings and large plant supports. No pruning is required, but it may need trimming after blooming to keep it in check. In fact, some clematis are better left unpruned to encourage maximum flower production. In this instance, pruning reduces the volume of flowers that appear in late spring.

Pruning for colourful stems and bark

Some trees and shrubs produce bold, colourful stems and bark, which can be enhanced by careful pruning to create dazzling effects, especially during the winter when the branches are bare.

Pictures clockwise from top left

Bright highlights Grown for its attractive white peeling bark, the birch *Betula utilis* var. *jacquemontii* is especially effective in the winter when silhouetted against an evergreen backdrop. When the tree is young, use secateurs in early summer to remove the lowest small branches. Then, when the stem has reached the height at which you want the branches to form, allow them to grow but continue to remove the smallest side branches. This will give you a simple yet strong, distinctive branch shape, and a clean white trunk.

Snakeskin decoration Unusual white striations on the green bark of *Acer* 'White Tigress' give rise to the tree's common name – snake-bark maple. To see these markings at their best, create a clear stem of between 1.2 and 1.8m (4 – 6ft) by removing the lowest branches with secateurs annually, until you have the required length of stem.

Show-stopping stems The dogwood *Cornus stolonifera* 'Flaviramea' is grown for its outstanding winter stem interest, with different cultivars ranging from green to orange and dark red. This dogwood is most effective when grown in groups of two or three plants. To achieve the striking winter stem interest, prune the plants annually in early spring using secateurs.

Burnished bark A member of the cherry family, *Prunus rufa* is grown for its ornamental mahogany coloured bark rather than its flowers, and is ideal for small gardens. The beautiful bark looks best when you can see through the branch structure. To achieve this, remove all the smaller and crossing branches from the main structure.

Beautiful brambles *Rubus cockburnianus* is an ornamental suckering bramble grown for its attractive winter stems, which are white and red in colour. This plant is both a beauty and a beast – the stems are covered in thorns and make an almost impenetrable barrier, so you will need to wear gloves and eye protection when pruning. To attain the attractive winter stem colour, cut the stems to the ground annually in early spring.

Pruning for fruit

Fruit brings welcome colour into the garden as well as edible treats. Fruit bushes and trees require a lot of pruning but the blossom and then colourful and delicious fruit make it all worthwhile.

Pictures clockwise from left

Colourful blueberries The bushes of this popular fruit are great value: they flower in the spring, fruit in the summer, and then provide lovely foliage colour in autumn. Blueberries fruit on branches produced the previous year. Prune the bushes during the winter, removing two or three of the oldest stems each year, as well as any weak, dead, or diseased growths. Also remove any of the lower branches that may lie on the ground when laden with fruit in the summer.

Decorative apples Apple trees are beautiful in blossom and when covered in fruits. When choosing an apple tree for your garden, bear in mind that different varieties grow at different rates, so look for one that suits the size of your garden and the space available. Prune apple trees in the winter to give an open, airy structure. Do not prune too hard as this stimulates vegetative growth at the expense of flower buds and fruit.

Productive pears Pear trees are suitable for small gardens if trained in a pyramid shape. To keep a tree small reduce the length of the main leader (the tallest stem at the top of the tree) in winter. Also remove any congested growths during the winter when you can clearly see the skeleton of the tree. Then, in late summer reduce the side branches by pruning them back to one leaf bud from the main stem. Pear trees will fruit without any pruning, but they can become too large for a small garden.

Wall-trained espaliers One of the most beautiful and artistic ways to grow an apple tree is to train it as an espalier against a wall, where pairs of branches are trained horizontally from the central stem. Apple espaliers are suitable for small gardens but require great care and maintenance. During the late summer, prune all the sideshoots, taking each one back to the first noticeable leaf above the main horizontal branch. As the plant grows older, the branches that produce fruit will become crowded and will then require thinning in the winter.

Choosing pruning tools

Using the right tool for the right job is one of the most important factors when pruning. Choose your tools carefully and look for good quality products that are safe to use and make sharp, clean cuts that won't damage your plants.

Secateurs There are two types of secateurs: anvil (*above*) and bypass (*right*). The cutting blade of anvil secateurs presses down on to a metal block edge, while the bypass's cutting blade passes the bottom blade in a scissor action. Bypass secateurs give a cleaner cut and are easier to use. Only use secateurs for cutting stems less than 1.5cm (½in) in diameter.

Pruning saw An essential tool, this saw has either a folding or fixed blade which can be replaced when it is worn or damaged. Pruning saws are good for awkward situations.

Long-armed saw Use this saw for cutting small branches above head height. Always wear eye protection and a safety helmet, and save large branches for the professionals.

Bow saw Only use this tool for cutting branches that have already been pruned and removed. The shape makes it unsuitable for use in difficult and awkward situations.

Loppers Often used for pruning branches that are too thick for secateurs – although a pruning saw is the ideal tool – or for reducing the length of branches and stems. When using loppers, don't employ excessive pressure, as you can easily twist and crush the pruned stem.

Long-armed loppers If you need to shorten stems, or remove dead or diseased material that is above head height, this is a useful tool. Never use long-armed loppers to cut stems more than 2.5cm (1in) in diameter as they can be quite difficult to control.

Electric hedge trimmer Useful for cutting most types of hedge. Always work from the bottom to the top, ensure the electric cable is behind you, use an emergency circuit breaker, and never use in damp or wet conditions. Wear ear defenders and always read the instructions before use.

Petrol hedge trimmer Usually much heavier than electric types, petrol trimmers can be tiring to use for long periods. They will saw through most hedges, and are useful for cutting those with thick sideshoots. Always wear ear defenders and read the instructions carefully.

Tool care and safety tips

Using the right pruning tools and correct safety equipment helps to ensure that pruning is safe and enjoyable. You will also protect yourself against accidents if your equipment is well maintained, and extend the life of your tools.

Cleaning secateurs

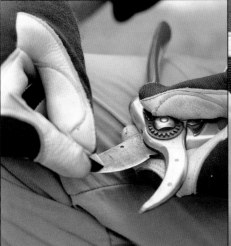

1 When pruning, plant sap dries and sticks to the blades, making them stiff. Scrape off the sap using a piece of metal with a straight edge, such as a metal plant label or penknife.

2 Then rub the blade with steel wool to remove any remaining dried sap and rust or other material. To prevent accidental cuts, wear gloves while cleaning your blades.

3 When the blade is clean, rub on some lubricating oil. This guards against rusting, and keeps the secateurs sharp and clean while they are being stored.

Cleaning pruning saws

1 When you have finished pruning, use a coarse brush to remove any sawdust lodged in the saw's teeth. If this is left it can harden and reduce the saw's cutting ability.

2 Next, use wire wool to rub both sides of the saw blade. This removes dried sap and dirt, which can also make the saw less efficient.

3 Before putting the saw away after cleaning, rub some lubricating oil onto it with a cloth to protect the blade from rusting.

Wear gloves Always wear sturdy gloves when pruning to protect your hands from sharp tools, and from cuts and scratches caused by thorny or sharp-edged plants.

Use protective goggles Protect eyes from dust, sawdust, and plant trimmings, especially when working above head height. Goggles also protect against thorns and shoots.

Keep electric wires behind you When using electric hedge trimmers, ensure that the cable is behind you so you cannot cut through it, and use an emergency circuit breaker.

Pruning your neighbour's plants Before pruning plants that are overhanging your garden, speak to your neighbours. You are more likely to reach an agreement about how much to cut off if you maintain a good relationship. However, branches that overhang your garden are classed by law as trespassing on your air space, and you do have the right to cut them back to your boundary, but no further. The branches that you have cut and any fruit that was on them should then be returned to your neighbour, who is classed as the plant's owner. You are not allowed to enter your neighbour's property, or to lean over it to prune your hedge, without seeking permission first.

Making ladders safe Use a tripod ladder, and ensure it is stable by fully extending the legs. Don't over-stretch or lean out to either side. If possible, ask someone to stand at the bottom.

Using platforms and ladders Before using this equipment, ensure each set of legs is on level ground and adjust if not. Do not over-stretch or lean out too far on either side.

The dangers of chain saws Always call in a qualified tree surgeon to cut down large branches that can be only safely removed with a chain saw. Do not attempt to use one yourself.

Essential pruning jobs

Most pruning tasks are performed annually, but those outlined here need immediate attention and are best tackled as soon as problems are seen.

Crossing and rubbing branches

Branches that have grown too close together and are rubbing against each other is a common problem. If you spot these, remove one of the branches, either the weakest one, or the stem that has suffered the most damage. Branches that rub each other can create open wounds through which disease may enter the plant, causing serious problems.

Removing suckers

A sucker is a vigorous strong growth that emerges from a point low down on a plant, close to the root system. If left, it can choke the plant or reduce its vigour. Such shoots are normally found on plants that have been grafted, such as roses, and usually look quite different to the rest of the plant. If seen early on, remove such a shoot by quickly tugging it away with a gloved hand, or if it has grown too large, remove the shoot using secateurs.

Cutting out reversed leaves

Reversion is when the leaves of a variegated plant turn pure green. If left to grow, these green shoots, which have greater vigour, can take over and spoil the appearance of the plant. When you see any shoots that are showing signs of reversion, remove them completely using secateurs, and make sure that you prune back to where the shoots are still all variegated. This can be done at any time of the year.

A sucker growing from below the graft (knobbly bulge) on a rose

Remove green shoots from variegated plants like *Euonymus* cultivars

Dealing with twin leaders

Twin leaders occur at the top of a tree when two stems of similar vigour are growing close together. Remove the weaker stem using secateurs. If left unpruned, the stems will try to grow away from each other, causing a weakness to develop. One stem may then break away from the tree, causing serious damage. Although this may not happen until the tree is much older, prompt action when the plant is young will prevent future problems.

Remove the weaker stem | A single leader has strength

Limiting frost damage

Buds and young shoots can be damaged when caught by spring frosts. Prune plants back to healthy, unfrosted buds to prevent dieback or diseases from starting at the frosted points. Most plants will then produce new growths lower down the stems. However, on some plants, such as *Hydrangea macrophylla*, frost may damage all the new flower buds produced on the previous season's growth, and you will lose the coming year's blooms.

Hydrangea macrophylla 'Libelle' with frost damage

Cutting out dead and diseased wood

Whenever you see dead or diseased wood on any tree or shrub, remove it immediately. If dead wood is left on a plant, disease can enter more easily and it may move down the stems, attacking healthy growths. Dead wood also looks unsightly. When a tree or shrub has been damaged, its natural defences will eventually form a barrier in the form of a slight swelling between the live and dead wood. In this instance, remove the dead wood above the barrier.

Dead wood on a hornbeam | Coral spot on a branch

Deadheading to promote flowering

The removal of dead flowerheads can encourage many repeat flowering plants, like roses, to produce more blooms. These dead flowers can be snapped off with the fingers, or removed using secateurs. On some shrubs, like rhododendrons, removing the dead flowers encourages the plant to produce more stems, rather than wasting its energy on making seeds. This enables the plant to produce more flowers the following spring.

A dying rose bloom can be easily snapped off by hand

Making pruning cuts

Trees, shrubs, and climbers grow in many different ways, and their shoots, buds, and stems may look completely different too. To avoid confusion, before you start pruning, try to identify the position and type of buds and shoots on your plant, and then make your cuts.

Identifying a shoot bud Buds come in many different shapes, sizes, and colours. Some are slight swellings or raised bumps on the stems; others may be a different colour from the rest of the stem, such as rose buds (*see right*). Buds are always produced at the point where leaves are growing, or have previously been attached to the stem. When pruning, you always cut immediately above a bud, which stimulates hormones in the plant to make the bud develop into a new stem.

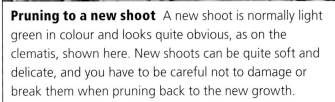

Pruning to a new shoot A new shoot is normally light green in colour and looks quite obvious, as on the clematis, shown here. New shoots can be quite soft and delicate, and you have to be careful not to damage or break them when pruning back to the new growth.

Pruning to new growth You can recognise the new growth on a plant because it looks much fresher than old wood. When pruning, cut off the old wood just above a new stem, using a sloping cut so that excess moisture runs away from the young growth.

Cutting opposite buds The buds of some plants, such as dogwoods (*Cornus*) and hydrangeas, are opposite each other. Prune immediately above a pair of buds with a flat, straight cut. When the buds grow they will produce two shoots growing in opposite directions from one another.

Cutting alternate buds The buds of plants such as roses and wisteria grow alternately along the stems. Try to prune to a bud that is facing outwards, away from the centre of the plant. Make a sloping cut immediately above the bud, so that excess moisture runs away from the bud.

Using a pruning saw If the stem you intend to prune is thicker than a finger, use a pruning saw to make the cut. Many stems are spoiled by attempting to cut them with incorrect tools. Pruning saws make a much cleaner cut than loppers. Always wear protective gloves.

Shearing When cutting shrubs or hedges with a dense habit, such as yew (*Taxus*) or box (*Buxus*), hand shears are the best tool for the job. Shears are also very useful for trimming lavenders and heathers. Make sure the shears are sharp and clean so you get a good clean cut.

Removing branches

It is very important to remove a branch correctly. Bad or rough cuts can reduce a plant's ability to heal itself, which may then allow disease to enter the wound. Eventually this can cause rotting, reducing the plant's potential lifespan.

Hard to reach branches Branches that are difficult to reach can lead the person who is pruning to take short cuts. Mistakes are more often made when one is attempting to prune from a distance. If the branch that needs to be pruned cannot be reached safely by a ladder, seek the help of a qualified and experienced tree surgeon. If a small branch is not too high, it may be possible to prune it with a long-armed lopper or pruning saw, following the same procedure shown opposite.

Torn branches A heavy branch is likely to tear when being pruned, as its weight will pull down the stem and rip it before you can complete your cut. If you don't have someone to hold the branch while you prune it, shorten it in stages before attempting the final cut. Also make an undercut first (*see Step 1, facing page*), which helps to prevent tearing when you cut through it from above.

Bad cuts Never cut flush to the trunk of the tree as this removes the tree's own healing system. It can look tidy to begin with, but the stem will not heal properly, and the open wound may then allow disease to enter the tree. Cutting branches flush with the trunk is one of the major causes of decay and ultimately death in trees.

How to remove a branch

1 Reduce the weight of a heavy branch by cutting it back in stages to leave a 15cm (6in) stump. Then make the final cut. To prevent tearing, first make an undercut where the branch starts to swell or about 3cm (1¼in) from the trunk.

2 Stop cutting when you are about half way through the branch. Then make another, slightly angled, cut from the top, just behind the crease in the bark where the branch meets the trunk. Ensure the upper cut meets the undercut.

Tip for success

3 This pruning method results in a clean cut, and leaves the plant's healing system intact. The cut surface will soon begin to shrink as the tree produces protective bark, which will eventually cover the exposed area.

When cutting a heavy branch, ask someone to help support the weight when you saw. This helps to prevent tearing. It can also stop the branch swinging or falling, and damaging the plant being pruned or the person who is pruning.

Spur pruning

Spur pruning encourages bud formation on trees, shrubs, and climbers. Where this rose has been spur pruned, it has produced three new stems, each of which will flower.

Spur pruning a rose

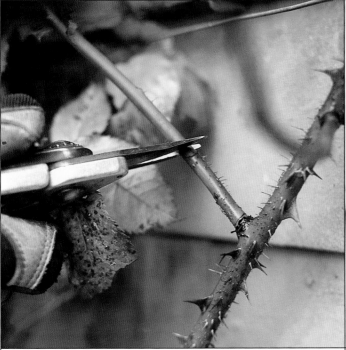

To spur prune a climbing rose, find a healthy side shoot growing from one of the main stems. Count two or three buds from the stem along the shoot. Make an angled cut immediately above this second or third bud, sloping away from it. Repeat further up the main stem.

After pruning, you will be left with short growths, which are described as "spurs". From the buds on these spurs two or three flowering stems will emerge, depending on how many buds were left on the spur.

Spur pruning wisteria

Spur prune wisterias in late winter. Using secateurs, shorten each new shoot that has grown the previous season, so that two or three healthy buds remain. Always make the cut immediately above the outermost bud and sloping away from it.

This picture shows the stems once they have been shortened to two or three buds. The buds on the short spurs will swell to produce flowers or flowering stems in late spring and early summer, producing cascades of sweetly scented purple or white blooms.

Pruning hydrangeas

Hydrangea paniculata flowers in late summer on stems it has made that same year. To keep the plants compact prune in early spring to promote new flowering wood. This also encourages larger flower panicles in the summer.

Hydrangea paniculata is an elegant plant with wonderful large cone-like flowerheads. Most have white flowers but there are also cultivars that are tinged with pink. They make excellent shrubs for the late summer garden.

1 In late winter or early spring, prune last season's stems to one or two buds from their base. Also take out any dead, diseased, crossing and weak branches.

2 Any large, unhealthy branches should be cut back into healthy wood or to the base using a pruning saw. This prevents disease from spreading to the rest of the plant and promotes the growth of new vigorous stems.

3 After pruning, you will be left with an open framework of branches. These will produce a mass of growth during the summer and an abundance of beautiful white flowers.

Hydrangea macrophylla, or mophead hydrangea, flowers in summer from buds that have already been set the previous summer. These buds are prone to frost damage in the spring months, and plants need careful pruning.

Hydrangea macrophylla produces sumptuous large flowerheads in blue, pink or white during the summer months, before *H. paniculata*. To ensure a good display, the developing flower buds need some frost protection throughout winter.

1 The hydrangea's old flowerheads help to protect the delicate new flower buds from frosts, so leave them on the plant during the winter months. The dried flowers also add structure and interest to the winter garden.

2 When the danger of hard frost has passed in late spring, remove the flowerheads by pruning the stems back to a pair of healthy buds, as shown.

3 Do not be tempted to prune too hard as this will remove many of the flower buds, which will have already formed on the stems that grew the previous year. New stems that grow in the coming year will bloom the following summer.

How to prune a smoke bush

Grown for their outstanding summer and autumn foliage, and tiny, cloud-like flowers, smoke bushes (*Cotinus*) are best pruned annually in the spring.

Other plants to prune this way

- *Catalpa bignonioides*
- *Cotinus coggygria*
- *Rhus chinensis*
- *Rhus typhina*
- *Sambucus nigra*
- *Weigela* 'Praecox Variegata'
- *Weigela* Wine and Roses

Foliage effects

Pruning hard encourages the plant to produce larger, more decorative leaves, although you may lose the smoke-like blooms.

1 Mature smoke bushes can outgrow their allotted location and suffer from dieback. Both problems are easily remedied by cutting plants back hard in the spring before the leaves appear.

2 First, remove any dead growth using a pruning saw. Also cut out diseased stems, taking them back to healthy growth. When removing large branches, cut them back in stages to ensure they do not tear.

3 To keep a cotinus small and compact, cut back all of the taller branches to about 60cm (2ft). Prune to healthy wood, which you can identify by checking that it is green in colour beneath the bark, and make sloping cuts.

4 Continue around the plant until you are left with a core structure of stems, each no higher than 60cm (2ft). New growth will soon start to sprout, resulting in plenty of fresh foliage that will provide exciting autumn colour.

Pruning witch hazel

With their fragrant, spidery flowers, witch hazels (*Hamamelis*) are wonderful shrubs in winter, but if left unpruned, they can become too large for a small garden.

Tip for success

Prune witch hazels just as the flowers are fading but before the leaves unfurl. Cut just above a healthy young sideshoot.

1 To reduce the size of this plant, in early spring prune back the taller branches by 30–50cm (12–20in). Try to keep in mind the overall shape you are aiming to achieve.

2 While pruning, step back occasionally to look at what you have cut out, and what still needs to be done. Always prune out old stems, leaving healthy young growth.

Tip for success

3 Occasionally you may find some crossing branches in the centre of the bush that are difficult to reach. If a branch is awkwardly positioned, it may be easier to cut upwards from below the branch.

If you are not sure how much to remove, reduce the length of the stems a little at a time. Stand back, and then prune more if needed, until you have created an attractive overall shape.

How to prune shrubby honeysuckle

Prune winter-flowering shrubs, such as *Lonicera x purpusii* 'Winter Beauty', in early summer. Remove the oldest flowering stems to encourage new, strong shoots to grow from the base.

Tip for success

It is much easier to use a pruning saw to cut through branches that are too thick for either loppers or secateurs.

1 First, reduce one-third of the oldest stems on the plant. Use loppers to cut back their length by about half, thereby decreasing the weight of the stem and preventing tearing, before you make the final cut closer to the ground.

2 With the loppers or a pruning saw, cut back to 30cm (12in) above the ground the stems that you have already pruned by half. Make a sloping cut immediately above a sideshoot, to allow rain to run off the cut surface.

3 Using secateurs, shorten the tallest of the new stems, which may be over 1.8m (6ft) high, by several centimetres (inches). This encourages buds further down the plant to shoot, creating a bushier plant with more flowers.

4 When you have finished pruning, you should still have some older stems that will produce flower buds the following winter. The strong young growths coming from the base will now have more room to develop.

Hard pruning a camellia

Evergreen shrubs, such as camellias, that have outgrown their position can be hard pruned in late spring or summer, just after they have finished flowering.

Other plants to prune this way

- *Aucuba japonica*
- *Elaeagnus pungens*
- *Erica arborea*
- *Escallonia*
- *Fatsia japonica*
- *Prunus laurocerasus*
- *Prunus lusitanica*
- *Viburnum tinus*

New growth

A year after pruning the plant will have produced a mass of young stems but may not flower for a further two or three years.

1 This plant has outgrown its location and now needs to be cut back hard. Camellias respond very well to severe pruning, a task best performed immediately after they have finished flowering in late spring or early summer.

2 Use a pruning saw to reduce the height of the plant. To prevent tearing, cut back large, heavy branches in stages, rather than cutting off long sections.

3 Loppers are ideal tools for pruning back awkwardly placed side stems, allowing you to reach them more easily. But the final cut close to the main branch must be made using a pruning saw, as it gives a cleaner cut.

4 Aim to reduce the plant height to about 60cm (24in). By the time you have finished, the camellia will resemble a small wooden stump, but it will not take long for new shoots to start growing.

Cutting back California lilacs and philadelphus

Most California lilacs (*Ceanothus*) have vivid blue flowers in early summer. If left unpruned, they can become large and untidy, but if cut back too severely, the plant will not regenerate. Prune immediately after flowering is finished.

1 Here you can see an evergreen *Ceanothus* in full bloom in early summer. To maintain its compact shape, it will need to be lightly pruned later in the summer, after it has finished flowering .

2 After flowering, you can more clearly see the branch structure of the plant. To keep it in good shape, cut back long, untidy branches by 22–30cm (9–12in), but leave some of the shorter stems unpruned.

3 Use secateurs to prune the branches, and make each cut immediately above a leaf bud. This will encourage the plant to produce growths from below the cut, resulting in a compact branching structure.

4 After pruning, the overall size of the plant is reduced, but it has not been cut back too severly, which would weaken it. If pruned like this annually, the *Ceanothus* will remain neat and bushy, suitable for a small garden.

Philadelphus has white scented flowers in early summer. Prune the plant after flowering to encourage the formation of new growths, which will bear flowers in the future. An annual prune also helps to contain the size of the plant.

1 In early summer, mock orange (*Philadelphus*) is a mass of white scented flowers. As soon as flowering has finished, cut back about a quarter of the oldest flowering stems to 15cm (6in) above the ground .

2 Cutting back hard some of the oldest stems promotes the formation of new shoots below the pruning cut, but do not be tempted to remove all the old stems, as this will reduce the volume of flowers the following summer.

3 Check the remaining old stems for young growths. These are best shortened rather than being hard pruned. Take off the top third of these young stems, and prune them back to new wood.

4 Finally, trim the tips of any strong young stems that are already present in the plant – some may be as tall as 2.5m (8ft). This encourages them to branch lower down, which results in more flowers.

How to prune a patio rose

Patio roses are small, repeat-flowering plants that can be grown in borders or containers. Prune them in early spring to encourage a mass of new shoots that will flower in the summer.

Tip for success

As well as pruning your rose every year, encourage it to keep flowering for longer by removing the blooms as they fade.

1 The aim of pruning is to reduce the plant's height by one-quarter to a half and to create an open shape. Cut back the outer stems, and then remove dead, diseased, and damaged growths, plus any weak and crossing stems.

2 Always prune above a strong outward-facing bud if possible. Ensure that the cuts are sloping so that rainfall runs away from the bud, reducing the chance of it rotting.

3 This strong stem is being cut back by one-half, which will encourage many strong flowering shoots to grow from it in the forthcoming summer.

4 As well as producing more flowering stems, the resulting simple framework allows air movement, which reduces the incidence of fungal diseases. Feed and mulch roses after pruning to further encourage healthy growth.

How to prune a shrub rose

Most modern shrub roses are repeat flowering and do not need to be pruned as hard as some roses, since they flower on older stems. Prune your shrub roses in early spring.

1 The aim of pruning a shrub rose is to create a strong structure and to remove congested stems that were produced the previous year. This improves air flow through the plant, which helps to prevent fungal diseases.

2 Cut off any dead, damaged, or diseased branches. Then remove any weak shoots not strong enough to support new flower growths. Also prune a few of the oldest stems down to the ground.

3 Reduce healthy main stems by a quarter, and prune some of the sideshoots by just a few centimetres (inches). Always cut above a healthy bud that faces outwards, away from the centre of the plant, if possible.

4 The pruned plant should be reduced in height by about a quarter, and have a strong, open, structure that appears uncluttered in the centre. By midsummer the plant should be covered in beautiful blooms.

Pruning other types of roses

Different types of roses have different pruning needs. Identify your roses and then follow these guidelines to ensure yours produce their best show.

Hybrid tea roses

This group of roses normally flowers more than once during the summer months. They respond well to hard pruning in early spring. First remove all dead, damaged, diseased, weak, and crossing stems, and then prune out the oldest stems, taking them back to the ground. Leave between three and five young, strong stems, which should be pruned to a height of 15cm (6in) above the soil. As a guide, stand your secateurs on the ground, and as these are normally about 15cm (6in) long, they will show you how far to prune back the stems. Always make a sloping cut above an outward-facing bud, if possible. In late autumn or early winter, reduce the height of the stems by one-third to reduce the risk of wind rocking the plant and damaging the roots.

Old garden roses

These roses normally have one flush of flowers each year. Prune in early spring, first removing any dead, damaged, diseased, weak, and crossing branches. They do not need severe pruning: aim to reduce the size of the plant by one-third. Always make a sloping cut above an outward-facing bud. In the autumn, cut back the stems by one-third to reduce the risk of wind rocking the plant and damaging the roots.

Examples of old garden roses

- *Rosa* 'Blanche Double de Coubert'
- *Rosa* 'Boule de Neige'
- *Rosa* 'Charles de Mills'
- *Rosa* 'De Rescht'
- *Rosa* 'Fantin-Latour'
- *Rosa* 'Frau Dagmar Hartopp'
- *Rosa* 'Louise Odier'
- *Rosa* 'Madame Isaac Pereire'
- *Rosa* 'Madame Pierre Oger'
- *Rosa* 'Maiden's Blush'
- *Rosa mundi*
- *Rosa rugosa*
- *Rosa rugosa* 'Alba'
- *Rosa* 'Souvenir de la Malmasion'
- *Rosa* 'William Lobb'

Examples of hybrid tea roses

- *Rosa* Alexander
- *Rosa* 'Blessings'
- *Rosa* Dawn Chorus
- *Rosa* 'Deep Secret'
- *Rosa* Elina
- *Rosa* Freedom
- *Rosa* Ingrid Bergman
- *Rosa* 'Just Joey'
- *Rosa* Lovely Lady
- *Rosa* Paul Shirville
- *Rosa* Peace
- *Rosa* Remember Me
- *Rosa* Savoy Hotel
- *Rosa* 'Silver Jubilee'
- *Rosa* Tequila Sunrise
- *Rosa* Troika
- *Rosa* Warm Wishes

Floribunda roses

Floribundas are repeat-flowering roses that produce clusters of blooms during the summer months. Pruning is very similar to hybrid tea roses, but not quite as hard. First, remove all dead, damaged, diseased, weak, and crossing stems. Your aim is to leave a framework of between six and eight of the strongest, youngest stems. Prune them to a height of between 20–30cm (8–12in), always make a sloping cut just above an outward-facing bud, if possible. In the autumn or early winter, reduce the height of the stems by one-third to reduce the risk of damage when wind rocks the plant and disturbs its root system.

Examples of floribunda roses

- *Rosa* 'Arthur Bell'
- *Rosa* 'English Miss'
- *Rosa* Fascination
- *Rosa* Fellowship
- *Rosa* 'Fragrant Delight'
- *Rosa* Iceberg
- *Rosa* Memento
- *Rosa* Pretty Lady
- *Rosa* 'Princess of Wales'
- *Rosa* Queen Elizabeth
- *Rosa* Remembrance
- *Rosa* Sexy Rexy
- *Rosa* Sunset Boulevard
- *Rosa* Tall Story
- *Rosa* The Times Rose
- *Rosa* Trumpeter

Extending flowering

Deadhead repeat-flowering roses throughout the summer to encourage them to bloom for a longer period. By removing the flowers, you prevent the plant from using its energy to form seed and stimulate it to produce more flowers instead. The easiest way to do this, and the way now practised in many large gardens, is to bend the stem just below the old flower, as shown, until it snaps off. The plant will soon start forming new flower buds. Alternatively, use secateurs to remove the flower and about 15cm (6in) of growth. The plant will then form more flowers buds, but it normally takes longer than the "snapping off" method.

Shearing lavender

Lavender (*Lavandula*) is a beautiful, aromatic shrub that can be grown on its own or as a low growing, colourful hedge. To maintain a good shape, it is best sheared twice a year.

Tip for success

After flowering, remove all the old flowerheads with secateurs. This stops the plant from putting all its energy into making seed.

1 To keep your lavender plants young, bushy, and healthy, cut them back in late winter or early spring using clean, sharp hedge shears.

2 Shear the lavender as close as possible without cutting into the old wood. This is very important as the old wood does not regenerate, which means that if you cut into it no new shoots will grow from the stems.

3 Here, you can see how the lavender has been cut just above where the new green shoots meet the old, brown wood. Shear to this point, and work systematically along and around the hedge, keeping it as level as possible.

4 This form of pruning encourages the lavender to become very bushy, and to produce a greater volume of flowers. The hedge then needs to be pruned again as the flowers fade in summer (see *Tip for success opposite*).

How to prune wall shrubs

Euonymus fortunei cultivars are vigorous plants that will grow even in poor soil. They often form rounded shrubs, but will also grow vertically, the variegated forms creating bright cladding for walls and fences. Prune plants in late spring.

1 As with all variegated plants, it is important to remove any growths that are showing signs of reversion, where stems of all-green leaves appear. Cut these back to variegated foliage using secateurs as soon as possible.

2 Using secateurs, cut back to a suitable length any very long growths that are hanging away from the wall and causing the plant to loose its neat shape.

3 To keep it neat and bushy, trim over the whole plant with hedging shears. Keep one eye on the overall shape to ensure you trim it as evenly as possible.

4 Remove any growths that are growing towards or into gutters or over doors and windows. When you have finished, the plant should resemble a closely clipped hedge growing against its supporting wall or fence.

Garrya elliptica is a useful evergreen shrub that produces long, pendulous catkins in the winter. It prefers to grow against the shelter of a wall for support and protection, and is best pruned in the spring, as the catkins are fading.

1 Any plant occasionally needs a prune to prevent it from growing too tall or wide. For a shrub trained against a wall, it also prevents it from becoming too heavy and pulling or falling away from its support.

2 Start by pruning the longest horizontal branches to reduce the width of the plant. Always make the cuts above a leaf bud or stem shoot to encourage new, fuller growth during the coming year.

3 Once you have trimmed the horizontal branches, start pruning the tall, vertical stems. Cut them back to a height that is appropriate for the position of the plant.

4 If the plant is pruned carefully, it should still retain its natural shape afterwards. The new growths that appear as a result of pruning will produce a good show of catkins the following winter.

How to prune a mahonia

When evergreens such as this mahonia have outgrown their allotted space they can be pruned back severely from midwinter to early spring, after flowering has finished.

Tip for success

To keep plants short and bushy and to encourage greater flower production, remove flowerheads immediately after flowering.

1 Prune back tall stems, removing a little at a time, rather than cutting back the whole growth in one go. At this stage cut the stems to about 60cm (2ft) high, keeping in mind the plant's balanced shape as you prune.

2 Once you have cut back the tall growths, look to see where you can make your final pruning cuts. At the same time, remove any damaged, diseased, or crossing stems, and cut out any old growths to leave 5 or 6 strong stems.

3 Cut back the remaining young healthy stems so that they are 30–40cm (12–16in) above the ground. If possible, ensure that all the cuts you make are slightly sloping to encourage the rain to run off.

4 Later in the year a mass of young shoots will grow from these shortened stems. The plant may not flower until two years after a severe pruning like this. Thereafter, to keep it bushy, follow the Tip for success (*see facing page*).

Pruning a holly bush

A well-shaped holly (*Ilex*) can provide a wonderful structural focal point in the garden all year round. To maintain their shape, it is best to prune holly bushes in early spring.

Holly hedge

Holly has thick, chunky growth so holly hedges are best trimmed in late summer using a petrol or electric hedge cutter.

1 To ensure that this young holly remains an attractive feature in the garden, it needs to be pruned annually, first to form a conical shape, and then to retain it.

2 Remove some of the lower branches to create space under the bush and a short, clear stem. This is known as "lifting the skirt" and produces a bolder appearance.

3 If two branches are growing closely together at the top of the plant and causing it to lose its conical shape, cut the weaker one – or the stem that is least vertical – above a shoot that is growing in line with the conical outline.

4 Work all around the bush, trimming back any branches that are too long, until you have a conical shape that is symmetrical and pleasing to the eye.

How to prune an apple tree

When carefully managed, an apple tree is highly ornamental, providing decorative blossom in the spring and a wealth of colourful fruit in the autumn. Prune in summer or winter.

1 Start by removing any branches that are crowding the centre of the tree. This will allow air to circulate, which reduces the risk of fungal infections during the summer. Also remove any dead, diseased, or damaged branches.

2 Cut the branches back to the collar. Make clean cuts with a sharp saw to reduce the risk of infection entering the wounds. Don't prune too hard, as it stimulates leafy growth at the expense of flowers and fruit.

3 Only reduce the height of the tree yourself if you can reach the top easily. Cut back any long branches by a half to one-third, or to a suitable side branch that, if possible, faces outwards to prevent any crossing branches.

4 When pruning back to a side branch, make an undercut first, and saw half way through the stem. Then make the final cut from above, sloping away from the side branch, to meet the undercut. This prevents the branch from tearing.

How to prune an apple tree *continued*

5 The sloping cut you make after removing a branch (*above*) allows moisture and rainfall to drain off the cut surface, reducing the risk of rotting. The remaining side branch should also point outwards.

6 Shorten any long, thin, whippy growths by cutting them back to short branches or spurs with a pair of secateurs. This encourages flower bud formation from these branches.

7 Where pruning cuts have been made in previous years, remove any short, weak, or crowded stems growing around the wound. These are of no use to the tree and divert energy from the main branches and flower stems.

8 Remove all branches that are crossing or are starting to grow from the outside of the tree into the centre. This helps to prevent branches from rubbing against each other in future, thereby reducing the risk of disease.

9 Continue to work around the tree, removing unwanted branches and taking care to make clean cuts. Step back from the tree to ensure you have created a balanced, simple framework, with an uncongested centre.

How to prune wisteria

Wisterias are beautiful plants for training up house walls and other structures. Prune these large, vigorous climbers twice a year, once in summer to keep the plant in check, and again in winter to help stimulate flowering.

Summer pruning

1 Wisterias are vigorous plants and during the summer after they have flowered, the plants produce very long tendril-like shoots that can block house windows or paths, or swamp their supporting structures.

2 To keep your wisteria tidy, reduce these shoots by two-thirds after the flowers have faded. This process may have to be repeated several times during the summer months as the plant continues to grow.

Winter pruning

1 In late winter, when the leaves have dropped, you will be able to see the effects of your summer pruning. The pruned stems will have developed new growth, which will look lighter in colour than older wood.

2 Spur prune all the stems that you pruned in the summer back to two or three healthy buds. These buds will then swell to become flower buds in spring.

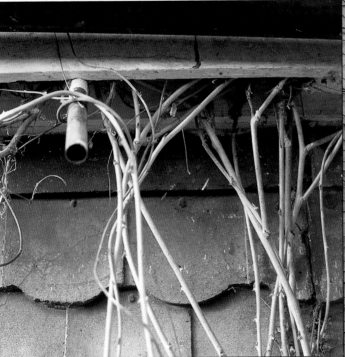

3 Also remove any stems that are growing into the eaves of the house, under roofing tiles, or around drainpipes. If left, they could cause damage to the house structure.

4 Ensure all stems are tied to sturdy wires on the house or plant supports, as wisteria is not self-clinging. The plant will look quite naked, but the buds will develop into a wall of scented flowers in late spring or early summer.

Cutting back clematis

Admired for their beautiful flowers, you can use clematis for an almost year-round show. They are divided into three groups, each with different pruning needs, so work out which one yours belongs to and follow these guidelines.

Group 1

Group 1 clematis are vigorous plants, and include *C. montana*, *C. alpina* and *C. armandii*. Flowering in late spring on the previous year's growth, they require very little pruning. Prune lightly immediately after they have flowered to contain their size, and remove dead, diseased, or damaged growth.

Group 2

This group of early summer-flowering clematis have large flowers that are produced from the previous year's growth. Many will also produce a second flush of flowers in late summer. Group 2 clematis require a light prune in early spring. Prune back the stems to a pair of healthy buds.

Group 3

Group 3 clematis include the small-flowered viticella and texensis types, *C. tangutica* and its cultivars, and some large-flowered hybrids. They bloom from midsummer to autumn on new season's growth and require hard pruning in early spring, or you can prune them more lightly.

Clematis montana (Group 1)

Clematis 'Nelly Moser' (Group 2)

Clematis 'Etoile Violette' (Group 3)

Clematis 'Frances Rivis' (Group 1)

Clematis 'H.E.Young' (Group 2)

Clematis tangutica (Group 3)

Pruning after planting

Help all groups of clematis to get established by pruning them after planting in spring, or in their first year immediately after flowering. Reduce the plant's height by one half, ensuring that you prune above a pair of healthy buds. This encourages the plant to produce growths from all the buds on the stem below the pruning cut, which will ultimately give you a much stronger plant. It also encourages root production, helping to develop strong, healthy growth. Take care when handling any clematis as the shoots can be very brittle.

Pruning Group 1

Immediately after flowering, give Group 1 clematis a light trim to help contain the size of the plant and to keep it looking tidy. Prune strong, leggy new season's growths, cutting above a pair of healthy buds. This will also help to show off the plant's attractive fluffy seedheads, but don't prune too hard or you will remove them. If a plant becomes too large, occasionally prune all stems back to 15cm (6in) from the ground in early spring. Montanas may not recover from this treatment, so only carry out drastic pruning if you have no choice.

Pruning Group 2

Prune Group 2 clematis in early spring when the buds are already in growth and new stems are visible. Work from the top of the plant, pruning each stem back to the first pair of healthy buds or growths. Remove any dead, diseased, or damaged wood. New growths will appear along the pruned stems, and these produce the flowers in early summer. If the plant has outgrown its site, hard prune all stems to 15cm (6in) from the ground in early spring. It may then not flower during the forthcoming summer, or it may bloom later in the season.

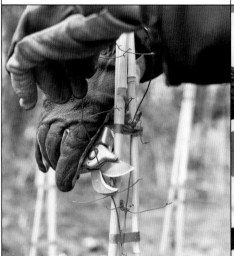

Prune above a pair of healthy buds

Cut away excess growth in spring

Prune lightly back to new growth

New growth soon emerges

Pruning helps to show off seedheads

Buds open below the pruning cuts

How to prune a Group 3 clematis

The late-flowering *Clematis* x *jouiniana* is extremely vigorous, and is suitable for clothing large supports or growing through substantial shrubs or small trees. As it belongs to pruning Group 3, it requires hard pruning in early spring.

1 This clematis has been grown over a large pyramid support made from birch twigs. Start pruning by removing all the loose growths that are covering the support.

2 Once all the stems have been removed from the support, you will have better access to the base of the plant. Prune back all long growths to give a manageable clump of short stems before making your final cuts.

3 Prune the growths hard back to one or two buds from the ground, as shown. Always make straight cuts just above a pair of healthy buds to reduce the risk of dieback.

4 You will be left with a mound of growths about 15cm (6in) high. To encourage healthy growth, add a little fertilizer and mulch. The plant will then grow 2–3m (6–10ft) and will be covered in flowers during late summer.

Lightly pruning late-flowering Group 3 clematis, such as this *Clematis tangutica*, encourages the plant to flower earlier.

Follow these simple steps to create a cascade of beautiful yellow nodding flowers throughout the summer.

1 In early spring and starting at the top of the plant, lightly prune back the main stems to fit the shape of the support. As with any pruning, also remove dead, damaged, or diseased stems as you work.

2 Then lightly prune the side stems back to the plant support. This will maintain the shape of the plant and encourage strong new growths that will flower in the summer. Make sure all cuts are made above two buds.

3 If there are strong young growths coming from the base of the plant, tie them in to the rest of the clematis so that they will not wave about in the wind and get damaged — clematis stems are brittle and easily broken.

4 When you have finished, the clematis should look as if it has had a light haircut, since you have just trimmed it back to the shape of the supporting structure.

Cutting back honeysuckle and ivy

Climbing honeysuckles (*Lonicera*) are grown for their beautifully scented flowers. Allow them to scramble over shrubs and trees in the garden, or encourage them to climb up supports, such as fences or trellises.

Climbing honeysuckles are easy to grow, and produce masses of sweetly scented blooms in summer. As they age, plants can become woody at the base, and look untidy and overgrown. Keep them in check and flowering prolifically by pruning regularly.

1 In spring, contain the size of a honeysuckle by removing long straggly growths and reducing the overall height of the plant by 30–50cm (12–20in).

2 Remove old, dead, damaged, or diseased stems. If your plant is very overgrown, cut all the stems back to about 15cm (6in) from the ground. New shoots will soon appear from the base, but you may lose the flowers that year.

3 Unless you gave the plant a hard prune, by late summer it will produce an even covering of flowers. If the plant has put on a lot of growth and is looking untidy, trim it again immediately after flowering has finished.

Ivies are versatile evergreen climbers that will grow in sun or shade, and adhere to almost any support or surface. In late spring or early summer, prune these vigorous plants to contain their spread, and to prevent stems clogging gutters.

1 The aim of pruning here is to reduce the plant's spread over the fence and to remove it from the tree trunk in front. Ivy can collect a lot of dust and dirt, so wear a dust mask when pruning if this affects you.

2 Working from the top of the fence panel, pull away long lengths of ivy. When you are happy with the amount removed, cut off the stems with secateurs. Also cut and pull away any ivy growing on tree trunks or other plants.

3 Remove ivy growing up walls and into house guttering. When removing ivy from walls you will reveal marks left by the roots, which help the ivy to cling to the surface. Use a stiff brush to remove the root residue.

4 The ivy has been cut back from the top of the fence by about 45cm (18in) to allow room for regrowth. It has also been removed from the tree trunk, resulting in a less cluttered and lighter part of the garden.

How to prune a rose on a tripod

Climbing roses, such as this *R.* 'White Cockade', can be trained over a wooden tripod to create a lovely focal point in a small space. Prune the rose in autumn or early spring.

Before pruning

The plant is a mass of stems, some of which are old and must be removed, while the younger stems need to be tied in.

1 Start by removing the rose stems from the tripod support. Cut all the ties that are holding the rose to the support, and then carefully unwind the stems, working down from the top of the plant.

2 Cut out any dead, damaged, or diseased wood. Then remove about one in three of the oldest stems by pruning them close to the base of the plant. Leave enough stems unpruned to cover the tripod.

3 With the unpruned older stems that you left to cover the tripod, spur prune the previous season's flowering stems, and tie them in. These spurs will produce flowering stems in the forthcoming summer.

4 Tie back the remaining young flexible stems using garden twine. To give the best coverage over the tripod, tie some in a clockwise and others in an anticlockwise direction.

Pruning rambling and climbing roses

Ensure a mass of flowers each year by pruning rambling and climbing roses during the autumn while their stems are still quite flexible. If you don't have time in autumn, these roses can also be pruned in late winter or early spring.

1 Remove one in three of the oldest flowering stems. These growths will be quite thick and should be cut back to almost ground level using a pruning saw or loppers.

2 Use sharp secateurs to spur prune the previous summer's flowering stems back to two or three healthy buds. These will then produce flowering stems during the forthcoming summer months.

Summer maintenance

3 Use garden twine or special rose ties to tie in all the stems. Bending flexible stems over and tying them onto horizontal supports or wires encourages the production of more flowering growths.

Do not attempt to prune a rambling rose in summer. Just tie in and support the long, strong new growths that have been produced, so that they are not damaged or broken. These are the stems that you will be cutting back when pruning and training in autumn.

This climbing rose has been carefully pruned and trained along horizontal wires that have been attached to the wall with vine eyes. Use galvanised wire and fix it at about 30cm (12in) intervals up the wall before planting your rose.

1 Cut all the ties that are holding the rose to the wires and pull the stems away from the wall. Remove one in three of the oldest flowering stems. Do not remove any of the strong new growths produced from the base of the plant.

2 Spur prune last season's flowering stems back to two or three healthy buds to encourage them to produce more flowering stems in the months ahead.

3 Tie all the remaining growths back onto the wires, and try to cover as much of the wall as possible. You may find some of the stems cross over one another but this won't be a problem as long as they don't rub.

4 Step back from time to time to ensure that you have tied the stems in a fan shape over the wall. By the time summer arrives, the plant will have produce more stems covered in leaves and flowers and the wall will be hidden.

Choosing a site

Growing vegetables in ideal conditions is not always possible, particularly if you have limited space, but it pays to find a sunny spot that is sheltered from the wind and easily accessible for watering and weeding.

Sheltered or sunny walls

A wall that faces the sun provides plants with protection from the wind and reflects the sun's heat back onto your crops during the day. It will also absorb heat and release it at night when the air temperature falls. A sheltered microclimate is ideal for growing heat-loving vegetables, such as tomatoes, aubergines, and peppers, so if you have one in your garden, make the most of it. Improve the soil, create a raised bed, or position pots at the base of the wall. Remember to keep plants well watered.

Tips for sunny walls
- Add supports, such as wire mesh, to the wall to secure tall and scrambling plants as they grow.
- Take advantage of a sunny wall as the perfect backdrop for tomatoes in a growing bag.
- Be adventurous and try growing more unusual crops, such as sweetcorn and chillies.

Small vegetable beds

Make the most of a small space by planning your crops carefully and squeezing as much variety into the plot as possible. Many vegetables are attractive plants in their own right, but add extra colour to the beds by including some flowers, too, which will not only look good but also help to attract pollinating insects. Planting vegetables close together also means that there is little bare soil on which weeds can establish, helping to minimize maintenance, but crop yields may be slightly reduced.

Tips for small vegetable beds
- Densely planted vegetables need a rich soil, so work in plenty of organic matter in autumn.
- Choose vegetable varieties with interesting colours and forms to add drama to your beds.
- Be wary of planting too close to tall hedges, which cast shade and take moisture from the soil.

A greater range of vegetables can be grown by a sunny wall.

Rows of vegetables packed tightly together will suppress weeds.

Growing under cover

Protecting crops from cold and wet weather in a greenhouse, cold frame, or under cloches gives them a head start in spring, extends the growing season into autumn, and allows a range of tender vegetables to be grown that may not perform well outdoors. Fitting large structures into a small garden can be difficult, so consider whether you have a suitable site before buying costly equipment. Site greenhouses and frames in full sun, away from overhanging trees, but sheltered from the wind as much as possible. Plants under cover rely on the gardener to provide adequate water and temperature control, which can amount to a lot of work, so make sure you have the time.

Tips for growing under cover

- Control greenhouse ventilation to regulate temperatures and remove damp air that can encourage disease. Automatic ventilation is a good investment.
- Use cold frames and mobile cloches for raising seedlings and protecting young plants.
- Where there is no space outdoors, try sowing seeds and growing heat-loving crops on a sunny windowsill.
- Install a water supply, such as a water butt, next to the greenhouse to make life easier.

Container growing

Filling pots, troughs, and windowboxes with a range of vegetables is one of the best ways for those with little or even no garden to harvest their own, homegrown produce. Tomatoes, salads, dwarf beans, herbs, and some root vegetables are just a few of the crops that will thrive in containers and can make attractive displays on patios, steps, and windowsills. Containers filled with good-quality compost are also useful in gardens with very poor soil or where soil-borne pests and diseases make vegetable growing difficult. However, containers can be expensive to buy and fill with compost, and without regular watering and feeding, plants will not perform well, so consider the practicalities before you begin.

Tips for container growing

- Keep costs down and be creative by making your own pots from galvanized metal bins or plastic containers.
- Good drainage is vital to prevent soil becoming waterlogged, so ensure pots have holes in their bases.
- Choose large pots, as they hold more soil, take longer to dry out, and suit many vegetables well.
- Look out for vegetable varieties suited to container growing, such as short, round carrots.

It is crucial to choose a site in full sun for your greenhouse.

Colourful crops, like this chard, are easy to grow in pots.

Making compost

Every gardener should find space for a compost heap or bin, as it turns garden and kitchen waste into a valuable source of organic matter to dig into soil or use as a mulch.

The final product Compost should be dark brown with a crumbly texture and pleasant, soil-like smell. The decomposition of bulky organic materials requires oxygen, moisture, and the right balance of carbon- and nitrogen-rich waste (*opposite*), which means that careful management is necessary. However, a successful compost heap is easy to achieve.

Different compost bin designs Your first task is to find a compost bin that suits the size of your garden and the amount of waste to be broken down. It is best to have two bins to allow the contents of one to be aerated by turning it into a second bin, which means that a new heap can be started in the first. The type of bin you choose depends on appearance, space, and cost considerations, but ensure that it has a loose-fitting cover to prevent waterlogging. Place your bin on bare soil, add compostable material, and let nature do the rest.

Wooden bins look good and can be bought or homemade. Choose a design with removable front slats for easy turning.

Plastic bins are relatively cheap and simple to install, but their design means that turning the contents can be tricky.

Bins constructed from wire mesh are particularly suitable for composting fallen leaves to make leaf mould.

What goes on the heap? Almost all plant waste from the garden can be composted, except for diseased material, perennial weeds, and meat and cooked waste, which attracts vermin. Nitrogen-rich (green) waste aids decomposition, but this must be balanced with carbon-rich (brown) waste to open up the structure of the heap and allow air to circulate. Aim to add a 50:50 mix of green and brown waste to your heap during the year.

What to add

- Carbon-rich woody prunings and hedge trimmings (which usually need to be shredded), plant stems, autumn leaves, shredded newspaper and cardboard.
- Nitrogen-rich grass clippings, herbaceous plant material, weeds, old vegetable plants, fruit and veg peelings, tea bags, coffee grounds.

Carbon-rich brown material adds bulk.

Chop up woody material before adding.

Making a compost trench

Kitchen waste, such as fruit and vegetable peelings, tea bags, and egg shells can also be composted in a long trench. The trench is best made during the autumn, when large areas of soil are often bare and the waste has time to break down before planting begins in spring. Vigorous plants, such as runner beans and squashes, respond particularly well to the high nutrient levels provided by kitchen left-overs.

Dig a trench about 30cm (12in) wide to one spade's depth and fill it with alternate layers of waste and soil. Then add a layer of soil on top. Allow at least two months before planting over the trench. As with any composting method, do not include meat or cooked waste because it may attract vermin.

Scatter waste on the bottom of the trench.

Fill with alternate layers of soil and waste.

Water-wise gardening

Hosepipe bans and water metering can cause problems during hot, dry summers, but the solution is to know how to use resources efficiently and to store your own supplies.

Keeping plants healthy Plants in dry soil are susceptible to disease and yield less, so it pays to keep soil moist. Watering thoroughly so the moisture penetrates deep into the soil is better than wetting the surface daily. Water in the evening or early morning to minimize evaporation.

Storing rainwater Water can be collected from the roofs of houses, garages, sheds, and greenhouses, and stored in water butts. These supplies of rainwater are a valuable alternative to mains water, although during hot summer months, rainfall rarely keeps up with demand.

A water butt is often easier than a mains tap to install in a convenient area of the garden, by a greenhouse or potting shed, for example. Make sure that you sit your water butt on a stack of bricks, slabs, or a purpose-made base, to allow a watering can to fit under the tap. Although many gardeners dislike the appearance of plastic butts, they are easy to disguise with ornamental planting, such as grasses and bamboo (*right*), or tall rows of runner beans.

Using grey water Water that has already been used in the home is usually suitable for watering plants in the garden. Normal household soaps and detergents do not damage plants but avoid bleaches and strong disinfectants. Allow hot water to cool before applying it to the soil.

Water the roots Pour water around the stem base, beneath the plant's foliage, so that it is absorbed into the soil around the roots where it is needed. The shade of the foliage also helps to prevent evaporation, and neighbouring weeds are not inadvertently watered, too.

Cloches and cold frames

Protect crops from pests and bring on their growth in cold weather by covering them with cloches or growing them in permanent cold frames.

Plastic bottle cloches Many plants benefit from protection in cool spring and autumn weather. Commercial cloches can be expensive, so large, clear plastic bottles, cut in half and placed over plants, are an effective alternative.

Corrugated plastic cloches Whole rows of plants can be covered using long, low tunnel cloches, which are left open at the ends for thorough ventilation or closed off when greater protection is required. No rain will reach cloched plants so remember to water them as necessary.

Rigid plastic cloches These large cloches are ideal for protecting blocks of young plants or more substantial crops, such as courgettes or early potatoes. The warm, dry atmosphere is also perfect for drying onion crops after harvest. Anchor these light structures to the ground.

Cold frames Usually permanent structures of brick with framed glass "lights", cold frames are useful for hardening off young plants and extending the productive season of crops such as salads and courgettes. Constructed in a sheltered, sunny spot, they are a good alternative to a greenhouse in a small garden, with the angled lights allowing water to run off and the maximum amount of light to reach the plants. A frame with a hard base is good for acclimatizing pot-grown plants to outdoor temperatures, while a bed of improved soil allows crops to be grown in the frame. Prop the lights open during the day to provide ventilation, and keep plants inside well watered.

Root crops

Cultivation tips

How to grow Easy to grow, most root crops simply need to be sown outdoors and kept free of weeds and pests to do well. With carefully selected varieties and successional sowing, you can harvest root crops all year.

Site and soil Many root crops like a well-drained, slightly acid soil that holds organic matter with some nutrients dug in. Potatoes, however, crop best on recently manured soil. Brassica root crops may succumb to club root on acid soils that have not been limed. Stony soils may cause malformation of long-rooted crops.

Sowing Most root crops can be grown from seed outdoors from early spring. Sow into drills at a depth of about 2cm (¾ in) Potatoes need a depth of 10cm (4in). Cover with soil and water in. Sow carrots, beetroot, turnips and radishes every few weeks for a continuous supply.

Care and potential problems Thin seedlings out, leaving strong plants to grow on at the correct spacing. Keep the surrounding soil weed-free and moist, watering in dry spells. Protect potato plants from frost and cover their lower stems and leaves with soil as they grow.

Roots in pots Carrots, beetroot, and radishes all grow happily in containers at least 25cm (10in) wide and deep – larger pots are needed for potatoes – as long as they are kept well watered. This is a good way to start the earliest crops under cover.

Growing potatoes through black plastic If earthing up potatoes sounds like too much effort, try planting your crop through holes cut in a layer of thick black plastic – push the edges into the soil to secure the plastic in place. This keeps out the light and helps warm the soil for a fast-maturing crop.

Crops to choose

Potato Early varieties suit small gardens since they are harvested by midsummer, whereas maincrops tie up the soil until mid-autumn.

Beetroot Not all beetroot are red, so you can choose unusually coloured varieties and opt for bolt-resistant types for early sowings.

Parsnip These roots will stand in the soil through winter with a covering of straw, but seeds need to be sown the previous spring.

Radish Sow radishes successionally for crops over a long season. Exotic hardy winter radishes can also be sown in summer.

Brassicas

Cultivation tips

How to grow Encompassing many of the hardiest winter crops, including cabbages and Brussels sprouts, this group also includes many summer favourites and oriental greens.

Site and soil Moist, well-drained, fertile soil suits most brassicas, so it is best to work in plenty of organic matter well in advance of planting. Lime should be added to soil with a pH lower than 6.8 to prevent clubroot. Brassicas prefer full sun, but will tolerate partial shade, while taller plants, such as Brussels sprouts, need to be staked on windy sites.

Sowing Most brassicas are best sown into an outdoor nursery bed under cover in spring and transplanted into their final positions as young plants. However, sow summer sowings of calabrese and kohlrabi directly into seedbeds in their final positions.

Care and potential problems Brassicas like cool weather and tend to bolt during hot, dry spells. Water transplants daily and mature plants once a week in dry weather. Cover the plants with fleece to prevent butterflies laying their eggs. Slugs, snails, aphids and whitefly all enjoy brassicas. Take measures to avoid clubroot.

Thwarting cabbage root fly Female flies lay their eggs at the base of young plants, so buy protective collars, or make your own out of thick paper. Use 15cm (6in) squares of paper and cut a slit and fit.

Coming back for seconds Broccoli and calabrese continue to produce secondary spears after the central one is cut, and frequent harvesting encourages even more. When harvesting summer cabbages, leave 5cm (2in) stumps and cut a cross 1 cm (½in) deep in the top. This will encourage a second crop to develop.

Crops to choose

Cauliflower Best on rich, heavy soils with plenty of manure. Snap outer leaves over each curd to protect them from sun and frost.

Kale Hardy and tolerant of poor soils, kale is easy to grow. Colourful, textured varieties brighten up the winter garden.

Brussels sprouts Harvest this classic winter vegetable from the base of the stem upwards, by snapping off each sprout by hand.

Kohlrabi Eat the swollen stems of these fast-growing exotics in salads or stir-fries. Harvest when no larger than a tennis ball.

Legumes

Pea and bean crops require less fertilizer than other vegetables because their roots are home to bacteria that take nitrogen from the air and fix it in the soil. Leave the nutrient-rich roots to break down in the soil after harvest.

Sugar snap peas ready for harvesting.

How to grow

Site and soil These climbing plants do best in full sun on fertile, slightly alkaline soil, improved with plenty of organic matter. Since they are susceptible to similar pests and diseases, practise crop rotation. Broad beans prefer clay soils, while other peas and beans do best on lighter soils. Provide shelter from strong winds.

Sowing and planting out All legume seeds need a warm soil in which to germinate, so wait until mid-spring to sow outdoors or start them off under cloches or in pots indoors. Successional sowings help to ensure a steady supply of produce. Erect appropriate supports before sowing or planting out to avoid damaging young plants.

Care and potential problems Beans are commonly grown up wigwams or rows of canes held together with string; peas scramble up chicken wire supported by canes or twiggy pea sticks. Beans may need coaxing up and tying into their supports, while peas hold on with tendrils.
  Keep plants well weeded, and mulch if possible. There is no need to water before flowering, unless plants are wilting. Begin watering generously when flowering starts to encourage pods to set. For bushier plants, pinch out growing tips when plants reach the top of their supports.
  Rodents love legume seeds, so sow indoors where this is a problem. Protect crops from pea moths by covering with fleece. Infestations of aphids are also common.

Harvest and storage Peas and beans are at their tastiest when small and freshly picked, so harvest frequently; this also encourages greater yields. Eating quality deteriorates quickly, even when crops are refrigerated, so either use straight away or freeze any excess as soon after harvest as possible. Borlotti beans can be left on the plant to mature, then dried and stored in a cool, dark place.

Sowing depths and spacing

CROP	SOWING DEPTH	SPACING	
		Plants	Rows
Broad beans	8cm (3in)	25cm (10in)	30cm (12in)
French beans, dwarf	5cm (2in)	10cm (4in)	45cm (18in)
climbing	5cm (2in)	15cm (6in)	45cm (18in)
Runner beans	5cm (2in)	15cm (6in)	45cm (18in)
Peas	4cm (1½in)	10cm (4in)	45–60cm (18–24in)

Cultivation tips

Discouraging blackfly on broad beans Blackfly are fond of the young, sappy growth at the tips of broad bean plants. Deter them by pinching out the tips when plants have plenty of flowers and the first pods have set.

Supporting runner beans Climbing French and runner beans need the support of sturdy canes, ideally at least 2.2m (7ft) tall, to hold up their lush growth. Wigwams of six or eight canes tied at the top are easy to construct.

Crops to choose

Colourful peas With violet flowers and pods, the mangetout pea 'Ezethas Krombek Blauwschok' adds colour to the productive garden.

Broad beans Rarely available fresh in the shops, these delicious beans are easy to grow and can be sown in autumn for a welcome late spring crop.

French beans Dwarf varieties of this heavy-cropping legume suit the small garden very well. They thrive in pots to yield plenty of gourmet beans.

Borlotti beans Grown in the same way as a climbing French bean, this beautiful Italian variety has pink-flecked pods. Eat the beans fresh or use them dried.

Alliums

Cultivation tips

How to grow Alliums include onions, leeks, and garlic. All are strongly flavoured and simple to grow on free-draining soils.

Site and soil A sunny, open site with fertile, well-drained soil is ideal for members of the onion family because they are prone to fungal diseases in damp conditions. Treat soil with a pH of less than 6.5 with lime, and don't grow them in the same place every year. Manure the ground a few months in advance to stop too much soft growth.

Sowing and planting out All alliums, except garlic, can be grown from seed. Sow in modules in early spring under glass for early crops, or outdoors for later crops. Harden off seedlings and plant out at the desired spacing, or thin direct-sown rows. The final spacing dictates the harvest size of the bulbs. Transplant leek seedlings when they are pencil-size. Drop them into holes 15cm (6in) deep and the width of a spade shaft. Water well, but do not back fill with soil. Succession sow spring onions. Onions and shallots can also be planted as sets (and garlic as cloves). Place sets 10cm (4in) apart in shallow drills.

Care and potential problems Water onions and shallots in very dry weather. Leeks respond well to regular watering and a mulch. All alliums are susceptible to fungal diseases, including onion white rot, downy mildew, and fusarium. Maintain good air flow around the plants and remove any infected material.

Harvest and storage Harvest leeks and spring onions when green, but allow the leaves of onions, shallots, and garlic to yellow and die down before lifting them. Store onions, shallots, and garlic on a wire rack until the leaves rustle; then hang them in a cool, dry place.

Crops to choose

Onions Small or heat-treated onion sets are less likely to bolt, so are a good choice for novices wanting a trouble-free crop.

Shallots A single shallot set will divide to produce a crop of several small, sweet bulbs, which are expensive in the shops.

Garlic Do not plant supermarket cloves; you will achieve better yields using virus-free stock of cooler-climate varieties.

Spring onions A quick, easy onion, ideal for the gaps between slower growing crops. Try one of the unusual red varieties.

Cucurbits

Cultivation tips

How to grow Vigorous and high-yielding, these plants, which include pumpkins, courgettes, and cucumbers are great fun to grow. Trailing varieties look good scrambling up a fence or over an arch. Some cucurbits may need hand pollination: female flowers have mini-fruit behind them, while male flowers grow on a thin stem. Remove male cucumber flowers in the greenhouse to prevent pollination and deformed, bitter fruits.

Site and soil Plants in the pumpkin family come from hot climates and thrive on well-drained soil enriched with organic matter. Once established, their growth can be rapid and extensive, so leave them enough space. Cucumbers do well in pots or growing bags.

Sowing and planting out These tender plants cannot tolerate frost and will not grow in the cold. Sow seeds indoors, in biodegradable pots to prevent root disturbance, and plant seedlings out when the weather improves. Harden seedlings off before planting out after the last frosts.

Care and potential problems Cucurbits require lots of watering. Cucumbers and squashes often benefit from support: cane wigwams, fan trellises, and wires in the greenhouse are all effective. Cucurbits are mostly pollinated by insects. Powdery mildew may occur and cucumber mosaic virus can cause deformed fruits. Red spider mite and whitefly can be a problem.

Harvest and storage Leave marrows, pumpkins, and squashes on the plant until they have a hard skin and cracked stem, and for longer, if possible, if they are to be stored. Cut with a long stem and cure in a warm room for several days, before storing somewhere cooler.

Crops to choose

Courgette Easy to grow and productive, courgettes usually have a bush, rather than trailing, habit, and suit small gardens.

Cucumber The smooth-skinned greenhouse types of cucumber are more difficult to grow than outdoor ridge varieties.

Summer squash Strangely shaped, soft-skinned squashes taste the same as courgettes and can be cooked in the same way.

Pumpkin A late summer bounty in the garden. Select varieties grown for flavour rather than size if they are for the kitchen.

Fruiting vegetables

These sun-loving crops are a popular choice for patio containers and warm windowsills. There are varieties to suit every size of garden and all kinds of climate, and the right selection will yield delicious late summer crops.

How to grow

Site and soil Provide a warm, sunny site, with light, fertile, well-drained soil for these tender crops. All, except sweetcorn, will flourish in containers, in a greenhouse or by a sunny wall. Warm the soil by covering with cloches or clear plastic before planting.

Sowing and planting out Sow crops under cover, at 16°C (60°F) or warmer, in early spring. Where small numbers are required, sow seeds into individual pots of multi-purpose compost, and cover with sieved compost. Keep growing seedlings in a well-lit place. Harden plants off in a cold frame or outside under fleece for a week before erecting supports and planting out in the final positions. Pots should be at least 25cm (10in) wide and deep, or you can use growing bags. Sweetcorn can be direct-sown outdoors in mild areas from mid-spring.

Care and potential problems Water well during flowering and when fruits are developing. Cordon tomatoes need tying into supports, and sideshoots that appear where leaves join the main stem should be pinched out. Pinch out the growing tips of aubergines and peppers to encourage compact growth. When fruits begin to set, apply a liquid fertilizer weekly. Aphids, red spider mite, and whitefly are common on crops grown under cover, as is botrytis (grey mould). Tomatoes are susceptible to blight, potato cyst eelworm, and viruses. Sweetcorn is a favourite with animal pests; mice eat seed in the soil, while birds, squirrels, and badgers can ruin crops.

Harvest and storage Pick aubergines while the skin is glossy. Uproot outdoor tomatoes and peppers before the first frost and hang in a greenhouse to ripen the last fruits. Check sweetcorn are mature when the silks turn brown by piercing a kernel; white juice shows ripeness.

Sowing depths and spacing

CROP	SOWING DEPTH	SPACING	
		Plants	Rows
Aubergines	1cm (½in)	45cm (18in)	60cm (24in)
Peppers (sweet and hot)	1cm (½in)	45cm (18in)	60cm (24in)
Tomatoes, bush	2cm (¾in)	60cm (24in	60cm (24in)
cordon	2cm (¾in)	45cm (18in)	60cm (24in)
Sweetcorn	4cm (1½in)	45cm (18in)	45cm (18in)

A truss of tomatoes, ripe for harvesting.

Cultivation tips

Watering tomatoes The best way to water tomatoes is to insert a pot, or plastic bottle cut in half with holes in the base, into the soil next to each tomato plant and water into it. This delivers moisture directly to the deeper roots and reduces evaporation rates.

Assisting sweetcorn fertilization Arrange plants in dense blocks where the pollen will be concentrated, to maximize the yield. These plants rely on the wind to disperse their pollen, and planting in this way encourages the best possible crop.

Crops to choose

Sweetcorn These plants look stately in flower beds and the freshly picked cobs, cooked seconds after harvest, taste fabulous.

Sweet pepper Easy to grow, the long, thin-walled varieties of grilling pepper look pretty on the plant and have good flavour.

Aubergine When pinched out to keep them bushy, aubergines make attractive plants for patio pots in warm areas.

Chilli pepper Easy to grow, these fiery fruits only ripen reliably under cover. Try them on a windowsill and freeze any excess.

Perennial and stem vegetables

Often disappointing when shop-bought, these vegetables are a gourmet treat when freshly picked. They are easy to grow, and perennial types also suit the ornamental garden. The stem vegetables celery and celeriac are not perennials.

Apply a fertilizer to asparagus in early spring.

How to grow

Site and soil Choose a sunny, open site, with deep, free-draining soil, and fork plenty of organic matter in before planting. Celery thrives only on very rich, moist soils, so if your soil is poor, you may do better with celeriac.

Sowing and planting out Asparagus and globe artichokes are difficult to grow from seed, so many gardeners start in spring with asparagus crowns and young globe artichoke plants. To plant asparagus, dig a trench 20cm (8in) deep and at the bottom make a central ridge with soil; spread the crown's roots over the ridge and cover with soil so that the tips are showing. Mulch with well-rotted manure. Plant globe artichokes in rows, with the leaf rosette above the soil. Simply bury Jerusalem artichoke tubers in the soil. Sow celery and celeriac seed indoors from mid-spring and harden off when they have five to six leaves, before planting out. Water plants in well. Self-blanching celery is an easy choice for beginners.

Care and potential problems Jerusalem artichokes may need support. Water and mulch globe artichokes in dry weather. Mulch the asparagus bed with organic matter, and apply fertilizer in early spring and after harvesting. Cut down when growth yellows in autumn. Water celery and celeriac weekly, and mulch with straw or compost. Globe artichokes may be attacked by black bean aphid, and Jerusalum types can spread invasively, so keep them in check. Fungal rots may affect all crops in wet weather.

Harvest and storage Harvest celery plants whole before the first frost. Celeriac is hardy and best left in the ground until required. Cut asparagus spears about 5cm (2in) below the soil surface when they are about 15cm (6in) tall. Cut the heads of globe artichokes while still tight. Unearth Jerusalem artichokes as and when required.

Sowing depths and spacing

CROP	SOWING DEPTH	SPACING	
		Plants	Rows
Celery	On surface	25cm (10in)	25cm (10in)
Celeriac	On surface	30cm (12in)	30cm (12in)
Asparagus	2.5cm (1in)	25cm (10in)	30cm (12in)
Globe artichoke	n/a	75cm (30in)	90cm (36in)
Jerusalem artichoke	10cm (4in)	30cm (12in)	30cm (12in)

Cultivation tips

Earthing up celery Trench celery is a traditional garden crop (*see left*). The stems are blanched by covering the stems with soil, known as "earthing up", to exclude light. Tie the stems together with string when the plant is 30cm (12in) tall, and pile earth around them to half their height. Repeat every three weeks until just the tops are showing in late autumn.

Mulching globe artichokes Globe artichokes, particularly young plants and those growing in cold areas, can be damaged by frost, so protect them during the winter by earthing up around them and covering the plant with a 15cm (6in) thick mulch of straw, or a double layer of horticultural fleece.

Harvesting young asparagus plants Patience is a virtue when establishing an asparagus bed. Resist harvesting the spears for the first two years after planting, to allow the plants to gather strength for future years. Harvest for six weeks in late spring in the third year and for eight weeks in the years that follow.

Crops to choose

Celery Self-blanching varieties are best grown close together in tight blocks or cold frames to produce tender, pale stems.

Celeriac This knobbly vegetable tastes much better than it looks and is delicious roasted, mashed, or in soups.

Globe artichoke A tall, easy-to-grow decorative plant with silvery foliage. The mature flower buds are a real delicacy.

Jerusalem artichoke The tubers are usually cooked but can be eaten raw. Plants are tall and make a good windbreak.

Salad and leafy vegetables and herbs

Everyone has room for a little pot of herbs or a windowbox of cut-and-come-again salad leaves. They are so easy to grow that you'll wonder how you managed before without all those fresh flavours on your doorstep.

How to grow

Site and soil Salad crops, chard, and many herbs tolerate most soils, except waterlogged, and don't demand a lot of soil preparation. However, spinach and oriental greens need a rich, fertile, non-acidic soil. All do well in containers and full sun, but lettuces need shade in high summer.

Sowing and planting out Leafy salads germinate quickly in warm conditions, but avoid extremes of heat or cold. Sow salads in modules under cover from early spring; sow spinach, Swiss chard, and pak choi outdoors in light shade. Successional sowings of small numbers of seeds help to guarantee a continuous supply of leaves. Plant out module-grown seedlings when their roots have filled the container, and water in well. Thin directly sown seedlings to the appropriate spacing.

Tender herbs, such as basil, are often grown from seed; hardy herbs are usually bought as young plants. Sow seeds under cover in early spring; plant out after the last frost.

Care and potential problems Keep rows of salads and leafy crops weed-free and don't let them dry out, to discourage bolting. Protect early or late crops from frost with cloches or fleece. Trim herbs regularly to keep them tidy and productive; water those in containers frequently.

Slugs and snails, as well as clubroot and caterpillars on brassicas, are the biggest problems. Lettuces are prone to fungal rots in wet weather; mildew can spoil spinach crops.

Harvest and storage Leafy salads are best eaten fresh. Cut hearting lettuces and pak choi at their base; pick leaves as needed from loose-leaf lettuces, cut-and-come-again crops, spinach, and chard. Use herbs fresh, or dry or freeze them.

Sowing depths and spacing

CROP	SOWING DEPTH	SPACING	
		Plants	Rows
Lettuce	1cm (½in)	15–30cm (6–12in)	15–30cm (6–12in)
Mizuna/mibuna	1cm (½in)	10–15cm (4–6in)	15cm (6in)
Rocket	1cm (½in)	15cm (6in)	15cm (6in)
Spinach	2.5cm (1in)	8–15cm (3–6in)	30cm (12in)
Chard	2.5cm (1in)	20cm (8in)	45cm (18in)
Basil	0.5cm (¼in)	20cm (8in)	20cm (8in)
Parsley	0.5cm (¼in)	20cm (8in)	30cm (12in)
Coriander	0.5cm (¼in)	20cm (8in)	30cm (12in)

Colourful red-leaved lettuce 'Great Dixter'.

Cultivation tips

Preventing lettuce and spinach bolting In hot weather and when the soil is dry, lettuces, spinach, and many other leafy crops, bolt, which is when plants run to seed and leaves become bitter (*see left*). Prevent or delay this by keeping the soil moist with regular watering and by planting summer crops in light shade rather than full sun.

Halting the spread of mint With its underground runners, mint can become an invasive nuisance in the garden, so it is best to grow it in a container or at least in a pot sunk into the soil. The latter will help to prevent it taking over, but may not confine it forever.

Propagating perennial herbs Renew the vigour of old woody perennial herbs by digging them up in late summer and dividing them. Using secateurs, cut the plants into small sections with plenty of healthy roots and leaves, which you can then replant. This works particularly well for thyme, chives, and oregano, but division is not suitable for shrubby herbs, such as sage and rosemary.

Crops to choose

Spinach A very nutritious crop and easy to grow. Harvest baby leaves to use in salads, or mature leaves for steaming.

Swiss chard This striking crop is grown for its coloured stems, which look good on the plate, and can be steamed or eaten fresh.

Apple mint Furry, with a mild, sweet flavour, this is the best mint for flavouring vegetables and to stroke as you walk past.

Purple sage This bushy, purple-tinged plant is so attractive that it is often planted in flowerbeds. It tastes good, too.

Sowing beetroot seeds outside

When sowing outdoors, the soil must be warm enough in spring for seeds to germinate (wait for the first weed seeds to sprout if you are unsure). Choose a dry day when the soil is moist to rake it to a fine, crumbly texture (tilth) for sowing.

Tip for success

For easy sowing, buy seeds that are attached at intervals to a biodegradable tape, which can simply be laid in the drill.

1   For a straight row, pull a string line tight across the seed bed and make a V-shaped drill by dragging the corner of a hoe along the string. Make the drill about 2.5cm (1in) deep for beetroot seeds (the depth varies for different crops).

2   Pour seeds into the palm of your hand and sow them one at a time at 5cm (2in) intervals along the row. (Spacings vary for different seeds according to their size; tiny seeds should be sown as thinly and evenly as possible.)

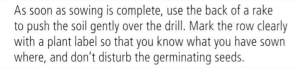

3   As soon as sowing is complete, use the back of a rake to push the soil gently over the drill. Mark the row clearly with a plant label so that you know what you have sown where, and don't disturb the germinating seeds.

4   Keep rows free of weeds. Remove excess seedlings by pulling them out with their roots, or pinching them off at soil level when they are large enough to handle. This ensures that the remaining plants have enough space.

Growing courgettes from plug plants

1 Buy compact, green plants with a healthy root system. Water well and plant out or pot on immediately to avoid checking their growth. Beware of buying courgettes and other half-hardy plants before the risk of frost has passed.

2 Carefully remove each seedling from its packaging and, holding the root ball rather than the delicate leaves, plant them into prepared soil so that the top of the root ball is just below soil level.

3 Gently firm the soil around each plant so that it is stable and water well to help it get established. Add a mulch of organic material around each plant (but not touching the stem) to retain soil moisture and prevent weeds.

4 Label, and add supports for plants that need them as they grow. Cloches are often useful to protect young plants from cold and windy weather. Continue to water the plants regularly until they are established.

Growing first early potatoes

1 In late winter, place your seed potatoes in egg boxes or trays with the maximum number of buds (eyes) pointing upwards. Stand the boxes in a cool, light place indoors for about six weeks to produce sturdy, dark sprouts (chitting).

2 When shoots reach about 2.5cm (1in) long, in early spring, mark a row on prepared soil. At 30cm (12in) intervals dig holes about 10cm (4in) deep and plant a single tuber in each, with its shoots pointing upwards.

3 Fill each hole with soil, rake over the row, and mark its position. A general purpose fertilizer can also be applied at the specified rate on either side of the row at this stage, or it may be worked into the soil before planting.

4 Tubers exposed to light will turn green, making them toxic and inedible. To avoid this, earth up the plants as they emerge by mounding soil around their stems to a height of around 15cm (6in).

Growing runner beans

Runner beans grow best in a rich, fertile soil, so prepare your site by digging in plenty of organic matter at least two weeks before planting. Plant scented flowers, such as sweet peas, nearby to attract pollinating insects to the garden.

1 Support is vital for these climbing plants. Build a wigwam from eight canes, ideally at least 2.2m (7ft) long, pushed firmly into the soil about 30cm (12in) apart, in a circle. Tie the canes securely at the top and again halfway down.

2 From late spring, when the soil is at least 12°C (54°F), plant two seeds at a depth of 5cm (2in) by each cane and water thoroughly. In cold areas or where the soil is heavy, sow the seeds in deep pots indoors in mid-spring.

3 After germination, remove the weaker seedling. Twist the remaining plant around its cane and tie it in with twine. A companion sweet pea plant will attract insects to the runner bean flowers, promoting a good crop.

4 It is important to pick runner beans regularly (at least twice a week), when they are young and tender, because over-mature pods are less appetizing and suppress the formation of new flowers.

Planting tomatoes in a growing bag

Growing bags dry out rapidly, but the volume of compost can be increased, and the need to water reduced, by planting into open-ended pots inserted into holes in the bag, as shown here.

Tip for success

Other summer crops, such as lettuce, suit growing bags, taking only 8–12 weeks from seed to the cropping stage.

1   Using a knife, carefully cut three openings in the top of the growing bag and cut drainage holes in the base. If using bottomless pots (buy ready-made, or make your own), insert them into the openings and fill with compost.

2   When the plants are hardened off and the first flowers are about to open, plant into the bag or the pots so that the top of the root ball is just below the compost surface. Firm the compost around the roots and water well.

3   Add canes or strong wires for support. Take care to pinch out all fast-growing sideshoots between the leaves and stem – they divert valuable energy away from fruit production. Apply a liquid tomato feed weekly.

4   Tie in the main stems with twine as they grow. Stop the plant growing taller by removing the growing tip, two leaves beyond the fifth or sixth cluster (truss) of fruit. This diverts the plant's energy into the last fruits of the season.

Growing chard in a container

A large pot filled with the glossy green leaves and neon-coloured stems of chard 'Bright Lights' will add colour to any patio. Harvest the baby leaves for salads when young, or allow them to mature for steaming and stir-frying.

Tip for success

Test different layouts in your container while the plants are still in their own pots to help create the best colour display.

1 Position the empty pot in a sunny, sheltered spot. Ensure the container has drainage holes, cover the base with a layer of crocks, and add multi-purpose compost to within about 2.5cm (1in) of the container's lip.

2 Water the young chard plants and carefully remove them from their pots, holding them by the roots rather than leaves. Gently tease out the roots to help them establish quickly and space them about 10cm (4in) apart.

3 Place the plants into holes made in the compost at the correct spacing, checking that the top of the root ball is just below soil level. Gently firm compost around each plant and water the container thoroughly.

4 Water the chard regularly to keep the large leaves firm and in good condition, especially during hot summer weather. You can also apply a nitrogen-rich feed to help maintain vigorous healthy growth.

Intercropping lettuce and sweetcorn

Planting a slow-growing and a fast-maturing crop together in a grid pattern is an efficient way to make the most of limited space. Lettuces can be grown among sweetcorn plants and picked before the cobs mature.

1 Measure and mark out a grid of 45cm (18in) squares. Use bamboo canes to mark the lines in the soil. This block arrangement is also ideal for maximizing the wind pollination of sweetcorn.

2 Transplant one young sweetcorn plant in the corner of each square. Firm the soil around the base of each plant. (Sweetcorn are tender plants, so may have to be raised from seed under cover.

3 Mix the lettuce seed with fine sand and scatter thinly in between the sweetcorn plants. Rake over carefully. The lettuces will mature in 8–12 weeks and fill the gaps in between the sweetcorn plants.

4 Thin the lettuce seedlings to 3–4 plants per square. Sweetcorn take at least 16 weeks to produce mature cobs, but the lettuce can be harvested long before the sweetcorn casts too much shade on them.

Planting a herb garden

This formal herb feature takes only a day to build and a season to mature. Here, bricks have been used to edge the beds and divide them into quarters. A potted bay tree forms the centrepiece.

1 Mark out a cross with pegs and string. Dig trenches following the string lines, just wider and not quite as deep as the bricks to allow space for the bricks to settle. Use a hammer handle to firm in the bricks.

2 Finish the last quarter and bed the bricks down securely, packing the soil firmly against them (no need to mortar them in). If you wish to have a plant in the centre of the feature, make sure that you leave space for it.

3 Arrange the plants in their pots before they go in the ground, so you can adjust the spacing if required. Water each plant thoroughly before removing it from its pot. Make planting holes and insert the plants. Water in well.

4 Finish off the design with a central plant – a bay tree, which can be clipped into shape, has been used here. Water all the plants regularly until they are fully established, especially in hot, dry weather.

Vertical vegetable garden

Vertical space is often under-used, but it has great potential in small gardens, increasing the space for growing a range of crops. Attaching pots of herbs and bush varieties of vegetables to a sturdy wire mesh can turn a bare sunny wall into a riot of colour, and they are simple to care for and convenient to harvest. Vigorous climbing beans, squashes, and nasturtiums can be planted in large containers at the base of the wall and are easy to train up the mesh for a fabulous, lush display.

Garden basics

Size 1.8x2.2m (6x7ft)

Suits Any sunny location with a wall or fence as a backdrop

Soil Light, multi-purpose compost

Site Wall in full sun

Shopping list

- 2 x aubergine 'Mohican'
- 3 x basil 'Sweet Genovase'
- 3 x basil 'Red Rubin'
- 3 x tomato 'Tumbling Tom Red'
- 1 x cucumber 'Masterpiece'
- 1 x courgette 'Tromboncino'
- 3 x runner bean 'Wisley Magic'

Planting and aftercare

Attach wooden batons to the wall and secure a sturdy wire mesh to them. Drill holes in the sides of plastic pots and windowboxes and thread galvanized wire through them before planting up. After the risk of frost has passed, fill the pots with a lightweight compost, plant up with hardened-off plants, secure pots to the mesh and arrange larger ones at the base of the wall. Leave space for plants to develop, and train climbing crops up the mesh. Water the plants frequently because they will dry out rapidly in their exposed position. Tie in climbing plants as they grow and harvest frequently to encourage further crops.

Aubergine 'Mohican'

Basil 'Sweet Genovase', 'Red Rubin'

Tomato 'Tumbling Tom Red'

Cucumber 'Masterpiece'

Courgette 'Tromboncino'

Runner bean 'Wisley Magic'

Hanging herb and vegetable basket

Vegetable gardening does not get much more convenient than picking juicy cherry tomatoes and fragrant herbs from just outside your back door. Hanging baskets are often associated with bedding plants, but why not try planting up a combination of cascading cherry tomatoes, vibrant nasturtiums, and delicious herbs instead? Kept well fed and watered, they will look great over a long season and provide tasty fresh produce for the kitchen as well.

Container basics

Size Basket at least 25cm (10in) in diameter

Suits Area close to the kitchen

Soil Multi-purpose compost

Site Wall in full sun and sheltered from strong winds

Shopping list

- 1 x chocolate peppermint 'Chocolate'
- 1 x parsley 'Forest Green'
- 1 x lemon thyme 'Golden Lemon'
- 1 x tomato 'Tumbler'
- 1 x chives
- 1 x nasturtium 'African Queen'

Planting and aftercare

Ensure that drainage holes have been made in the base of the basket. Place a layer of lightweight compost in the bottom of the basket, then position the plants, still in their pots, to see where they will look best. Remember that trailing plants should be near the edge. Once you have settled on a design, water the plants well, remove them from their pots, and place in the basket. Fill the gaps with compost, firming round the plants, and water the basket thoroughly. Hang it on a sturdy hook and water regularly. Once tomatoes begin to set, apply a liquid tomato feed weekly.

Peppermint 'Chocolate'

Parsley 'Forest Green'

Lemon thyme 'Golden Lemon'

Tomato 'Tumbler'

Chives

Nasturtium 'African Queen'

Cut-and-come-again windowbox

Even without a garden it is possible to grow a good supply of tasty baby salad leaves. Cut-and-come-again salads are one of the quickest and easiest crops to grow from seed and, when grown in a windowbox, could not be more convenient to care for and harvest. Try growing your own mix of lettuce, oriental greens, and rocket to create a peppery salad, which tastes wonderfully fresh when it has gone from plant to plate in a matter of seconds.

Windowbox basics

Size 50x15cm (20x6in)

Suits Window ledge where a windowbox can be secured

Soil Good, multi-purpose compost

Site Window ledge with access for watering, in full sun or partial shade

Shopping list

- 1 x packet mibuna seeds
- 1 x packet mizuna seeds
- 1 x packet lettuce 'Oakleaf' or 'Salad Bowl Mixed' seeds
- 1 x packet rocket seeds

Planting and aftercare

Choose a window ledge in sun or partial shade, which can be reached easily for watering and harvesting. Ensure the windowbox is secured and has drainage holes in the base. Add a layer of crocks to the box and fill it to within 2cm (¾in) of the top with multi-purpose compost. Mix the different seeds together in a bowl and sow thinly from the palm of your hand from mid-spring until late summer. Cover with a thin layer of compost and water well. Germination is rapid and the first leaves can be cut with scissors after 3–5 weeks, leaving a 5cm (2in) stump to regrow. Two or three further harvests can be cut at 3–5 week intervals. Water the windowbox regularly for a healthy crop.

Mibuna

Mizuna

Lettuce 'Oakleaf'

Additional plant idea

Rocket 'Rocket Wild'

Decorative climbing display

Few flower and vegetable combinations could be more eye-catching than this mix of exotic purple blooms and bulging orange squashes. The vigorous growth of squashes is perfect for training up a fence and provides an interesting contrast to the delicate foliage of the climbing passion flower and cup and saucer plants. All of these plants flourish in summer heat, so will perform best in warmer areas with a long growing season.

Border basics

Size 2x2m (6x6ft)

Suits Vegetable or ornamental garden with a fence or trellis as a backdrop

Soil Fertile, moist, but well-drained

Site Border in front of fence or trellis in full sun

Shopping list

- 1 x squash 'Uchiki Kuri' or 'Jack Be Little'
- 1 x passion flower (*Passiflora caerulea*)
- 1 x cup and saucer plant (*Cobaea scandens*)

Planting and aftercare

Sow squash and cup and saucer plant seeds under cover in mid-spring, either in a warm room or a heated propagator. Passion flowers are readily available as plants and will persist as perennial climbers in warm gardens. Attach wires or trellis to a bare fence, so the climbing plants can be tied in or use their own tendrils for support.

Once the risk of frost has passed, plant the young plants about 30cm (12in) away from the base of the fence, about 45cm (18in) apart, and water them well. Tie the stems to the supports when they are long enough, after which the passion flower and cup and saucer plant should find their own way, while the squash may need further tying in. Water the squashes regularly once fruits have formed.

Squash 'Uchiki Kuri'

Passion flower (*Passiflora*)

Cup and saucer plant (*Cobaea*)

Alternative squash

Squash 'Jack Be Little'

Exotic vegetable raised bed

If you have a sheltered, sunny wall that absorbs the sun's heat during the day and warms the surrounding air at night, take advantage of this microclimate to grow exotic crops. This raised bed has been filled with heat-loving tomatoes, peppers, aubergines, and feathery-leaved chickpea plants, as well as cucumbers and sweet potatoes that scramble up the wall. Some of these vegetables only crop well in hot summers, but they make attractive curiosities that are fun to try.

Border basics

Size 2x1m (6x3ft)

Suits Any style of garden

Soil Fertile, moist, but free-draining

Site Border in front of a wall in full sun, in warm regions

Shopping list

- 1 x aubergine 'Moneymaker'
- 1 x cucumber 'Carmen'
- 1 x sweet pepper 'Gypsy'
- 1 x tomato 'Summer Sweet'
- 1 x chickpea 'Principe'
- 1 x sweet potato 'Beauregard'

Planting and aftercare

Sow seeds of tomatoes, cucumbers, sweet peppers, and aubergines under cover in spring. Once the risk of frost has passed, harden the young plants off and plant them out in the raised bed. It is a good idea to soak the chickpeas in regularly changed water for a few days until they sprout before planting them in their final positions. Plant the sweet potato "slips" with about 5cm (2in) of stem above the soil and, as with the other young plants, water well. Attach wire mesh to the wall and train the cucumber and sweet potato stems through it. Once the first fruits have set, feed weekly with a tomato food that is high in potash. Crops should be ready to harvest in late summer.

Aubergine 'Moneymaker'

Cucumber 'Carmen'

Sweet pepper 'Gypsy'

Tomato 'Summer Sweet'

Chickpea 'Principe'

Sweet potato 'Beauregard'

Courtyard vegetable garden

Even a modest corner of the garden can be enough to grow an interesting range of vegetables that will crop well over a long season. Here, cordon tomatoes and runner beans have been trained up the wall and fence to make the best use of the vertical space. Edging the path is a densely sown crop of cut-and-come-again lettuce. Red cabbage and sweetcorn will extend the harvest into late summer and early autumn; the courgette in the pot until mid-autumn.

Border basics

Size 4x2m (12x6ft)

Suits Courtyard garden

Soil Fertile, moist, but free-draining

Site Corner of garden, sheltered by a wall or fence, in full sun

Shopping list

- 3 x tomato 'Gardener's Delight'
- 3 x runner bean 'Liberty'
- 1 x courgette 'Burpee's Golden'
- 9 x sweetcorn 'Swift'
- 1 x packet lettuce seed 'Salad Bowl Mixed'
- 3 x cabbage 'Marner Early Red'

Planting and aftercare

Prepare the area by digging in plenty of organic matter, ideally in autumn. Buy plug plants or, where there is space under cover, sow tomato, runner bean, red cabbage, and sweetcorn seeds in pots, harden them off, and plant out after the risk of frost has passed. Plant tomatoes in a growing bag because they thrive on the rich compost, adding canes for support and pinching out sideshoots as they grow. Give the runner beans wires to climb up. Plant sweetcorn in a block to aid pollination, and direct-sow a few lettuce seeds regularly to ensure a continuous crop. Water young plants in, and continue watering and feeding regularly those in growing bags.

Tomato 'Gardener's Delight'

Runner bean 'Liberty'

Courgette 'Burpee's Golden'

Sweetcorn 'Swift'

Lettuce 'Salad Bowl Mixed'

Cabbage 'Marner Early Red'

Pretty potager

Formal patterns and exquisite colour combinations characterize the French-style potager, where vegetables look as attractive as ornamental plants.

Planting a potager is not difficult, but it does require careful planning to select and arrange coloured varieties that mature to provide interest throughout the year. Here, sweetcorn and runner beans add valuable height to a scheme dominated by grey and purple foliage.

Border basics

Size 6x8m (20x25ft)

Suits An area with easy wheelbarrow access and a water supply

Soil Fertile, moist, and free-draining

Site Large open plot in full sun, with shelter from strong winds

Shopping list

- 1 x packet runner bean 'Liberty' seed
- 1 x packet sweetcorn 'Lark' seed
- 1 x packet cabbage 'Red Jewel' seed
- 1 x packet broad bean 'The Sutton' seed
- 1 x packet kale 'Red Russian' seed
- 1 x pack shallot 'Golden Gourmet' sets

Planting and aftercare

Prepare the soil by adding plenty of well-rotted manure the autumn before planting. Draw out your design on paper, calculating the number of plants required to fill each row and what they can be replaced by once harvested. Plant the seeds in spring, harden off where required, and transplant into neat rows in early summer, adding supports for the runner beans. Water the young plants well, tie climbers to their supports, and protect from pests as necessary. Harvest crops as they mature and plan to have replacement plants ready to fill the empty ground as soon as possible to maintain the garden's appearance.

Runner bean 'Liberty'

Sweetcorn 'Lark'

Cabbage 'Red Jewel'

Broad bean 'The Sutton'

Kale 'Red Russian'

Shallot 'Golden Gourmet'

Garden allies

Some wild creatures help to pollinate plants, break down compost, and prey on pests, so make these friendly visitors welcome in your garden.

Busy bees The flowers of many vegetables, such as runner beans, need to be pollinated by insects in order to set their crop. Bees are excellent pollinators, so include ornamental flowers in your vegetable garden to entice them in.

Friendly pest predators

Not all insects found in the vegetable garden are pests, and many of them prey on harmful insects that can destroy entire crops if left unchecked. It is, therefore, well worthwhile encouraging the good guys into your vegetable plot to try to achieve a natural balance and keep pest numbers low. Remember, too, that many pesticide sprays, even organic ones, kill beneficial insects as well as pests, so are best used only as a last resort.

Hoverflies Sometimes mistaken for bees, adult hoverflies are great pollinators, while the larvae feed voraciously on insect pests.

Ladybirds The adults are familiar friends, but the less appealing larvae enjoy nothing better than feasting on juicy aphids.

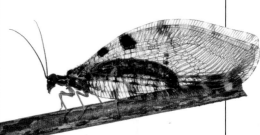

Lacewings The delicate appearance of the adult lacewing belies the enormous appetites of its larvae for common garden pests.

Helpful animals and birds

Although they may be elusive, many larger garden residents, such as birds and hedgehogs, can be a gardener's best friend, feeding on slugs and all kinds of other unwelcome visitors. Birds soon flock to gardens where food is provided, and different species will pick off insects and even feed on snails during a visit. Create suitable habitats for all kinds of creatures and they will repay you with a healthier and more productive garden.

Song thrushes These birds break snails from their shells, so plant a berry-bearing shrub or tree on your patch to give them winter food, too.

Brandling worms Smaller and redder than the usual earthworm, these creatures rapidly reduce vegetable matter to compost.

Frogs and toads Even a small pond can become home to a number of frogs and toads, which will help to keep the slug population in check.

Gallery of weeds

Perennial weeds

Field bindweed (*Convolvulus arvensis*) This climber, with its pretty white flowers and heart-shaped leaves, will regrow from the tiniest fragment of root and quickly spread.

Bramble (*Rubus*) A scrambling shrub, with long, arching, prickly stems, that can rapidly become invasive and hard to remove. The stems also re-root at the tips.

Creeping buttercup (*Ranunculus repens*) This low-growing plant with yellow flowers spreads by runners that form a dense mat of shallow roots, which are relatively easy to remove.

Couch grass (*Agropyron repens*) This leafy grass spreads incredibly fast by tough, underground roots that can be hard to dig up intact. It will regrow from any pieces left in the soil.

Dandelion (*Taraxacum officinale*) Catch the rosettes of toothed leaves while small and easy to remove – once the tap root grows and the seeds have dispersed, the job is much harder.

Dock (*Rumex*) Large pointed leaves and tall flower spikes grow above a fleshy tap root that extends deep into the soil and takes considerable effort to remove once established.

Ground elder (*Aegopodium podagraria*) The creeping roots make this a pernicious garden weed, easily recognized by its elder-like leaves and clouds of white flowers.

Stinging nettle (*Urtica dioica*) The coarse, jagged leaves are covered with stinging hairs. The bright yellow, creeping roots are easy to see, but a challenge to remove.

Horsetail (*Equisetum*) Almost impossible to eradicate, the dark brown, bootlace-like roots of these feathery plants can extend several metres underground.

Annual and biennial weeds

Annual meadowgrass (*Poa annua*) This insignificant-looking, low-growing grass colonizes any available space, including cracks in paving, so remove it before it sets seed.

Ragwort (*Senecio jacobaea*) The yellow daisy flowers of this tall plant are produced in its second year, followed by fluffy white seeds that colonize open ground.

Common chickweed (*Stellaria media*) Rather delicate, with charming little white, star-like flowers, this weed establishes and sets seed rapidly, and its sprawling habit smothers seedlings.

Groundsel (*Senecio vulgaris)* The white fluffy seeds of this weed float on the breeze, so can probably be found in every garden. Remove plants before the tiny yellow flowers mature.

Shepherd's purse (*Capsella-bursa pastoris*) A rosette of cut-edged leaves gives rise to a spike of small white flowers, which quickly form heart-shaped seed capsules.

Hairy bittercress (*Cardamine hirsuta*) Best pulled up as a seedling, when it has small, watercress-like leaves, because the flower stem rapidly forms long seed pods.

Cleavers (*Galium aparine*) This scrambling weed is covered with little hooked bristles that enable it to climb through plants. Uproot it rather than pulling the stems.

Fat hen (*Chenopodium album*) The grey-green, diamond-shaped leaves of this common weed are easily recognized. It quickly grows tall, with a loose flower spike at its tip.

Plantain (*Plantago*) Low-growing rosettes of almost leathery leaves turn up in beds, paving, and lawns. Remove them before the little bottlebrush flowers are produced.

Dealing with pests

Every garden has its share of pests, so don't panic and reach for the insecticide spray at every sighting. Healthy plants can usually tolerate them, and some are also food for beneficial insects, which you can encourage into your plot.

A healthy balance Help plants stay healthy by providing plenty of water and a rich, well-drained soil, and prevent a build-up of pests by planting each crop in a different part of the garden every year. Encourage beneficial creatures, such as birds, hoverflies, and frogs, with suitable food and habitats. This helps achieve a natural balance, where predators keep pest numbers at an acceptable level, and there is less need for chemical intervention.

Control strategies Check plants regularly and pick off any unwelcome arrivals immediately. If you anticipate a problem, put a barrier, such as horticultural fleece for carrot fly, in place, or grow companion plants alongside the crop to entice beneficial insects or confuse pests. If necessary, use chemical sprays in the evening when bees and other beneficial insects are not flying. Sticky sheets are useful in the greenhouse, as are biological controls, which introduce a predatory organism to kill the pests.

Sticky sheets in the greenhouse help to control air-borne pests.

Keeping out animal pests

Large animal pests can devastate a vegetable plot overnight, so where you anticipate a problem, the best way to stop them reaching your plants is to create a physical barrier. Deer and rabbits need fences to keep them at bay, but there are a number of cheap and easy ways of outwitting slugs, snails, mice, and pigeons.

- Halved plastic bottles with copper tape around the base protect young plants from slugs, snails, and birds.
- Netting supported with canes or wire keeps out birds; a fine net separates egg-laying butterflies from brassicas.
- Tightly secured netting deters burrowers like rabbits (*see opposite*), which eat roots, brassicas, and peas.

Plastic bottles and copper tape deter slugs.

Prevent bird damage with netting.

Horticultural fleece keeps out carrot fly.

Gallery of pests

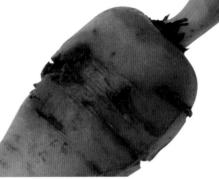

Aphids Sap-sucking insects (greenfly, blackfly) weaken growth and carry diseases. Encourage birds and insect predators, pick off small groups, or use a suitable insecticide.

Rabbits Keep these voracious vegetable eaters out of the garden with a small-meshed fence that extends 30cm (1ft) underground to prevent them from burrowing in.

Carrot fly Cover crops with horticultural fleece, sow carefully to reduce the need for thinning, or grow resistant varieties to prevent carrot fly larvae tunnelling into roots.

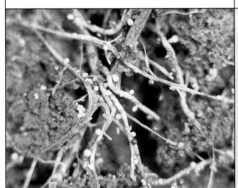

Potato cyst eelworm These microscopic, sap-sucking nematodes cause potato leaves to discolour and die. Avoid replanting the same crop where an infestation has occurred.

Caterpillars Different parts of various plants may be damaged by caterpillars. Pea moth caterpillars (*above*) live inside the pods. Net crops to exclude egg-laying adults.

Flea beetles These tiny black beetles eat round holes in the leaves of brassicas, turnip, radish, and rocket. Keep them at bay by covering seedlings with horticultural fleece.

Whitefly Treat glasshouse whitefly with the biological control *Encarsia formosa* (parasitic wasp), and the brassica whitefly with a suitable insecticide.

Red spider mite Small mites cause mottling on leaves, particularly in the greenhouse. Mist plants to increase humidity, and use a predatory mite *Phytoseiulus persimilis*.

Slugs and snails Protect vulnerable plants, and try beer traps and torch-lit hunts to control numbers. Nematode biological controls are less harmful to other animals than slug pellets.

Dealing with diseases

Just like people, strong, healthy plants are more able to fight off infection than weak, malnourished ones. Here's how to keep yours fighting fit.

Prevention is better than cure Good cultivation is as much a part of fighting diseases as recognizing and treating them, and with few fungicides now available to the amateur, preventative measures are essential.

Plants require a ready supply of nutrients and water to sustain healthy growth, so add plenty of organic matter to the soil to release nutrients and help retain moisture. Additional watering may also be needed, particularly in hot weather. It is important not to forget plants under cover and in containers, which rely on regular watering and feeding to sustain them. Damp conditions and poor air circulation can encourage fungal problems, such as damping off of seedlings, so use free-draining compost and provide good ventilation when sowing indoors.

A tidy plot also helps to keep diseases at bay. Ensure that sources of infection, such as dead leaves, harvested plants, and nearby weeds, are removed at the first opportunity. Burn or bin any diseased material; don't compost it because infection could spread.

Although not easy in a small garden, it is advisable to practise crop rotation, where related groups of crops are grown together and moved to a new bed each year, helping to prevent the build-up of diseases in the soil. Where diseases are known to be a problem, try growing resistant varieties. Be aware that plants brought into your garden can introduce disease, so check any purchases or gifts carefully before planting.

Deficiency, not disease Signs of nutrient deficiency, such as yellowing leaves and blossom end rot on tomatoes and peppers, are often mistaken for diseases. Learn to recognize these disorders, so that you can act quickly and minimize their effects. Sometimes the remedy is as simple as improving the water supply; other problems may need fertilizer added to the soil.

Use fresh seed compost and new or sterilized pots and trays to prevent damping off disease.

Keep the plot well watered to encourage vigorous, healthy growth that is less susceptible to all kinds of infection.

Add lime to acid soils before planting brassicas to increase the pH level and reduce the incidence of clubroot.

Gallery of diseases and disorders

Potato/tomato blight Brown patches on leaves, fruits, and tubers, caused by a fungus that thrives in warm, wet weather. Grow resistant varieties or spray with copper-based fungicide.

Sclerotinia Fungus that causes brown, slimy rot with fluffy, white growth, predominantly on stems and fruits of various vegetables. Remove and burn or bin affected plants.

Magnesium deficiency Older leaves of various vegetables show yellowing between veins, especially on acid soil or after heavy rains. Apply Epsom salts to the soil or as a foliar spray.

Clubroot This soil-borne slime mould infects brassicas, causing swollen, distorted roots, wilting foliage, even death. Ensure good drainage, lime acid soil, and choose resistant varieties.

Blossom end rot Dry conditions affect calcium uptake, which causes sunken, black patches at the tips of tomatoes and sweet peppers. Correct with adequate, regular watering.

Powdery mildew A wide range of crops are affected by these fungi, causing powdery white growth on leaves in dry soil conditions. Water the soil well, but not over the leaves.

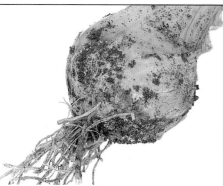

Onion white rot This fungus persists in the soil for up to seven years and causes fluffy white growth on bulbs and roots and yellowing of leaves. Remove and burn infected plants.

Rust Orange or brown spots appear on the leaves and stems of various vegetable crops, particularly in damp weather. Remove infected leaves and grow resistant varieties.

Botrytis A fluffy, grey mould (or whitish spots on tomatoes) that enters plants through wounds or flowers. Remove dead and infected plant material to reduce risk of infection.

Tall plants for sun (Ab–Cy)

Abutilon *x* suntense

This spectacular evergreen shrub is a fine choice for a sunny, sheltered site by a wall or fence. The hairy, grey-green leaves are shaped like those of a grapevine. In late spring, clusters of large, open, purple or white flowers cover the plant for many weeks.

H: 4m (12ft), **S**: 2m (6ft)
❀❀ ◊ ☼

Acacia dealbata

Reaching tree-sized proportions, this quick-growing evergreen has fern-like, sea-green foliage. In sheltered spots, it produces scented, puffball-shaped, yellow flowers in late winter. If it grows too large, it can be pruned to size in spring.

H: 15m (50ft), **S**: 6m (20ft)
❀❀ ◊ ☼ ♈

Arbutus unedo

The strawberry tree is one of the best evergreen trees for a small garden. Shrubby when young, it has glossy, dark green leaves and bell-shaped, white or pink flowers in late autumn, followed by strawberry-like fruits. The bark is reddish-brown.

H: 10m (30ft), **S**: 6m (20ft)
❀❀❀ ◊ ☼ ♈

Betula utilis *var.* jacquemontii

With its light canopy and slender form, this silver birch suits small sites well. In winter, the dazzling white trunk with its peeling bark provides interest; catkins and young leaves are an attraction in spring. The leaves turn butter-yellow before falling.

H: 15m (50ft), **S**: 7.5m (23ft)
❀❀❀ ◊ ◊ ☼ ◐

Buddleja davidii '*Dartmoor*'

Buddlejas are easy to grow and attractive to butterflies. In mid- to late summer this graceful selection has reddish-purple, cone-shaped flowerheads on long, arching stems, giving a weeping appearance. Prune in spring to keep under control.

H: 3m (10ft), **S**: 2m (6ft)
❀❀❀ ◊ ☼ ♈

Cestrum parqui

An unusual shrub that is ideal for a warm, sunny wall. Its greenish-yellow flowerheads, which are scented at night, appear from spring until the frosts. In cold areas, the plant may die to the ground, but will usually grow again from the root.

H: 3m (10ft), **S**: 2m (6ft)
❀❀ ◊ ☼ ♈

Clematis 'Alba Luxurians'

One of the most rewarding clematis, this plant bears masses of small green-tipped white flowers with black anthers. Mature plants scramble up trellis to cover a wall or fence, but may overwhelm shrubs or small trees. In late winter, cut back to 20cm (8in).

H: 5m (14ft), **S**: 1.5m (5ft)
❄❄❄ ◊ ☼ ♈

Clematis cirrhosa

Both evergreen and winter-flowering, this scrambling climber needs a sunny position, but proves a quick-growing, easy plant. The shiny leaves make a good foil to the creamy, bell-shaped flowers, which can be speckled with red inside; fluffy seedheads follow.

H: 6m (20ft), **S**: 3m (10ft)
❄❄ ◑ ◊ ☼

Clematis 'Perle d'Azur'

This plant makes an excellent addition to a small garden. It produces blue blooms in succession from midsummer to autumn. The flowers are tinged violet as they open, but fade to blue as they age. Prune stems to 20cm (8in) in late winter.

H: 3m (10ft), **S**: 1.5m (5ft)
❄❄❄ ◊ ☼

Cornus kousa var. chinensis

This must rank as one of the best garden plants. White or pink spring flowers with showy bracts are followed by red, strawberry-like fruits. Mature plants become more tree-like and the flower displays ever more spectacular.

H: 7m (22ft), **S**: 5m (15ft)
❄❄❄ ◑ ☼ ♈

Cotinus coggygria 'Royal Purple'

For lovers of coloured foliage, this large shrub is a good choice. The rich red-purple leaves offset pale-coloured flowers at the back of a border. In summer, wispy flowerheads may be produced; in autumn, leaves gradually turn scarlet before falling.

H: 5m (15ft), **S**: 4m (12ft)
❄❄❄ ◑ ◊ ☼ ◐ ♈

Cynara cardunculus

The cardoon makes a fine plant even in small gardens, with its architectural form, silver-green foliage, and purple, thistle-like flowers, which attract bees. Place at the back of a border or use as a feature plant for a sunny corner. It dies to the ground in winter.

H: 2m (6ft), **S**: 1.2m (4ft)
❄❄ ◊ ☼ ♈

Tall plants for sun (Ja–Tr)

Jasminum nudiflorum
Of all winter-flowering plants, this jasmine, usually grown as a climber, is perhaps the most reliable. Small, bright yellow flowers appear all winter on leafless, dark green stems. Hard frost will claim some blooms, but more are produced in mild spells.

H: 4m (12ft), **S**: 4m (12ft)
❄❄❄ ◊◊ ☼ ◑ ♔

Juniperus communis 'Hibernica'
This conifer brings contrast, structure, and backbone to the small garden. With blue-green, prickly needles and a dense-growing, compact habit, it eventually forms a column several metres high, standing out from rounded and horizontal growth.

H: 5m (15ft), **S**: 60cm (24in)
❄❄❄ ◊◊ ☼ ◑ ♔

Mahonia x media 'Buckland'
A useful shrub with glossy evergreen foliage, architectural form, and sweetly scented, bright yellow flowers held in spikes during the darkest winter months. The leaves are spiny; weeding beneath these plants is best done wearing gloves.

H: 4m (12ft), **S**: 3m (10ft)
❄❄❄ ◊◊ ☼ ◑ ♔

Malus 'John Downie'
This compact crab apple is perhaps the best of its kind for a profusion of ornamental fruit in late summer. Yellow and orange in colour, and large, the apples stand out from the deciduous foliage. In spring, pure white blossom opens from pink buds.

H: 10m (30ft), **S**: 6m (20ft)
❄❄❄ ◊ ☼ ◑ ♔

Olea europaea
The olive has become viable for temperate gardens, thanks to milder winters. It needs a sheltered site and as much sun as possible. It then makes a noble specimen with evergreen, silver-green foliage and a grey trunk. Small white flowers appear in summer.

H: 6m (20ft), **S**: 5m (15ft)
❄❄ ◊ ☼

Photinia x fraseri 'Red Robin'
Evergreen photinia is at its glorious best in spring when the new bright copper-red growth appears; the large, smooth leaves retain a reddish tinge as they mature. It can be used as a hedge, since it responds well to pruning, and is quite compact.

H: 3m (10ft), **S**: 3m (10ft)
❄❄ ◊ ☼ ◑ ♔

Prunus x subhirtella 'Autumnalis Rosea'

This tree suits those who like to enjoy the garden all year. Delicate, starry, pale pink flowers are produced between autumn and spring. New spring growth is bronze-green, turning dark green as the leaves expand.

H: 8m (25ft), **S**: 6m (20ft)
✷✷✷ ◊ ◑ ☼ ♈

Robinia pseudoacacia 'Frisia'

This deciduous tree's golden foliage provides dramatic contrast to other plants and illuminates dark town gardens. Plants are usually grafted and have thorny, brittle stems; remove any suckers with green leaves that appear from the base.

H: 15m (50ft), **S**: 8m (25ft)
✷✷✷ ◑ ☼ ♈

Romneya coulteri

The tree poppy is a distinguished perennial that sends up tall yet slender, unbranched stems with silvery leaves that in mid- to late summer are topped by huge, scented, gold-centred flowers with delicate white petals.

H: 2m (6ft), **S**: 2m (6ft)
✷✷✷ ◊ ☼ ♈

Solanum crispum 'Glasnevin'

This glamorous relation of the potato has scrambling stems, and makes a beautiful wall shrub. Small purple flowers with yellow centres appear in bunches all summer and associate well with clematis and roses. Plants respond well to a light trim in spring.

H: 4m (12ft), **S**: 2m (6ft)
✷✷ ◊ ☼ ♈

Sorbus cashmiriana

With its open growth habit, delicate foliage, and pink flowerheads in early summer, this tree is a good choice. In autumn and early winter, the canopy is resplendent with clusters of shiny white fruits the size of small marbles that linger after the leaves have fallen.

H: 8m (25ft), **S**: 6m (20ft)
✷✷✷ ◊ ◑ ☼ ◑ ♈

Trachelospermum asiaticum

This evergreen climber is an excellent plant for the smaller garden; it does best in a sheltered spot. Small glossy leaves form dense cover up walls or over fences, and from early summer, clusters of starry, strongly scented cream flowers appear.

H: 4m (12ft), **S**: 3m (10ft)
✷✷ ◊ ◑ ☼ ◑ ♈

Tall plants for shade (Ac–St)

Acer palmatum *var.* dissectum *Dissectum Atropurpureum Group*

This is one of the most popular of small Japanese acers, with rich purple foliage. Slow-growing, it eventually forms a low, mounded shrub. The delicate leaves may be damaged by drying winds, so give it some shelter.

H: 2m (6ft), **S**: 3m (10ft)

❆❆❆ ◊ ◐ ☀

Camellia sasanqua

Most camellias bloom in spring but those of *C. sasanqua* open in late autumn. There are many cultivars, with scented single or semi-double flowers in white or pink. Train stems against a sheltered wall to protect the flowers from frost. Needs acid soil.

H: 4m (12ft), **S**: 2m (6ft)

❆❆❆ ◊ ◐ ☀ ☀

Cercis canadensis '*Forest Pansy*'

One of the most desirable of all deciduous shrubs, this is grown for its heart-shaped, rich purple foliage and clusters of purple, pea-like flowers in spring. In autumn, the leaves develop orange tints before falling. Grow it in a sheltered position.

H: 3m (10ft), **S**: 3m (10ft)

❆❆❆ ◊ ☀ ◐ ♈

Daphne bholua '*Jacqueline Postill*'

It is worth spending time finding a good spot for this evergreen daphne. In winter, it bears a profusion of waxy pink flowers with an intoxicating perfume that carries on the wind. It is best planted in a sheltered spot.

H: 3m (10ft), **S**: 1.5m (5ft)

❆❆ ◊ ◐ ☀ ♈

Dicksonia antarctica

This tree fern is one of the most recognizable of exotic plants. Its bright green fronds unfurl from tight croziers that appear from the tip of the slow-growing trunk. These plants need shelter, moisture, and protection in cold winters.

H: 6m (20ft), **S**: 4m (13ft)

❆❆ ◊ ☀ ♈

Fatsia japonica

Few hardy plants provide more impact than fatsia, with its large, leathery, hand-shaped leaves. In autumn, heads of white flowers are followed by drooping bunches of shiny, black berries. It develops an elegant, upright habit with age.

H: 3m (10ft), **S**: 2m (6ft)

❆❆ ◊ ◐ ☀ ◐ ♈

Hydrangea quercifolia

Most hydrangeas are grown for their showy flowerheads, but this species is better known for its oak-like foliage, which develops dramatic autumnal colours before falling. Creamy-white, conical flowerheads are long-lasting. It remains a compact shrub.

H: 1.5m (5ft), **S**: 1m (3ft)
❄❄❄ ◊ ☼ ☼ ♀

Ilex aquifolium 'Silver Queen'

This slow-growing holly is a reliable performer. It eventually forms a large, cone-shaped shrub with prickly evergreen leaves edged with silver. An undemanding shrub for a dark corner or shaded border, it is a male plant and will not produce berries.

H: 12m (40ft), **S**: 3m (10ft) or more
❄❄❄ ◊ ◊ ☼ ☼ ♀

Lonicera periclymenum 'Graham Thomas'

This is one of the best honeysuckles. It is shade-tolerant, free-flowering, and well scented, especially in the evening. Creamy-yellow, tubular flowers appear in early summer and throughout the season.

H: 4m (12ft), **S**: 3m (10ft)
❄❄❄ ◊ ◊ ☼ ☼ ♀

Phyllostachys

Beloved of garden designers, this bamboo is an excellent, well-behaved, clump-forming plant. *P. nigra* has rich ebony stems that contrast well with the bright green foliage. Remove lower branchlets and older stems to show off the colour of the stems.

H: 7m (22ft), **S**: 5m (15ft)
❄❄❄ ◊ ◊ ☼ ☼ ♀

Sambucus racemosa 'Plumosa Aurea'

In spring and summer, this deciduous shrub is furnished with delicate, gold feathery foliage; the young shoots are tinged bronze. It is best if the stems are cut down annually to about 60cm (24in) in early spring.

H: 3m (10ft), **S**: 2m (6ft)
❄❄❄ ◊ ◊ ☼ ☼

Stewartia monadelpha

Stewartias are deciduous trees, often developing mottled trunks and impressive autumnal tints before leaf fall. This species is one of the more widely available, producing white summer flowers like those of a small camellia. Grow it in a sheltered spot.

H: 20m (70ft), **S**: 5m (15ft)
❄❄❄ ◊ ☼ ☼

Medium-sized plants for sun (Ac–Co)

Acanthus mollis
With mounds of glossy architectural foliage and handsome prickly spires of purple flowers, this perennial will add a touch of drama to any garden. The large, rich green leaves that emerge in early spring may be damaged by frosts.

H: 2m (6ft), **S**: 2m (6ft)
❄❄ ◊ ☼ ◐

Allium hollandicum 'Purple Sensation'
This bulb flowers after the spring bulbs but before summer flowers get going. Rounded, metallic purple flowerheads are carried on tall, slender stems that punctuate lower plantings. Plant in drifts in spring.

H: 1.2m (4ft), **S**: 20cm (8in)
❄❄❄ ◊ ☼ ♈

Angelica archangelica
This herbaceous plant flowers, sets seed, and dies in two years. In its first year, it produces unremarkable clumps of large, divided leaves, but in the second year, it is transformed. A stout stem is topped by football-sized heads composed of bright green flowers.

H: 2.5m (8ft), **S**: 1.2m (4ft)
❄❄❄ ◐ ☼ ◑

Aster turbinellus
Reaching its best in early autumn, this aster has mauve daisy flowers held aloft on slender stems. The yellow-centred blooms are produced in profusion, creating a dainty effect. The stems may need extra support; position any canes or twigs early.

H: 1m (3ft), **S**: 1m (3ft)
❄❄❄ ◊ ◐ ☼ ♈

Berberis thunbergii f. atropurpurea 'Dart's Red Lady'
Berberis are tough and easy to grow, but some make first-rate flowering or foliage plants. This deciduous cultivar with viciously spiny stems is grown for its richly coloured red leaves, making a good foil for other garden plants.

H: 1.2m (4ft), **S**: 2m (6ft)
❄❄❄ ◊ ◐ ☼ ◑

Bupleurum fruticosum
This is a fine shrub for a sunny spot, forming a mound of silver-green evergreen foliage, and producing delicate heads of tiny, bright yellow flowers all summer. It thrives in dry, chalky soil and also in the open in mild coastal areas.

H: 2m (6ft), **S**: 2m (6ft)
❄❄ ◊ ☼

Buxus sempervirens

Box has a long history in cultivation, thanks to its evergreen nature and good response to clipping. Use as topiary, a low hedge, or shape it to add formality. 'Marginata' (pictured) has yellow-edged leaves. Dislikes waterlogged soil.

H: 3–4m (10–12ft) if unclipped, **S**: 2m (6ft) ❄❄❄ ◊ ◑ ☼ ☀ ♈

Canna 'Striata'

Thanks to their exotic flowers and bold foliage, cannas make great plants for a sunny garden. 'Striata' has yellow-striped green leaves and orange flowers in summer. Lift the rhizomes and keep frost-free, or protect with a thick mulch in winter.

H: 2m (6ft), **S**: 1m (3ft) ❄ ◑ ☼ ♈

Chimonanthus praecox

In summer, this deciduous shrub is unremarkable; in winter, small rounded buds swell and open to waxy, creamy-yellow, bell-shaped flowers with a purple centre. Their spicy perfume gives the plants its common name of wintersweet.

H: 3m (10ft), **S**: 2m (6ft) ❄❄❄ ◊ ☼

Choisya ternata Sundance

This neat shrub is popular due to its golden evergreen foliage, which is lightly aromatic, as are the sprays of white flowers. It is best grown in some shade when it becomes lime-green and has an illuminating presence. Dislikes waterlogged soil.

H: 2m (6ft), **S**: 1.5m (5ft) ❄❄ ◊ ☼ ☀ ♈

Cistus x hybridus

This easy, evergreen shrub is a sight to behold in early summer. For two to three weeks, it is smothered in masses of single, white flowers with a yellow eye. Cistus are not long-lived, but they will endure drought for a while.

H: 1.2m (4ft), **S**: 1.5m (5ft) ❄❄ ◊ ☼

Correa 'Dusky Bells'

This charming, winter-flowering plant is worth growing in a sheltered, sunny position. Low and shrubby, it has small, evergreen leaves and bears pinkish-red, bell-shaped flowers with protruding anthers in mild spells during winter. It needs shelter.

H: 1m (3ft), **S**: 60cm (24in) ❄❄ ◊ ◑ ☼ ♈

Medium-sized plants for sun (Cr–Hi)

Crocosmia x crocosmiiflora 'Venus'
The common montbretia has strappy leaves topped by sprays of orange flowers in late summer, but there are many rather more desirable selections. *C. x crocosmiiflora* 'Venus', with gold and red flowers, is a good example.

H: 50cm (20in), **S**: 60cm (24in)
❄❄ ◊ ◗ ☼ ◐

Dahlia 'Bishop of Llandaff'
This popular old cultivar produces velvety, red, single flowers above purple foliage. It is compact, making it good for the smaller plot, and a fine companion for other late-flowering perennials. Lift the plant in winter and keep the tubers frost-free.

H: 1.2m (4ft), **S**: 60cm (24in)
❄ ◊ ☼ ♛

Deutzia x rosea 'Campanulata'
This compact, deciduous shrub makes a good undemanding plant for the smaller garden. It has upright, twiggy growth and hairy leaves. The blooms, which are bell-shaped and white with a pink tinge, remain beautiful for several weeks.

H: 1.2m (4ft), **S**: 1.2m (4ft)
❄❄❄ ◊ ◗ ☼ ◐

Dierama pulcherrimum
The wand flower or angel's fishing rod is aptly named. In summer, long arching sprays of large, bell-shaped flowers appear from tufts of tough, strappy, evergreen leaves. Flowers are usually pink but sometimes white or even dark purple.

H: 1.5m (5ft), **S**: 60cm (24in)
❄❄ ◊ ☼

Echinacea purpurea
The cone flower is a most appealing herbaceous plant, producing pinky-purple daisy-like flowers with a large, dark central cone, tinged orange. The flowers are held on stout stems, although sideshoots carry later blooms that appear well into autumn.

H: 1.2m (4ft), **S**: 60cm (24in)
❄❄❄ ◊ ☼

Euphorbia characias
This evergreen perennial is a superb early summer-flowering plant, with rounded heads of lime-green bracts surrounding insignificant flowers. The sea-green, lance-shaped leaves are carried on fleshy stems that bleed a milky toxic sap if cut.

H: 1.5m (5ft), **S**: 1m (3ft)
❄❄ ◊ ◗ ☼

Euphorbia *x* martinii

This spurge is a good choice, being of compact but upright growth and particularly effective in flower. The green blooms have red centres and appear in spring on tall, rounded, airy heads, carried on purple stems with dark evergreen leaves.

H: 60cm (24in), **S**: 60cm (24in)
❊❊❊ ◊ ☀ ♛

Grevillea *'Canberra Gem'*

For much of the year, this unusual evergreen shrub is quietly attractive, clad in narrow, almost needle-like, bright green leaves. In summer, it is transformed with exotic-looking, pink-red flowers dangling here and there. It needs acidic soil.

H: 1.5m (5ft), **S**: 1.5m (5ft)
❊❊ ◊ ☀ ♛

Hebe *'Midsummer Beauty'*

The length of its floral display makes this evergreen hebe worthy of space in the garden. In midsummer, long spikes of violet and white flowers are produced. They have a delicate fragrance and continue into autumn, even winter, if the weather is mild.

H: 2m (6ft), **S**: 2m (6ft)
❊❊ ◊ ◗ ☀ ◑ ♛

Helenium *'Moerheim Beauty'*

This late-flowering border perennial is deservedly popular. From mid- to late summer to early autumn, it produces shuttlecock-shaped, daisy-like flowers in rich marmalade shades on stout upright stems. Deadheading ensures a later flush of blooms.

H: 1.4m (4½ft), **S**: 1m (3ft)
❊❊❊ ◊ ◗ ☀ ♛

Hemerocallis *'Corky'*

A clump-forming perennial with narrow, strappy foliage. Slender stems appear in summer, carrying clusters of orange-yellow, funnel-shaped flowers, each displaying a red tinge to the outside. The blooms last just a day but are soon followed by others.

H: 60cm (24in), **S**: 60cm (24in)
❊❊❊ ◊ ◗ ☀ ◑ ♛

Hibiscus syriacus *'Oiseau Bleu'*

Few shrubs better this hibiscus in full bloom. Just as many other plants are fading, it produces a profusion of 8cm- (3in-) wide, open bell-shaped flowers of rich blue – a rare colour so late in the season. The flowers last until early autumn.

H: 2.5m (8ft), **S**: 1.5m (5ft)
❊❊❊ ◊ ☀ ♛

Medium-sized plants for sun (In–Ph)

Inula hookeri

This clump-forming perennial should be more widely grown. It produces beautiful yellow flowers with slender petals that appear from midsummer at the tips of soft stems bearing hairy oval leaves. In late autumn, the shoots can be cut to the ground.

H: 60cm (24in), **S**: 60cm (24in)
❄❄❄ ◌ ☀

Iris laevigata

This plant is perfect for moist areas, growing well even in standing water. The sword-shaped foliage provides a contrast to other shrubby growth. In early to midsummer, flowering stems bear a succession of beautiful blooms, usually lavender-blue in colour.

H: 50cm (20in), **S**: 30cm (12in)
❄❄❄ ◌ ◌ ☀ ☀ ⚱

Iris sibirica 'Perry's Blue'

Siberian irises are good for ground that does not dry out. In spring, slender, strappy foliage erupts from clumps, followed by tall, branched, flowering stems. These bear dainty sky-blue flowers with white markings, 6cm (2½in) across, over several weeks.

H: 1m (3ft), **S**: 50cm (20in)
❄❄❄ ◌ ◌ ☀ ☀

Lavandula stoechas

With its aromatic foliage and long-lasting flowers, French lavender lends a Mediterranean feel to sunny gardens. The flowerheads have distinctive purple "ears", or bracts, held on stems above the narrow, greyish-green leaves. Grow in a sheltered spot.

H: 60cm (24in), **S**: 60cm (24in)
❄❄ ◌ ☀ ⚱

Lilium regale

This is an easy lily to grow. Fleshy stems furnished with narrow leaves appear in spring and grow rapidly. Large buds swell and burst to reveal silver-white, trumpet-shaped flowers with protruding stamens and a wonderful scent.

H: 1.5m (5ft), **S**: 30cm (12in)
❄❄❄ ◌ ☀ ☀ ⚱

Lobelia tupa

In spring, this exotic-looking plant produces fleshy, red-flushed shoots with large, rather downy leaves. In late summer, heads of red, tubular flowers open over several weeks, and last well into autumn. Cut stems to the ground after the first frosts.

H: 2m (6ft), **S**: 1m (3ft)
❄❄ ◌ ◌ ☀

Melianthus major
A remarkable foliage plant, with dramatic, blue-silver, deeply cut leaves that look superb in a white border or with contrasting purple foliage. Usually it is cut to the ground by frost, and should be covered with a thick mulch to protect the roots.

H: 2m (6ft), **S**: 1m (3ft)
❄❄ ◐ ◔ ☼ ♈

Miscanthus sinensis 'Zebrinus'
With its tall stems and strappy foliage, this ornamental grass is a favourite. The leaf blades are marked with broad yellow stripes, giving the plant a remarkable appearance, especially when grown in full sun, which helps intensify the markings.

H: 2m (6ft), **S**: 1m (3ft)
❄❄❄ ◐ ☼ ☼

Nandina domestica
A most useful shrub, this plant ticks all the boxes. It has a delicate yet architectural form with large, divided leaves that develop attractive autumnal tints. In early summer, sprays of white flowers appear, followed by clusters of orange berries that persist into winter.

H: 2m (6ft), **S**: 2m (6ft)
❄❄❄ ◊ ☼ ☼ ♈

Pennisetum setaceum 'Rubrum'
This delightful grass is a tender perennial, ideal for a container in a sunny spot during summer. Best treated as an annual, it will produce purple fluffy flowerheads (known as "cats' tails") held on arching stems, above rich red foliage.

H: 1m (3ft), **S**: 60cm (24in)
❀ ◐ ◊ ☼

Perovskia 'Blue Spire'
This delicate-looking, shrubby plant is a good choice for a sunny, dry position. It forms an upright bush with strongly aromatic, silver-green foliage. From late summer until autumn, clouds of violet-blue flowers are produced.

H: 1.2m (4ft), **S**: 1m (3ft)
❄❄❄ ◊ ☼ ♈

Phlomis russeliana
A dependable, useful perennial with large, soft, heart-shaped leaves that cover the ground well, even in winter. In early summer, attractive stout stems of soft yellow flowers appear. After flowering, these stems provide structure into autumn and winter.

H: 1m (3ft), **S**: 1.2m (4ft)
❄❄❄ ◐ ◊ ☼ ☼ ♈

Medium-sized plants for sun (Ph–We)

Phormium 'Yellow Wave'

This tried-and-tested phormium is graceful and compact. Its broad, evergreen, strappy foliage is lavishly marked with yellow, set against green, each blade arching gracefully to give established clumps an elegant appearance.

H: 1.2m (4ft), **S**: 1m (3ft)
❄❄ ◊ ◐ ☼ ☼ ♆

Pinus mugo 'Ophir'

This compact, slow-growing pine is ideal for the smaller garden, growing well even in a container. Its short branching stems are covered in dense bristles and it will form a large shrub. However, it is most attractive in winter when its needles turn bright gold.

H: 1.5m (5ft), **S**: 1.5m (5ft)
❄❄❄ ◊ ☼

Pittosporum tobira

With its shiny, evergreen leaves and heads of cream-coloured, sweetly scented summer flowers, this plant should be seen more often. It grows throughout the Mediterranean, so is a good choice for those who like to be reminded of warmer climes.

H: 2m (6ft), **S**: 2m (6ft)
❄❄ ◊ ☼ ♆

Rosa x odorata 'Mutabilis'

A most beautiful rose that flowers from late spring until late autumn. Clusters of dainty, single flowers open a warm orange-yellow and turn rich pink with age. The young stems and leaves of this compact, but open, bush are tinged purple.

H: 1m (3ft), **S**: 1m (3ft)
❄❄ ◊ ☼ ♆

Rosa xanthina 'Canary Bird'

This rose is one of the earliest to bloom – in late spring. It produces a profusion of single, sunshine-yellow flowers, which have a light perfume, and has attractive apple-green foliage. A second reduced display appears in autumn.

H: 2m (6ft), **S**: 2m (6ft)
❄❄❄ ◊ ☼ ♆

Rosmarinus officinalis

This dense evergreen has strongly aromatic foliage and attractive blue flowers in spring and sometimes autumn. It will grow well in pots, is drought-tolerant, and responds well to trimming. It is a useful herb for cooking.

H: 1.5m (5ft), **S**: 1.5m (5ft)
❄❄ ◊ ☼

Salvia officinalis '*Purpurascens*'
Purple sage is a useful plant for the smaller garden: it is easy, quick-growing, and has aromatic, oval, soft, purple leaves. The plant forms ground-covering mounds, and in summer sends up flowering stems with small purple blooms.

H: 1m (3ft), **S**: 1m (3ft)
❄❄ ◊ ☼ ☗

Salvia x sylvestris '*Mainacht*'
Many salvias are first-rate plants for their summer flowers; this compact selection is useful in the smaller plot. Its early summer flowers are of an intense purplish-blue that is unusual for the time of year. They are carried in profusion in stiff upright spikes.

H: 1m (3ft), **S**: 50cm (20in)
❄❄ ◊ ☼ ☗

Stipa gigantea
The perennial giant oat, although large, is manageable in almost any garden. It forms a low hummock of long, narrow leaves, and in summer, produces tall stems bearing transparent golden flowerheads that shimmer in the breeze.

H: 2m (6ft), **S**: 1m (3ft)
❄❄❄❄ ◊ ◑ ☼ ☗

Trachycarpus wagnerianus
This is the perfect hardy palm for smaller plots, as it is slow-growing and compact. The plant forms a trunk gradually and is furnished with fan-shaped, dark, evergreen, deeply pleated leaves that give it a most refined appearance.

H: 2m (6ft) after 10 years, **S**: 2m (6ft)
❄❄❄ ◊ ◑ ☼ ◑

Verbena bonariensis
This "must-have" perennial is a useful plant even in small gardens because, although tall, it has a transparent quality, allowing views to planting behind. It is long-flowering, with heads of purple blooms appearing in summer and lasting into autumn.

H: 2m (6ft), **S**: 60cm (24in)
❄❄ ◊ ☼ ☗

Weigela '*Eva Rathke*'
These shrubs are grown for their spring and early summer blossom. This compact selection forms a dense shrub. Dark red flower buds appear in profusion in late spring and open to crimson, funnel-shaped flowers. Remove oldest stems after flowering.

H: 1.5m (5ft), **S**: 1.5m (5ft)
❄❄❄ ◊ ☼ ◑

Medium-sized plants for shade (Ac–De)

Acer shirasawanum 'Aureum'

This slow-growing, compact plant is striking, especially in late spring and early summer when its foliage is at its best. As the golden leaves expand, they resemble little oriental fans, seen to best effect in shade where they stand out from other planting.

H: 1.5m (5ft) after 10 years, **S**: 1m (3ft)

❄❄❄ ◊ ◐ ☼ ◑ ♈

Anemanthele lessoniana

This grass is better known as *Stipa arundinacea*. It makes a neat clump of fairly broad, evergreen foliage, the leaves arching attractively. In late summer, tiny flowers are produced. In autumn, the clump develops russet tints, adding to its desirability.

H: 1.2m (4ft), **S**: 1.2m (4ft)

❄❄ ◊ ☼ ◑

Anemone x hybrida 'Honorine Jobert'

There are few perennials to match this noble plant in late summer. Vigorous clumps of bold, divided foliage build steam through the summer until flowering stems appear, topped by sprays of single, white flowers.

H: 1.5m (5ft), **S**: 60cm (24in)

❄❄❄ ◊ ◑ ☼ ♈

Aquilegia McKana Group

A cottage-garden favourite, this perennial is a good choice for its spring flowers in a wide range of different colours. The clumps of foliage develop in spring and are soon topped by distinctive flowers lasting for several weeks.

H: 1m (3ft), **S**: 50cm (20in)

❄❄❄ ◊ ☼ ◑

Aruncus dioicus

This large, but easy-to-grow perennial is suited to moist sites. In spring, shoots soon form hummocks of leafy stems. By midsummer, plumes of tiny creamy-white flowers appear. They are held in handsome flowerheads and last for several weeks.

H: 2m (6ft), **S**: 1.2m (4ft)

❄❄❄ ◊ ◑ ☼ ◑

Astilboides tabularis

A plant of great beauty, this species' main feature is its large, parasol-like leaves, each roughly circular, with the leaf stem attached to the centre. Soft green and delicate in early summer, they darken as the season progresses. White flowers appear in late summer.

H: 1.5m (5ft), **S**: 1m (3ft)

❄❄❄ ◊ ◑ ☼

Aucuba japonica

This evergreen deserves recognition as one of the best hardy shrubs for year-round appeal. It will also withstand mistreatment. Its large oval leaves are spangled with golden spots. In spring, heads of red-purple flowers appear that develop into crimson berries.

H: 2.5m (8ft), **S**: 2.5m (8ft)
❀❀❀ ◊ ◊ ◊ ☼

Berberis darwinii

This spiny evergreen is one of the most spectacular spring-flowering shrubs and deserves a spot at the back of a border. The glossy foliage is an attractive foil to the clusters of bright orange flowers that cover the plant, followed later by blue berries.

H: 2m (6ft) after 10 years, **S**: 2m (6ft)
❀❀❀ ◊ ◊ ☼ ♉

Camellia japonica *'Bob's Tinsie'*

This plant is a favourite, thanks to its unusual flowers and neat, compact habit. The glossy, oval, evergreen foliage is a good foil to the small, cup-shaped, red flowers that appear in abundance throughout spring.

H: 1.5m (5ft), **S**: 1m (3ft)
❀❀❀ ◊ ◊ ☼ ♉

Cornus sanguinea *'Winter Beauty'*

This shrub is grown for the colour of its twigs. In summer, it is forgettable, but once the leaves turn butter-yellow in autumn, the show begins. The stems are bright orange-yellow, the younger shoots tinged red, making the plant look like a glowing flame.

H: 2m (6ft), **S**: 2m (6ft)
❀❀❀ ◊ ☼ ☼

Cotoneaster horizontalis

This shrub has much to recommend it. In spring, the soft green foliage is the attraction, followed by pink-white flowers in summer. In autumn, the leaves turn crimson before they fall; in winter, the stems are often peppered with red berries.

H: 2m (6ft), **S**: 2m (6ft)
❀❀❀ ◊ ◊ ☼ ☼ ♉

Desfontainia spinosa

At first glance, this plant resembles a compact holly with its small, dark, spine-edged leaves. In summer, it has a trick up its sleeve: long, tubular, pendent, red and yellow flowers appear, and are of great beauty, especially against the dark foliage.

H: 1m (3ft), **S**: 60cm (24in)
❀❀ ◊ ☼ ♉

Medium-sized plants for shade (Di–Le)

Dicentra spectabilis

The bleeding heart is a popular plant for light shade. Fleshy shoots emerge as winter ends and are easily damaged by late frosts. The soft foliage, which dies down in midsummer, is topped by arching sprays of pink and white flowers that last for several weeks.

H: 1m (3ft), **S**: 60cm (24in)
❄❄❄ ◊◑ ☼ ♈

Digitalis purpurea

The foxglove is easy to grow, thrives in shade, and seeds freely. It is usually a biennial, which means it lives two years, building up a rosette of large oval leaves in the first, and producing its tall flower spike in the second. The flowers are usually purple or white.

H: 2m (6ft), **S**: 60cm (24in)
❄❄❄ ◑ ☼ ◑

Geranium *x* oxonianum *'Claridge Druce'*

This herbaceous plant is one of the toughest, and ideal for dry shade. It develops a mound of foliage that is often semi-evergreen, above which appear bright pink flowers from spring until late autumn.

H: 1.2m (4ft), **S**: 1m (3ft)
❄❄❄ ◊◑◑ ☼ ◑

Hedychium densiflorum

This hardy ginger makes a fine late-flowering perennial. In summer, it develops vigorous, fleshy shoots that grow quickly and display lush foliage. At the tips of each shoot appear spikes of scented, orange flowers that are produced well into autumn.

H: 1.2m (4ft), **S**: 2m (6ft)
❄❄ ◊◑ ☼ ◑

Helleborus argutifolius

This evergreen perennial is a useful plant, growing well in shade and filling gaps with its handsome serrated foliage, held on rather shrubby stems. In winter, bright green, open flowers appear. After flowering, stems wither and yellow and should be cut out.

H: 1m (3ft), **S**: 1m (3ft)
❄❄ ◊◑ ☼ ◑ ♈

Hosta *'Jade Cascade'*

This huge, sturdy yet elegant hosta is well named. The long, pointed, rich green leaves, up to 30cm (12in) long, are strongly veined and held in a distinctive, downward-facing way on tall leaf stems. In early summer, tall spires of lilac blooms appear.

H: 1.2m (4ft), **S**: 1.1m (3½ft)
❄❄❄ ◊ ◑

Hosta sieboldiana

This large hosta has fine foliage. The leaves, which emerge from blue, tooth-like shoots in spring, are blue-grey at first, developing a green tinge as they age. Mature clumps make large mounds of puckered leaves 30cm (12in) long and as much across.

H: 1m (3ft), **S**: 1m (3ft)
❄❄❄ ◐ ☼

Hosta 'Sum and Substance'

A spectacular hosta cultivar that is one of the largest and easiest to grow of all, with huge golden-green leaves, especially bright as they first emerge in spring. In summer, tall spikes of lavender flowers appear. This hosta is also relatively slug-resistant.

H: 75cm (30in), **S**: 1.2m (4ft)
❄❄❄ ◐ ☼ ♔

Hydrangea macrophylla 'Lanarth White'

This hydrangea forms a rounded dome of growth. The flattened heads are composed of tiny blue or pink fertile flowers surrounded by pure white florets, and appear in late summer. The flowers show up best in shade.

H: 1m (3ft), **S**: 1m (3ft)
❄❄❄ ◊ ◐ ☼ ♔

Ilex crenata var. latifolia

This holly looks rather like box, but it is quicker growing. It responds well to trimming and can be kept as a low hedge. Other selections include *I. crenata* 'Golden Gem', which has glowing yellow foliage and makes a superb plant for shade.

H: up to 1.5m (5ft), **S**: 1.5m (5ft)
❄❄❄ ◊ ◐ ☼ ☼

Iris foetidissima

A UK native, this perennial is great for shade, even under trees and shrubs. The lance-shaped foliage remains in good condition in winter, and in spring, purple flowers appear. The orange seeds, which remain showy all winter, are the main talking point.

H: 1m (3ft), **S**: 60cm (24in)
❄❄❄ ◊ ◐ ☼ ♔

Leucothoe fontanesiana 'Rainbow'

A clump-forming evergreen shrub with an attractive, arching, fountain-shaped habit. The leaves are splashed and flecked with cream, pink, and orange. In summer, white, bell-shaped flowers hang from the stems.

H: 1.5m (5ft), **S**: 1.2m (4ft)
❄❄❄ ◐ ☼

Medium-sized plants for shade (Le–Vi)

Leycesteria formosa

An excellent shrub for a range of situations, including dry shade. In summer, clusters of pinky-purple flowers hang from arching stems amid lush oval leaves. By autumn, purple berries develop. The green stems are attractive in winter.

H: 1.5m (5ft), **S**: 1.2m (4ft)
❄❄❄ ◊◊ ☼ ◑ ♆

Ligularia dentata 'Desdemona'

This leafy perennial is a dramatic choice for moist sites. Clumps of large, rounded leaves flushed with purple are held on long stems, which appear from the ground in spring. These are followed by tall stems with orangy-yellow, daisy-like flowers.

H: 1.2m (4ft), **S**: 60cm (24in)
❄❄❄ ◊◊◊ ◑ ♆

Osmunda regalis

A large, deciduous fern, ideal for moist areas. In spring, croziers unwind from the ground and fresh, bright green fronds unfurl. Clumps provide an architectural element in summer; in autumn, they turn bright yellow.

H: 1.2m (4ft), **S**: 1m (3ft)
❄❄❄ ◊◊◊ ◑ ♆

Pieris 'Forest Flame'

This evergreen shrub is grown for its dramatic, bright red shoots and sprays of white, bell-shaped flowers. The flowers appear in early spring before the scarlet shoots. As the leaves mature, they fade to pink before turning green. It needs acidic soil.

H: 2.5m (8ft), **S**: 2m (6ft)
❄❄❄ ◊ ◑ ♆

Primula florindae

The largest and most spectacular of primulas, this perennial resembles a giant cowslip. Clumps of broad, soft green leaves 30cm (12in) long develop in spring, followed by tall flower stems that carry scented, bell-shaped flowers in yellow or orange.

H: 1.2m (4ft), **S**: 60cm (24in)
❄❄❄ ◊ ☼ ♆

Rhododendron 'Olive'

This evergreen rhododendron needs a sheltered position and acid soil to do well. The small, green, oval leaves serve as a good foil to the clusters of bright mauve-pink, funnel-shaped flowers up to 4cm (1½in) across. These are produced in late winter.

H: 1.5m (5ft), **S**: 1m (3ft)
❄❄❄ ◊ ☼

Rhododendron 'Persil'

This plant is a wonderful sight in late spring. Heads of large, scented, white flowers with a yellow flash in the centre appear at the same time as the soft, hairy leaves. The flowers last for several weeks, and show up well in shade. The plant needs acidic soil.

H: up to 2m (6ft), **S**: 2m (6ft)
❄❄❄ ◗ ☼ ◑ ♈

Ribes sanguineum 'Brocklebankii'

This compact flowering currant is most attractive in spring, the pink flowers appearing at the same time as the yellow leaves – to spectacular effect. This plant shows up well in shade and grows better out of sun because the leaves can scorch.

H: 1.5m (5ft), **S**: 1m (3ft)
❄❄❄ ◌ ◗ ◑

Sarcococca hookeriana *var.* digyna

Evergreen, compact, and winter flowering, this shade-loving plant is ideal for small gardens. The narrow leaves are shiny and the plant forms a dense, rounded mound. In winter, small, white tassels appear: these have a delicious, spicy scent.

H: 1m (3ft), **S**: 1m (3ft)
❄❄❄ ◌ ◗ ◑ ☼ ♈

Skimmia x confusa 'Kew Green'

With its glossy, pointed leaves, this skimmia cultivar is one of the most reliable. The large, conical, greenish-cream flowerheads, produced in early spring, have a delicious scent. This is a male plant; for berries, a female or hermaphrodite plant is required.

H: 1m (3ft), **S**: 1.5m (5ft)
❄❄❄ ◗ ☼ ♈

Viburnum davidii

This evergreen shrub, which forms a low mound, is a plant for all seasons. The oval leaves are attractively pleated and rich green. In summer, large heads of small, white flowers appear. Bright blue berries follow, provided male and female plants are grown.

H: 1m (3ft), **S**: 2m (6ft)
❄❄ ◌ ◗ ☼ ♈

Viburnum tinus 'Eve Price'

A compact and free-flowering evergreen plant that makes an ideal backdrop at the back of a border. It forms dense cover and has small, green, oval leaves. Heads of pink-tinged flowers are displayed through winter and spring.

H: 2m (6ft), **S**: 2m (6ft)
❄❄❄ ◌ ◗ ☼ ◑ ♈

Short plants for sun (Al–Di)

Allium schoenoprasum

Chives are not only useful in a herb garden – they are also an easy-to-grow choice for a flower garden and ideal as border edging. The narrow, blue-green leaves are especially attractive when topped by pinkish-mauve flowers that last several weeks.

H: 30cm (12in), **S**: 20cm (8in)
❄❄❄ ◊ ☼

Artemisia alba 'Canescens'

This useful front-of-border perennial, with its silver leaves, should be more widely grown. The lacy foliage is held on stems that tend to sprawl, covering the soil well. Cut plants to the ground in a cold winter, and new shoots will appear in spring.

H: 30cm (12in), **S**: 30cm (12in)
❄❄ ◊ ☼ ♆

Aster 'Coombe Fishacre'

In early autumn, few plants can compete with asters. This selection has a long flowering period and is well suited to smaller gardens. The blooms are daisy-like, pink with a darker eye, and appear in a multitude, lasting until the frosts.

H: 60cm (24in), **S**: 60cm (24in)
❄❄❄ ◊ ☼ ♆

Astrantia major

These beautiful perennials are becoming popular, thanks to the range now available. Clumps of leaves appear in spring and are topped by dainty flowers held on tall stems. The showy white or pink bracts resemble petals and encircle the true flowers.

H: 45cm (18in), **S**: 30cm (12in)
❄❄❄ ◑ ☼ ☀

Bergenia purpurascens

This perennial has beautiful foliage and flowers. It is more compact and has a longer season of interest than most bergenias, so it is better suited to small gardens. The glossy foliage develops rich purple tints in winter; in spring, pinkish-purple flowers appear.

H: 30cm (12in), **S**: 60cm (24in)
❄❄❄ ◊ ☼ ◑ ♆

Calluna vulgaris 'Silver Knight'

For silver foliage, few heathers create a better effect than this shrubby, evergreen plant. When mature, it produces a wonderful wispy silver cloud of dense, quite upright, but ground-covering, growth. Although easy to grow, it must have acid soil.

H: 30cm (12in), **S**: 60cm (24in)
❄❄❄ ◊ ◑ ☼

Campanula glomerata

One of the simplest campanulas to grow, this low, spreading perennial makes good summer ground cover, and self-seeds freely. From early summer until autumn, heads of bell-shaped blue or white flowers appear on short stems.

H: 30cm (12in), **S**: 1m (3ft)
❄❄❄ ◊ ◖ ☼ ☀

Catananche caerulea

This sun-loving perennial is grown for its lavender-blue flowers, which look rather like pale cornflowers, produced in summer and autumn. The blooms are held on a wiry stalk above clumps of silvery foliage. They combine well with other pale-coloured plants.

H: 60cm (24in), **S**: 30cm (12in)
❄❄ ◊ ☼

Ceratostigma plumbaginoides

Easy to grow, this low shrub flowers when most other plants have finished. It spreads at the root and, under ideal conditions, forms a large clump. The rich blue flowers are held in clusters above the leaves, which turn red before falling.

H: 30cm (12in), **S**: 60cm (24in)
❄❄ ◊ ☼ ♆

Cerinthe major

Growing swiftly from seed, this annual develops into a low bush, covered in blue-silver leaves. Long-lasting, purple, bell-shaped flowers appear in late spring, giving an attractive, almost iridescent appearance. It self-seeds freely.

H: 45cm (18in), **S**: 30cm (12in)
❄❄❄ ◊ ☼

Convolvulus cneorum

This evergreen, low-growing shrub is grown both for its soft, bright silver foliage and the multitude of white, cup-shaped flowers that appear in summer. Each flower lasts little more than a day but the bush is covered in blooms for weeks.

H: 50cm (20in), **S**: 1m (3ft)
❄❄ ◊ ☼ ♆

Diascia barberae '*Blackthorn Apricot*'

Often grown as an annual, this plant is perennial in the right position. Although cut to the ground in winter, new stems appear in spring to make a small sprawling clump. The stems bear peach-coloured flowers all summer.

H: 30cm (12in), **S**: 30cm (12in)
❄❄ ◊ ☼ ♆

Short plants for sun (Er–Ge)

Erica carnea 'Foxhollow'

There are many winter-flowering heathers but this is a favourite, bearing small, pale pink, bell-shaped flowers throughout the coldest weather. The needle-like, pale green leaves become tinged with red in winter. A good low-growing plant.

H: 20cm (8in), **S**: 60cm (24in)
❄❄❄ ◊ ◐ ☼ ♧

Erigeron karvinskianus

The little Mexican daisy is a welcome plant in many gardens, often growing in gaps in paving or out of dry stone walls – anywhere hot and dry. The small pink-tinged white daisy flowers appear from early summer to winter on low sprawling plants.

H: 20cm (8in), **S**: 60cm (24in)
❄❄ ◊ ☼ ♧

Erysimum 'Bowles' Mauve'

This is a superb plant for injecting colour into cottage garden-style planting in spring and summer. It forms an evergreen, shrubby plant with grey-green leaves. In spring, the flowering stems are soon covered with purple flowers.

H: 60cm (24in), **S**: 60cm (24in)
❄❄ ◊ ☼ ♧

Euphorbia cyparissias 'Fens Ruby'

This low-growing perennial is a useful, if somewhat invasive plant, grown for its foliage and spring flowers. In spring, purplish-green shoots appear, producing delicate foliage. As the season progresses, small, lime-green flowers develop.

H: 30cm (12in), **S**: 2m (6ft)
❄❄❄ ◊ ◐ ☼

Euphorbia rigida

This sprawling plant is superb in a sunny rockery. Fleshy stems arise from a central crown, then grow along the ground in an almost snake-like fashion, holding narrow, triangular blue-silver leaves. Lime-green flowers appear in early summer.

H: 20cm (8in), **S**: 60cm (24in)
❄❄ ◊ ☼

Francoa sonchifolia

In a sunny, warm area, this perennial makes good ground cover. The fleshy leaves grow from a creeping stem, which in mid- to late summer sends up tall stems, well above the foliage, of pale pink flowers spotted with darker pink.

H: 60cm (24in), **S**: 60cm (24in)
❄❄ ◊ ☼ ◐

Fuchsia *'Genii'*

This compact, hardy fuchsia is a reliable cultivar. It produces masses of pendent purple and red flowers in late summer and autumn, until the first frosts. The blooms are held against bright yellow leaves, adding to the plant's impact.

H: 60cm (24in), **S**: 60cm (24in)
❄❄ ◊ ☼ ◑ ♔

Gaura lindheimeri

A delicate-looking perennial for the front of a sunny border that produces wands of open, white flowers held on slim stems from midsummer until mid-autumn. Hard frosts will kill the top growth but fresh shoots appear in spring if protected in winter.

H: up to 1m (36in), **S**: 1m (3ft)
❄❄ ◊ ☼ ♔

Geranium *'Ann Folkard'*

This hardy geranium is appealing for both flowers and foliage. The leaves are hand-shaped and bright gold in colour, especially when young; they become greener as they age. Large, open, bright magenta flowers with dark centres are produced all summer.

H: 60cm (24in), **S**: 1m (3ft)
❄❄❄ ◊ ☼ ◑ ♔

Geranium *Rozanne* ('*Gerwat*')

One of the finest of all hardy geraniums, this selection has trailing, non-rooting stems that cover the ground from late spring, producing masses of large, open bright blue flowers from early summer well into autumn. Cut back stems in winter.

H: 45cm (18in), **S**: 60cm (24in)
❄❄❄ ◊ ☼ ◑

Geum coccineum

This clump-forming perennial is a fine summer-flowering plant. It forms a rosette of toothed green leaves, and attractive, open, saucer-shaped, orange-red flowers with yellow stamens for several weeks. Plants like sun but not overly dry soil.

H: 50cm (20in), **S**: 30cm (12in)
❄❄❄ ◊ ◉ ☼ ◑

Geum rivale

A European native, the little water avens is attractive for wet areas in perhaps wilder patches of the garden. This perennial forms clumps of leaves, and over several weeks in early summer produces dusky pink and red bell-shaped flowers.

H: 50cm (20in), **S**: 30cm (12in)
❄❄❄ ◊ ◉ ☼

Short plants for sun (Ha–Pe)

Hakonechloa macra 'Aureola'

This ornamental grass is a fine garden plant. It forms a low clump of gold and green striped foliage. The plant spreads slowly from slender rhizomes and will grow in a range of situations, including sun, as long as the soil is moist.

H: 30cm (12in), **S**: 40cm (16in)
❀❀❀ ◌◑ ☼◐☀ ♈

Helianthemum 'Rhodanthe Carneum' ('Wisley Pink')

This low-growing plant is ideal for sunny rockeries. Plants are evergreen with small, oval, silvery foliage. In early summer, silver-pink flowers with a soft yellow eye appear. They last a day, but are produced in profusion.

H: 30cm (12in), **S**: 50cm (20in)
❀❀❀ ◌ ☼ ♈

Hemerocallis 'Golden Chimes'

A dainty day lily, ideal for the small garden because it is compact and free-flowering. In summer, flowering stems appear from clumps of narrow, arching leaves. The bright yellow, open, trumpet-shaped flowers have brownish-red reverses.

H: up to 1m (3ft), **S**: 50cm (20in)
❀❀❀ ◌ ☼ ◐ ♈

Hypericum olympicum

An ideal plant for open, sunny positions, this low-growing shrub is a fine sight in summer. The small leaves are grey-green and a good foil to the open, starry, golden-yellow flowers produced in clusters at the ends of the stems.

H: 30cm (12in), **S**: 50cm (20in)
❀❀❀ ◌ ☼ ♈

Iris unguicularis

Few herbaceous plants are of interest in winter but this evergreen iris is a stellular performer. For much of the year it is unremarkable, but in mild spells during winter, delicate lavender-mauve flowers with yellow markings open, lasting several days.

H: 30cm (12in), **S**: 60cm (24in)
❀❀❀ ◌ ☼ ♈

Lychnis flos-cuculi

The ragged robin is a European native. It is a short-lived perennial that sends up tall flowering stems in early summer. The flowers are open, starry, usually pale pink, sometimes white, with long narrow petals. Plants grow well in damp shade.

H: 75cm (30in), **S**: 30cm (12in)
❀❀❀ ◌◑ ☼ ◐

Narcissus *'Jetfire'*

There are many narcissi to choose from but this selection, with its elegant and brightly coloured early spring blooms, is a favourite. The flower petals are rich gold and reflexed, while the trumpet is a contrasting reddish-orange.

H: 22cm (9in), **S**: 10cm (4in)
❄❄❄ ◊ ☼ ◐ ☼ ♀

Nepeta *x* faassenii

Useful and easy, catmint is a clump-forming plant with spreading stems and blue-green, soft, aromatic foliage that is attractive to cats. In summer, sprays of blue flowers appear. If the plant is cut back after flowering, it will produce a second crop.

H: 50cm (20in), **S**: 50cm (20in)
❄❄❄ ◊ ☼ ♀

Oenothera speciosa

Low-growing and sun-loving, this plant spreads freely at the root, especially in light soil, producing short, upright stems. The large, cup-shaped, pink flowers open from pointed buds and are short-lived, but appear in great profusion throughout summer.

H: 30cm (12in), **S**: 50cm (20in)
❄❄❄ ◊ ☼

Osteospermum *'Sunny Serena'*

A tender perennial, grown for its dazzling daisy flowers in summer and well into autumn, this plant is well suited to container cultivation or filling gaps in sunny beds and borders. Remove blooms as they fade and apply feed regularly if in a pot.

H: 60cm (24in), **S**: 30cm (12in)
❄ ◊ ☼

Penstemon *'Alice Hindley'*

With its shimmering, pale mauve-violet flowers carried in upright flowerheads, this is one of the most desirable penstemons. Oval leaves are carried on woody stems that should not be cut back until spring when new shoots arise from the base of the plant.

H: 75cm (30in), **S**: 50cm (20in)
❄❄ ◊ ☼ ♀

Penstemon *'Andenken an Friedrich Hahn'*

A most popular penstemon, this plant is better known as *P.* 'Garnet'. Loose but upright flowerheads of rich red, tubular blooms appear throughout summer and well into autumn, until the first frosts.

H: 75cm (30in), **S**: 60cm (24in)
❄❄ ◊ ☼ ♀

Short plants for sun (Pe–Za)

Persicaria affinis 'Superba'

For ground cover, there are few plants to match this perennial, particularly in late summer and autumn when the the blooms open pale pink and age to crimson, giving a fine two-tone look on the same plant. Rust-brown leaves carpet the ground in winter.

H: 30cm (12in), **S**: 60cm (24in)
❄❄❄ ◑ ◌ ☼ ◑ ♉

Phlox 'Chattahoochee'

A low-growing perennial that is ideal for the front of a border or a rockery. In early summer, flowers are carried in clusters. They are a delightful rich lilac colour with a central reddish-purple eye, and are produced in profusion.

H: 30cm (12in), **S**: 60cm (24in)
❄❄❄ ◌ ☼ ◑

Pittosporum tenuifolium 'Tom Thumb'

This evergreen makes a great addition to the smaller garden, with its compact form and mahogany coloured foliage. The leaves are particularly attractive in spring as green new growth emerges, giving the plant a two-tone effect.

H: up to 1m (3ft), **S**: 60cm (24in)
❄❄ ◌ ☼ ♉

Pulsatilla vulgaris

The pasque flower is one of the most beautiful spring flowers. The fern-like foliage forms a small clump, while its star-shaped flowers are usually rich purple, but can be pink, red, or white, and have a boss of golden stamens. The plant prefers a chalky soil.

H: 30cm (12in), **S**: 20cm (8in)
❄❄❄ ◌ ☼ ♉

Rudbeckia fulgida *var.* sullivantii 'Goldsturm'

Perennials that flower in autumn are valuable and this plant is also compact. Its daisy-like flowers, with narrow, golden petals and a black central cone, open atop stout stems, which should be cut to the ground after flowering.

H: 60cm (24in), **S**: 60cm (24in)
❄❄❄ ◌ ◑ ☼ ♉

Sedum 'Herbstfreude'

With its succulent grey-green stems and foliage, this plant is well adapted to withstand hot sun and drought. In late summer, flat heads of rust-red flowers open, lasting for several weeks; the dry flowerheads remain attractive into winter.

H: 60cm (24in), **S**: 1m (3ft)
❄❄❄ ◌ ☼ ♉

Sisyrinchium striatum 'Aunt May'

This choice plant earns its keep. All year, the rapier-like foliage, striped lengthways with cream and grey-green, provides striking contrast to more rounded shapes. In early summer, spikes of primrose-yellow flowers open in succession.

H: 60cm (24in), **S**: 30cm (12in)
❄❄ ◊ ☼ ♆

Stachys byzantina 'Big Ears'

This selection of the common lambs' ears has large, oval leaves, which are covered with silvery-white "wool". The low-growing plant is particularly attractive at the front of a pale-coloured border. In summer, erect spikes of mauve flowers appear.

H: 60cm (24in), **S**: 1m (3ft)
❄❄❄ ◊ ☼

Stipa tenuissima

This perennial grass is a good choice for the garden as it is beautiful for much of the year. In spring, the bright green growth is attractive, but in summer, the flowerheads give clumps a fluffy appearance, and as the seeds form, plants become straw-coloured.

H: 60cm (24in), **S**: 30cm (12in)
❄❄ ◊ ☼ ♆

Veronica gentianoides 'Tissington White'

A good plant for early summer, this low-growing perennial carpets the ground with its shiny oval leaves. Numerous spikes of grey-white flowers arise in late spring and remain attractive for several weeks.

H: 60cm (24in), **S**: 60cm (24in)
❄❄❄ ◊ ◐ ☼ ♆

Vinca difformis

Periwinkles are popular ground-covering plants, but this species is more refined than many. The flowers are the plant's star turn. They are produced through much of winter and spring and are pale blue to nearly white and propeller-shaped.

H: 60cm (24in), **S**: 1.2m (4ft)
❄❄ ◊ ☼ ◑ ♆

Zauschneria californica

Spectacular in flower, this plant needs a hot situation to grow well, but is an excellent choice for a sunny corner. It forms a low plant with small grey-green leaves. In late summer, sprays of vibrant, orange-red flowers appear, each bloom shaped like a small fuchsia.

H: 60cm (24in), **S**: 60cm (24in)
❄❄ ◊ ☼

Short plants for shade (Al–He)

Alchemilla mollis

Commonly known as lady's mantle, this perennial thrives in the shade. The soft green leaves form a mound of growth, and have a charming way of catching water droplets. In summer, heads of lime-green small flowers appear.

H: 30cm (12in), **S**: 60cm (24in)
❄❄❄ ◗ ☼ ♉

Arum italicum *subsp.* italicum *'Marmoratum'*

This perennial is grown for its winter foliage. Leathery leaves, richly veined in silver-white, appear in late autumn. The green flowers in summer are uneventful, but later displays of red berries (poisonous) are attractive.

H: 60cm (24in), **S**: 30cm (12in)
❄❄❄ ◌ ◗ ☼ ♉

Brunnera macrophylla *'Dawson's White'*

This compact perennial needs a cool, moist position. The hairy, heart-shaped leaves, margined with white, are particularly attractive with the sprays of blue flowers that are carried on stems above the foliage.

H: 30cm (12in), **S**: 30cm (12in)
❄❄❄ ◌ ◗ ☼

Carex elata *'Aurea'*

With vibrant fountains of rich, golden, grassy foliage, this clump-forming deciduous perennial is a desirable plant for moist, even wet, soil in shade. Here, it shines out from darker plants, especially in spring when the leaves are young.

H: 70cm (28in), **S**: 45cm (18in)
❄❄❄ ◗ ● ☼ ♉

Cornus canadensis

A seldom-seen ground-cover plant that spreads by rhizomes in acidic soil. The leaves are held around short stems, and showy white flowerheads are borne in early summer. Each has four "petals" that are actually bracts, and may be followed by red berries.

H: 20cm (8in), **S**: 1m (3ft)
❄❄❄ ◗ ☼ ♉

Corydalis flexuosa

This dainty perennial is easy to grow in a cool corner. It comes into growth early, fleshy shoots producing fern-like leaves. The electric-blue flowers are held in clusters and look rather like shoals of little fish. After flowering, plants often die down quickly.

H: 20cm (8in), **S**: 60cm (24in)
❄❄❄ ◗ ☼ ♉

Cyclamen hederifolium

This is an essential plant for its autumn flower displays. The plant grows from a corm just below the surface of the soil, sending up masses of pink or white flowers, followed by attractive leaves that are marked with silver or darker green.

H: 10cm (4in), **S**: 20cm (8in)
❄❄❄ ◌ ◐ ☼ ♈

Daphne laureola *subsp.* philippi

This upright bushy evergreen is slow-growing and suited to the smaller plot. The leaves are shiny and clustered towards the tops of the stems, from where, in late winter, strongly perfumed, green bell-shaped flowers appear, followed by black berries.

H: 60cm (24in), **S**: 1m (3ft)
❄❄❄ ◌ ◐ ☼

Epimedium *x* versicolor

These easy-to-grow, clump-forming perennials are good for shaded spots under shrubs. The dainty, divided foliage is attractive, especially in spring, and is often bronze-tinged. Clusters of yellow, orange, or pink flowers appear at the same time.

H: 20cm (8in), **S**: 30cm (12in)
❄❄❄ ◌ ◐ ☼ ♈

Galanthus nivalis

The first flowers of the common snowdrop are a sign to gardeners that spring is on the way. These plants grow well in shade and will quickly bulk up to form large clumps, which need to be split regularly to keep them flowering.

H: 10cm (4in), **S**: 20cm (8in)
❄❄❄ ◌ ◐ ☼ ♈

Geranium macrorrhizum

This is one of the lower-growing hardy geraniums, good for planting under larger shrubs and forming dense ground cover with its soft aromatic foliage. In spring, short stems produce clusters of pink, mauve, or white flowers over several weeks.

H: 30cm (12in), **S**: 60cm (24in)
❄❄❄ ◌ ◐ ☼

Helleborus *x* hybridus

Also known as Lenten roses, these perennials are very popular spring plants. In late winter, new shoots emerge; the nodding flowers appear first, followed by the leaves. The flowers come in many colours except blue, and they last for weeks.

H: 50cm (20in), **S**: 30cm (12in)
❄❄❄ ◌ ◐ ☼

Short plants for shade (He–Uv)

Heuchera 'Plum Pudding'

This foliage plant makes an attractive addition to a shady border. The rounded, evergreen, wavy-edged leaves are purple-red with silver markings that give the plant a metallic shimmer. In summer, spires of flowers are held above the foliage.

H: 60cm (24in), **S**: 30cm (12in)
❄❄❄ ○ ◑ ☀

Lysimachia nummularia 'Aurea'

This perennial's brightly coloured foliage means it can be used in the garden to dramatic effect. The golden, oval leaves are held on stems that grow flat on the ground, forming a dense mat. Yellow, cup-shaped flowers appear in summer.

H: 3cm (1¼in), **S**: 1m (3ft)
❄❄❄ ○ ◑ ● ☀ ☀ ♔

Meconopsis cambrica

The delightful Welsh poppy is a welcome plant in many gardens; its fresh foliage and flowers make a wonderful show in shaded positions. The flowers, carried on slender stems above the leaves, appear in shades of yellow or orange.

H: 50cm (20in), **S**: 30cm (12in)
❄❄❄ ○ ◑ ☀ ♔

Omphalodes cappadocica 'Cherry Ingram'

This little perennial is a delight in spring. Its small leaves form a compact clump that starts early into growth. Starry, mauve-blue flowers are carried in small spires and are beautiful for several weeks.

H: 20cm (8in), **S**: 30cm (12in)
❄❄❄ ○ ◑ ☀ ♔

Ophiopogon planiscapus 'Nigrescens'

A useful perennial that can be combined with many other plants. It is clump-forming and evergreen with almost black, grass-like foliage. In summer, small, mauve flowers appear, followed by black berries.

H: 15cm (6in), **S**: 20cm (8in)
❄❄❄ ○ ◑ ☀ ♔

Pachysandra terminalis

This evergreen, ground-covering plant is one of few that will grow in dry shade under shrubs and trees. Its toothed leaves form a mat of growth that prevents weeds; the plant spreads via underground runners. In summer, white flowers appear.

H: 20cm (8in), **S**: 60cm (24in)
❄❄❄ ○ ◑ ☀

Primula pulverulenta

This perennial must have moist, rich soil to thrive. The leaves emerge in spring before the flowerheads. The stout stems, which are covered in a chalky white coating, are striking and contrast well with the rounded heads of small, reddish-purple blooms.

H: 60cm (24in), **S**: 30cm (12in)
❄❄❄ ◐◑ ☼ ♈

Primula vulgaris

The common primrose is a worthy garden plant and will grow in shady borders under trees and shrubs, in cool rockeries, or naturalized in rough grass. In early spring, a succession of yellow, or sometimes white, or even pink, flowers open over many weeks.

H: 15cm (6in), **S**: 20cm (8in)
❄❄❄ ◐ ☼ ♈

Pulmonaria 'Sissinghurst White'

With attractive, bell-shaped flowers produced over many weeks in spring, and silver-green foliage, these perennials are excellent garden plants. This dependable selection has white flowers that show up well in shade.

H: 20cm (8in), **S**: 60cm (24in)
❄❄❄ ◐ ☼ ♈

Saxifraga fortunei

This perennial is remarkable for its late-flowering habit, although some selections bloom during summer. It is a clump-forming plant with handsome, glossy, hand-shaped leaves. Showy flowerheads of white flowers appear before the frosts.

H: 50cm (20in), **S**: 30cm (12in)
❄❄❄ ◐◑ ☼

Tiarella cordifolia

A good ground-cover plant, this perennial spreads from runners, colonizing small areas. The hand-shaped leaves are soft and tinted purple. Small, white, pink-tinged flowers are held in short spires during spring.

H: 20cm (8in), **S**: 60cm (24in)
❄❄❄ ◐◑ ☼ ♈

Uvularia grandiflora

A most elegant perennial that bears flowers in mid-spring. Tall, slender stems with oval leaves arise, from which dangle bell-shaped, yellow flowers with long twisted petals. It is not an easy plant and likes a cool moist soil with added organic matter.

H: 60cm (24in), **S**: 30cm (12in)
❄❄❄ ◐◑ ☼ ♈

Trees, large shrubs, and hedging

Acer palmatum '*Sango-kaku*'

This elegant Japanese maple is a shade-loving deciduous tree for all seasons. In spring and autumn the palmate leaves are distinctly yellow, and in winter the bright lacquer-red stems make a striking feature. Provide shelter and fertile soil.

H: 6m (20ft); **S**: 5m (15ft)
❄❄❄ ◊ ☼ ☼ ♔

Amelanchier *x* grandiflora '*Ballerina*'

A small spreading tree for acid, clay-rich soils and exposed sites. White blossom smothers the bare branches in spring followed by red, ripening to black, fruits. The oval leaves, bronze tinted in spring, colour red in autumn.

H: 6m (20ft); **S**: 8m (25ft)
❄❄❄ ◊ ☼ ☼ ♔

Arbutus unedo

This evergreen with flaky red-brown bark forms a large shrub or small tree in sheltered gardens. Lily-of-the-valley-like blooms appear in early winter and the rounded fruits, ripening red in autumn, give rise to the common name, strawberry tree.

H: 8m (25ft); **S**: 8m (25ft)
❄❄❄ ◊ ☼ ♔

Betula utilis *var.* jacquemontii

For winter garden impact, plant this white-barked Himalayan birch as a multi-stemmed tree or a cluster of three saplings. Cultivars, including 'Jermyns' and 'Grayswood Ghost', have even brighter bark. Long catkins dangle in early spring.

H: 18m (60ft); **S**: 10m (30ft)
❄❄❄ ◊ ◊ ☼ ☼ ♔

Camellia *x* williamsii

An evergreen, shade-loving shrub that flowers through mid- and late spring and drops its spent flowers neatly. Single to fully double blooms are white through to deep pink and cultivars are suitable for large pots or as wall shrubs. Requires acid soil.

H: 2–5m (6–15ft); **S**: 1–3m (3–10ft)
❄❄❄ ◊ ☼ ♔

Cornus controversa '*Variegata*'

Tiered whorls of branches create a distinctive architectural profile, and with bright green and white foliage and flat heads of white flowers in early summer, this charming tree makes a beautiful focal point. Requires neutral to acid soil.

H: 7m (23ft); **S**: 7m (23ft)
❄❄❄ ◊ ◊ ☼ ☼ ♔

Cornus kousa *var.* chinensis *'China Girl'*

This small conical tree, for neutral to acid soils, has tiny green flowers in early summer, surrounded by creamy-white, petal-like bracts. Fleshy red fruits develop later, followed by purple-red autumn leaves.

H: 7m (22ft); **S**: 5m (15ft)
❄❄❄ ◊ ☼ ◐

Crataegus laevigata *'Paul's Scarlet'*

Like many hawthorns, this hardy tree with a long season of interest is suitable for exposed sites. 'Paul's Scarlet' has a mass of raspberry red blossom in late spring followed by a crop of red berries loved by birds.

H: 8m (25ft); **S**: 8m (25ft)
❄❄❄ ◊ ◊ ☼ ◐ ♈

Cupressus sempervirens *Stricta Group*

The narrow columns of Italian cypress act like exclamation marks. Informal groups also work well in Mediterranean-style gravel gardens, casting little shade. Maintain a single leading shoot when plants are young.

H: 20m (70ft); **S**: 3m (10ft)
❄❄❄ ◊ ☼ ♈

Fagus sylvatica

Beech makes an excellent hedge or windbreak, holding on to its coppery autumn leaves through winter; the new spring foliage is bright green. Plant bare-root hedging between late autumn and early spring. Trim once in late summer. Chalk tolerant.

H: 1.2–6m (4–20ft); **S**: 1.2–2m (4–6ft)
❄❄❄ ◊ ◐ ☼ ◐ ♈

Fatsia japonica

The false castor oil plant is a shade-loving evergreen that adds a tropical or contemporary touch with its glossy, hand-shaped leaves and branched flowerheads in autumn. Plant in late spring in a sheltered spot. Remove frost-damaged leaves in spring.

H: 1.5–4m (5–12ft); **S**: 1.5–4m (5–12ft)
❄❄ ◊ ☼ ♈

Ilex *x* altaclerensis *'Golden King'*

Sparkling in winter sunshine with its glossy, almost spineless, yellow-edged leaves, this holly makes a neat conical shape with little pruning. Despite its name, 'Golden King' is female and, with male pollen in the vicinity, produces crops of red berries.

H: 6m (20ft); **S**: 4m (13ft)
❄❄❄ ◊ ☼ ◐ ♈

Trees, large shrubs, and hedging

Magnolia x loebneri 'Leonard Messel'

This rounded tree or large shrub blooms on bare branches in mid-spring. The eye-catching flowers are lilac pink and produced in abundance. Provide fertile, moisture-retentive soil and shelter from wind. Tolerates lime.

H: 8m (25ft); **S**: 6m (20ft)

❄❄❄ ◐ ☼ ◐ ♈

Mahonia x media 'Charity'

As well as upright flower clusters in late autumn and blue-black berries loved by birds, 'Charity' is strikingly architectural with whorls of large, evergreen, spiny leaves. 'Winter Sun' blooms through winter. Prune lightly after flowering to keep compact.

H: 5m (15ft); **S**: 4m (12ft)

❄❄❄ ◐ ☼ ♈

Malus x robusta 'Red Sentinel'

Crab apples are two-season plants offering both blossom and attractive fruits. 'Red Sentinel' is very hardy and bears white flowers in late spring followed by small yellow-red glossy fruits that turn dark red with age and last well into winter.

H: 7m (22ft); **S**: 7m (22ft)

❄❄❄ ◐ ☼ ♈

Photinia x fraseri 'Red Robin'

Although this evergreen can be kept fairly compact through spring and summer pruning, it makes an excellent back of border plant or informal hedge. The new growth is bright coppery red and large heads of tiny white flowers appear in late spring.

H: 5m (15ft); **S**: 5m (15ft)

❄❄❄ ◐ ◐ ☼ ◐ ♈

Phyllostachys nigra

Black bamboo produces a column of slender arching stems, glossy black when mature and contrasting with the light green leaves. Associate with other architectural plants or grow in a pot. Thin out weak canes from the base and cut off low side shoots.

H: 3–5m (10–15ft); **S**: 2–3m (6–10ft)

❄❄❄ ◐ ☼ ◐ ♈

Prunus x subhirtella 'Autumnalis Rosea'

Perfect for the smaller garden, this cherry bears tiny clusters of delicate, double pale pink flowers during mild periods from autumn through to spring. The leaves are narrow, bronze when young, and the habit airy.

H: 8m (25ft); **S**: 8m (25ft)

❄❄❄ ◐ ☼ ♈

Rhamnus alaternus *'Argenteovariegata'*

A white-variegated form of Italian buckthorn with contrasting black stems, this dense evergreen makes a handsome wall shrub. In a sheltered spot it can also be grown freestanding, clipped into a broad cone or dome.

H: 5m (15ft); **S**: 4m (12ft)
❄❄ ◊ ☼ ♈

Sorbus aria *'Lutescens'*

A compact, oval-headed whitebeam, the unfurling felted leaves are silvery-white becoming light sage with white undersides. In late spring, prominent clusters of white flowers appear, followed by dark red fruits. An ideal lawn specimen. Tolerates chalk.

H: 10m (30ft); **S**: 8m (25ft)
❄❄❄ ◊ ◖ ☼ ◑ ♈

Sorbus vilmorinii

This dainty Chinese rowan eventually forms a small tree. The dark glossy green divided leaves turn rich red-purple in autumn, and late spring flowers produce drooping clusters of crimson berries, ageing to pink and white. Likes deep, fertile, acid soils.

H: 5m (15ft); **S**: 5m (15ft)
❄❄❄ ◖ ☼ ◑ ♈

Taxus baccata

Clipped as a hedge, the shade-loving common yew produces a smooth, dense finish. Cut once in late summer. Plant bare-root plants in the dormant season, ideally before Christmas, and container plants all year round. The whole plant is poisonous.

H: 2–4m (6–12ft); **S**: 1–1.5m (3–5ft)
❄❄❄ ◊ ◖ ☼ ◑ ♈

Viburnum x bodnantense *'Dawn'*

In frost-free periods, from late autumn to spring, this upright deciduous shrub produces clusters of pink blooms with a strong scent of sweet almonds. It is happy on clay and requires little pruning. 'Deben' and 'Charles Lamont' are similar cultivars.

H: 3m (10ft); **S**: 2m (6ft)
❄❄❄ ◖ ☼ ◑ ♈

Viburnum tinus *'Eve Price'*

This compact and tough evergreen tolerates a wide range of soils and flowers from early winter to mid-spring. Flower clusters are pink in bud, opening white and honey-scented, and these are followed by blue-black berries that are attractive to birds.

H: 3m (10ft); **S**: 3m (10ft)
❄❄❄ ◊ ◖ ☼ ◑ ♈

Climbers

Clematis *'Bill MacKenzie'*
This vigorous cultivar flowers from midsummer to late autumn and bears intriguing 'lemon peel' blooms with dark red centres. Fluffy silver seedheads follow, and the foliage is light green and feathery. Prune stems almost to the ground in early spring.

H: 7m (22ft)
❋❋❋ ◊ ☼ ☼ ♈

Clematis *'Etoile Violette'*
From midsummer through to autumn, violet-purple nodding blooms are produced on the new season's growth. As with all viticella clematis, hard prune in early spring to about 30cm (12in) from ground level, just above a pair of fat buds.

H: 5m (15ft)
❋❋❋ ◊ ☼ ☼ ♈

Clematis *'Markham's Pink'*
This dainty, double-flowered clematis has rose-pink blooms from spring to early summer and silvery ornamental seedheads. It is ideal for decorating a trellis, covering a low wall, or training up a shrub or small tree. Prune only to remove dead stems.

H: 2.5m (8ft)
❋❋❋ ◊ ☼ ☼ ♈

Clematis *'Perle d'Azur'*
Profuse in bloom, this sky-blue, small-flowered clematis shines from midsummer to autumn even on a north-facing wall. Prune back to about 30cm (12in) from ground level in spring, just above strong buds. 'Prince Charles' is more compact.

H: 5m (15ft)
❋❋❋ ◊ ☼ ☀

Euonymus fortunei *'Silver Queen'*
Though usually grown as ground cover, euonymus cultivars will climb walls and fences, self-clinging via aerial roots. 'Silver Queen' makes dense, bushy wall cover, adding light to a shady aspect, and the white edges turn pink in winter. Trim to neaten.

H: 6m (20ft)
❋❋❋ ◊ ◊ ☼ ☀

Hedera helix *'Glacier'*
The grey-green, three- to five-lobed leaves of this English ivy are marbled with a variable white margin that is brightest in good light. Self-clinging stems make a close-knit wall or fence covering, and it can be pruned at any time to control spread.

H: 2.5m (8ft)
❋❋❋ ◊ ◊ ☼ ☼ ♈

Hydrangea anomala *subsp. petiolaris*

Although this deciduous, self-clinging climber takes a few years to begin climbing and flowering in earnest, it is a stunning sight on a shady wall when covered in its white midsummer blooms. It has yellow autumn foliage.

H: 15m (50ft)

❄❄❄ ◐ ☀ ◑ ⚱

Parthenocissus henryana

This well-behaved form of Virginia creeper develops silvery veins and red tints in partial shade but has better autumn colour in full sun, when the leaves turn crimson before falling. It clings to vertical surfaces via sticky-ended tendrils. Prune to control size.

H: 10m (30ft)

❄❄❄ ◐ ☀ ◑ ⚱

Pileostegia viburnoides

An evergreen, self-clinging climber that thrives in sheltered sites on fertile soil. The architectural leaves are long, leathery and pointed and, in late summer and autumn, frothy sprays of white flowers appear. May take a few years to reach flowering size.

H: 6m (20ft)

❄❄ ◌ ☀ ◑ ⚱

Schizophragma integrifolium

This self-clinging, deciduous hydrangea relative blooms in midsummer and bears heads of tiny fertile flowers surrounded by showy sterile bracts. *Schizophragma hydrangeoides* 'Roseum' ⚱ has pink bracts. Shade the roots and provide initial support.

H: 12m (40ft)

❄❄ ◐ ☀ ◑ ⚱

Trachelospermum jasminoides

Confederate or star jasmine is an evergreen twining climber with small, fragrant, white pinwheel blooms in midsummer. Thrives in a hot, sheltered site. Provide wire supports. Growth may be slow at first. *Trachelospermum asiaticum* ⚱ is similar.

H: 9m (28ft)

❄❄ ◌ ☀ ⚱

Vitus vinifera *'Purpurea'*

The leaves of this deciduous vine are intricately cut and a rich red-purple shade, becoming darker in autumn when clusters of unpalatable small, round, purple grapes ripen. Provide support for the tendrils to cling to and plant on fertile soil.

H: 7m (22ft)

❄❄❄ ◌ ◐ ☀ ⚱

Medium-sized shrubs

Acer palmatum *var.* dissectum
Dissectum Atropurpureum Group
Purple-red, finely cut foliage, which
turns a vibrant red in autumn, covers
the arching stems of this slow-growing
deciduous shrub. Like other Japanese
maples it prefers rich, moisture-
retentive soil and a sheltered site.

H: 2m (6ft); **S**: 3m (10ft)
✳✳✳ ◊ ☼ ☀

Aucuba japonica *'Variegata'*
Spotted laurel is a shade-loving
evergreen whose gold-splashed leaves
lighten gloomy corners. Tolerant of
pollution, it is ideal for town gardens.
Female forms, like 'Crotonifolia' ♛ and
'Variegata', have bright red berries.
Remove frost-damaged tips in spring.

H: 3m (10ft); **S**: 3m (10ft)
✳✳✳ ◊ ◊ ☀

Buddleja *'Lochinch'*
This butterfly bush has silvery-white
stems and grey-green leaves that
make a lovely foil for the pale
lavender flowerheads, which appear
from mid- to late summer. Each tiny
bloom has an orange 'eye'. Prune
back hard in early spring.

H: 2.5m (8ft); **S**: 3m (10ft)
✳✳✳ ◊ ☼ ♛

Ceanothus *x* delileanus
'Gloire de Versailles'
A deciduous Californian lilac, this
bushy shrub flowers prolifically from
midsummer to mid-autumn. The
blooms are a soft powder-blue and
work well in a mixed border. Prune
to a low framework in mid-spring.

H: 1.5m (5ft); **S**: 1.5m (5ft)
✳✳✳ ◊ ☼ ♛

Choisya *'Aztec Pearl'*
This rounded, evergreen Mexican
orange blossom has glossy narrow
leaves that produce an airy effect.
Flowering abundantly in late spring,
with a second late-summer show,
its star-shaped blooms are pink-tinged
white and fragrant.

H: 2.5m (8ft); **S**: 2.5m (8ft)
✳✳✳ ◊ ◊ ☼ ☀ ♛

Choisya ternata *Sundance*
Lime-coloured and slow-growing,
this popular, neat evergreen makes a
vibrant addition to a shady border; it
rarely flowers. On drier soils or in full
sun, the foliage is golden. Avoid poor
soils, and frost-prone or exposed
sites. A good container plant.

H: 2.5m (8ft); **S**: 2.5m (8ft)
✳✳✳ ◊ ◊ ☼ ☀ ♛

Cornus alba *'Sibirica'*

This slowly suckering dogwood has red autumn foliage and lacquer-red winter stems. Plant in groups for maximum impact, and prune hard in early spring to promote plenty of new growth with vibrant colour. Tolerates waterlogged clay.

H: 3m (10ft); **S**: 3m (10ft)
❄❄❄ ◊ ◖ ☼ ◐ ♈

Cornus alba *'Spaethii'*

Variegated dogwoods provide foliage contrast in mixed borders and help to lighten evergreen plantings. When established, prune out one third of the oldest growth in early spring to promote the cherry-red winter stems. Remove all-green shoots.

H: 3m (10ft); **S**: 3m (10ft)
❄❄❄ ◊ ◖ ☼ ◐ ♈

Daphne bholua *'Jacqueline Postill'*

This late winter-flowering evergreen daphne is hard to beat for fragrance, especially when planted in a spot sheltered from wind. The small but numerous blooms are deep purple-pink outside and white within. Mulch to retain moisture.

H: 2–4m (6–12ft); **S**: 1.5m (5ft)
❄❄❄ ◊ ☼ ◐

Escallonia laevis *'Gold Brian'*

This compact cultivar is grown mainly for its attractive bright, lime-green to gold, glossy foliage. A reliable evergreen for most gardens, it resents exposure to cold, drying winds. Deep pink blooms are produced during summer. Pruning is rarely required.

H: 1.2m (4ft); **S**: 1.2m (4ft)
❄❄❄ ◊ ◖ ☼ ◐

Fargesia murielae *'Simba'*

An excellent dwarf form of bamboo, 'Simba' is well behaved either in the border or in a large container. The fluttering leaves clothing the upright stems are a fresh, light green. Thin out weak stems, and some older than three years, to maintain an airy habit.

H: 2m (6ft); **S**: 60cm (24in)
❄❄❄ ◊ ☼ ◐ ♈

Hebe *'Great Orme'*

A long-flowering hebe with tapering, rich pink, fading to white blooms from midsummer to autumn. The stems are purple, contrasting attractively with the narrow, glossy, mid-green leaves. Ideal for town or seaside gardens with shelter from cold winds.

H: 1.2m (4ft); **S**: 1.2m (4ft)
❄❄ ◊ ☼ ♈

Medium-sized shrubs

Hebe salicifolia
A hardy species, this narrow-leaved hebe flowers between early summer and mid-autumn. Tapering white or lilac-tinged blooms are borne on upright to arching stems clothed in light green leaves. *Hebe* 'Spender's Seedling' is similar but more compact.

H: 2.5m (8ft); **S**: 2.5m (8ft)
❄❄❄ ◊ ☼

Hydrangea arborescens *'Annabelle'*
The blooms of this long-flowering American hydrangea first appear in early summer; they are fresh apple-green in bud, expanding to form very large creamy-white domes. They then make attractive papery heads in autumn. Prune lightly in spring.

H: 2.5m (8ft); **S**: 2.5m (8ft)
❄❄❄ ◐ ☼ ☼ ▽

Hydrangea paniculata
With abundant cone-shaped creamy-white heads in late summer, forms of *H. paniculata* are ideal for the mixed border; pink tints often develop in autumn, especially in cultivars like 'Unique' ▽. Prune to a low framework each spring for larger blooms.

H: 3m (10ft); **S**: 2.5m (8ft)
❄❄❄ ◐ ☼ ☼

Hydrangea *'Preziosa'*
This compact hydrangea has dark mahogany stems and red autumn tints. Late-summer flowers beautifully combine young, pale pink blooms with mature heads of deep red, tinted purple on acid soils. Trim shoot tips to the first fat buds in spring.

H: 1.5m (5ft); **S**: 1.5m (5ft)
❄❄ ◐ ☼ ☼ ▽

Hydrangea serrata *'Bluebird'*
A lacecap type with narrow, tapered leaves, this dainty hydrangea bears porcelain-blue heads over a long period through summer into autumn. 'Grayswood' ▽ with mauve blooms, acquiring raspberry tints in autumn, is slightly taller at 2m (6ft).

H: 1.2m (4ft); **S**: 1.2m (4ft)
❄❄ ◐ ☼ ☼ ▽

Juniperus x pfitzeriana *'Sulphur Spray'*
The arching to upright branches of this juniper are covered in feathery sprays of pale sulphur-tinted foliage, the colouring most pronounced at the shoot tips. Stems may be removed to control height and spread.

H: 1.5m (5ft); **S**: 1.5m (5ft)
❄❄❄ ◊ ◐ ☼ ▽

Nandina domestica
Heavenly bamboo is an evergreen or semi-evergreen shrub with upright stems. The divided leaves are tinted coppery red when young and develop strong red-purple tones in winter. Midsummer flower sprays are white, developing into orange-red berries.

H: 2m (6ft); **S**: 1.5m (5ft)
❄❄ ◊ ◖ ☼ ♈

Olearia x haastii
This small-leaved evergreen is neat and compact and thrives in sheltered town gardens or in seaside areas. The leathery leaves have a white felted reverse. Frothy heads of tiny white, yellow-centred daisies appear between mid- and late summer.

H: 2m (6ft); **S**: 3m (10ft)
❄❄ ◊ ☼

Osmanthus x burkwoodii
In mid-spring this small-leaved evergreen is smothered in clusters of tiny white tubular blooms with a strong perfume. A compact shrub, it doesn't require pruning but can be clipped immediately after flowering to form simple topiary shapes.

H: 3m (10ft); **S**: 3m (10ft)
❄❄❄ ◊ ◖ ☼ ◑ ♈

Phormium 'Alison Blackman'
A New Zealand flax with olive-green-centred leaves carrying gold stripes with a narrow red margin. Tall flower shoots sometimes appear in summer. Tougher than many other coloured-leaf cultivars. 'Sundowner' has similar colouring but is larger.

H: 1.4m (4½ft); **S**: 1.4m (4½ft)
❄❄ ◊ ◖ ☼

Phormium tenax Purpureum Group
Ideal for a dramatic focal point in the border, members of this group have tapering, strap-shaped leaves that arch at the tip and, when mature, produce towering, rod-like flower stems. The cultivars 'Platt's Black' and 'All Black' are particularly dark.

H: 2m (6ft); **S**: 2.5m (8ft)
❄❄ ◊ ◖ ☼ ♈

Physocarpus opulifolius 'Diabolo'
Use this dark purple-leaved form of the deciduous ninebark for foliage contrast in the mixed border. The leaves are tri-lobed and toothed, and in early summer dome-shaped heads of pale pink blooms appear. Spring prune for larger leaves.

H: 2–2.5m (6–8ft); **S**: 2.5m (8ft)
❄❄❄ ◊ ◖ ☼ ◑ ♈

Medium-sized shrubs

Pittosporum *'Garnettii'*
These New Zealand natives make useful evergreen backdrops or wall shrubs for sheltered town gardens and seaside plots. 'Garnettii' has mahogany stems with grey-green, white-edged leaves, pink-tinged in winter, and dark purple, scented spring blooms.

H: 3m (10ft); **S**: 2m (6ft)
❄❄ ◊ ☼ ♉

Rhododendron yakushimanum
An evergreen for acid soil that makes a neat dome shape. It produces rose-pink buds in spring that open to large heads of white and pale pink bell-shaped blooms. The new leaf growth, covered in a colourful felting of light cinnamon, is also a feature.

H: 2m (6ft); **S**: 2m (6ft)
❄❄❄ ◊ ☼ ◑ ♉

Rosa glauca
Even when not in flower, this shrub rose makes an attractive foil for flowers in the mixed border. Arching red-purple stems bear soft purple-grey leaves and, in summer, single cerise-tinted blooms appear, later producing dark red spherical hips.

H: 2m (6ft); **S**: 1.5m (5ft)
❄❄❄ ◊ ◊ ☼ ◑ ♉

Rosa rugosa *'Alba'*
A shrub rose with apple-green, virtually disease-free foliage and yellow autumn colour. All summer, flushes of large, single, fragrant white blooms appear, each with a yellow eye. Showy tomato-red hips follow, which are attractive to finches.

H: 2m (6ft); **S**: 2m (6ft)
❄❄❄ ◊ ☼ ◑ ♉

Sambucus nigra *'Black Lace'*
(syn. *'Eva'***)**
Aptly named, this deciduous elderberry has finely-cut, purple-black foliage and, if only lightly pruned, flat plates of pink summer blossom and black berries. Prune to a low framework in early spring to keep compact.

H: 3m (10ft); **S**: 3m (10ft)
❄❄❄ ◊ ☼ ◑

Sarcococca hookeriana *var.* **digyna**
The upright stems of this suckering evergreen shrub are clothed in shiny, narrow, tapering leaves. In winter, tiny blooms with tufts of cream anthers release a pervasive perfume, giving rise to the common name of sweet box. Shiny black berries follow.

H: 1.5m (5ft); **S**: 2m (6ft)
❄❄❄ ◊ ☼ ◑ ♉

Skimmia japonica *'Rubella'*

This glossy, evergreen woodlander has showy cones of crimson flower buds that develop in autumn and open to sweetly fragrant white blooms in spring. This cultivar is male so does not produce berries. It is slow-growing, and needs shelter and fertile soil.

H: 1.5m (5ft); **S**: 1.5m (5ft)
❄❄❄ ◐ ☼ ☀ ♔

Syringa meyeri *'Palabin'*

This dwarf lilac has fragrant, lavender-pink blooms in late spring and early summer and small oval leaves. It thrives on neutral to alkaline soils. *Syringa pubescens* subsp. *microphylla* 'Superba' ♔ flowers intermittently from spring to autumn.

H: 2m (6ft); **S**: 1.5m (5ft)
❄❄❄ ◌ ◐ ☼ ☀ ♔

Taxus baccata *'Standishii'*

Ideal for lightening a shady area or as a focal point amongst ground cover, this golden-leaved yew makes a compact column over time. Prune back competing leading shoots to reduce spread. *Taxus baccata* 'Fastigiata Aureomarginata' ♔ is larger.

H: 1.5m (5ft); **S**: 60cm (24in)
❄❄❄ ◌ ◐ ☼ ☀ ♔

Viburnum x burkwoodii *'Anne Russell'*

In mid- and late spring this compact, deciduous viburnum produces domed heads of waxy textured, sweetly fragrant blooms that are pink in bud, opening white. Red fruits and colourful tints feature in autumn.

H: 2m (6ft); **S**: 1.5m (5ft)
❄❄❄ ◐ ☼ ☀ ♔

Viburnum davidii

This evergreen has handsome dark leaves, held on red leaf stalks, with distinctive, deeply grooved, parallel veins giving a pleated effect. Small flower clusters in late spring produce lustrous blue berries on female shrubs when both sexes are present.

H: 1m (3ft); **S**: 1.5m (5ft)
❄❄❄ ◐ ☼ ☀ ♔

Weigela florida *'Foliis Purpureis'*

The bronzy-purple foliage of this compact, deciduous weigela is its main feature. In late spring and early summer, clusters of crimson buds open to funnel-shaped blooms with pale pink interiors, and these contrast well with the dark leaves.

H: 1m (3ft); **S**: 1.5m (5ft)
❄❄❄ ◐ ☼ ☀ ♔

Low shrubs, shorter perennials, and ground-cover plants

Acorus gramineus *'Ogon'*

This variegated Japanese rush produces fans of grassy foliage with bold gold and green stripes. Often grown as a marginal plant in ponds, this variety also thrives on fertile, moisture-retentive soil and makes an excellent foliage container plant.

H: 25cm (10in); **S**: 15cm (6in)

❄❄❄ ◐ ● ☼ ☼

Anaphalis triplinervis *'Sommerschnee'*

Pearly everlasting is a clump-forming perennial with felted, grey-green, lance-shaped leaves. From mid-to late summer it bears ball-shaped flowers made of pure white papery bracts. Avoid very dry soil in summer.

H: 70cm (28in); **S**: 60cm (24in)

❄❄❄ ◌ ◐ ☼ ◑ ♈

Armeria maritima

Varieties of sea pink or thrift are drought-tolerant evergreens that make fine grassy tussocks. The abundant white, pink or red-purple flowers of *A. maritima* are borne in spherical clusters between late spring and early summer.

H: 20cm (8in); **S**: 30cm (12in)

❄❄❄ ◌ ☼

Artemisia schmidtiana *'Nana'*

Both the species and the dwarf form 'Nana' create low domes of bright, silvery-green, filigree foliage. Close-planted to form an evergreen carpet, they are ideal as drought-tolerant ground cover or to front a dry border. The flowers are insignificant.

H: 8cm (3in); **S**: 30cm (12in)

❄❄❄ ◌ ☼ ♈

Artemisia stelleriana *'Boughton Silver'*

The white-felted foliage of this low evergreen is intricately cut and looks more like lace than leaf. Use it to fill gaps between other plants, especially towards the front of the border, or to provide textural contrast in a container.

H: 15cm (6in); **S**: 45cm (18in)

❄❄❄ ◌ ☼

Arum italicum *'Marmoratum'*

From late autumn through to mid-spring, the marbled, arrow-shaped leaves of lords and ladies cover the ground. In spring, pale green flowers appear followed by gleaming spikes of autumn berries. Good on heavier soils, it needs moisture in sunshine.

H: 30cm (12in); **S**: 15cm (6in)

❄❄❄ ◐ ☼ ◑ ♈

Astilbe *'Bronce Elegans'*
This pretty, dwarf astilbe has finely cut, rich copper foliage in spring and feathery pink plumes from mid- to late summer. Plants form creeping herbaceous colonies and are suitable for the front of a border. Tolerates full sun given plentiful moisture.

H: 30cm (12in); **S**: 25cm (10in)
✽✽✽ ◐ ◐ ☼ ☼ ☼ ♈

Bergenia cordifolia *'Purpurea'*
This evergreen elephant's ears has magenta bell-shaped flowers in late winter and rich purple-red leaf tones through autumn and winter. Its large, glossy, rounded leaves make a strong contrast with grassy foliage plants. *Bergenia purpurascens* ♈ is similar.

H: 60cm (24in); **S**: 75cm (30in)
✽✽✽✽ ◐ ☼ ☼ ☼ ♈

Carex flagellifera
One of the New Zealand sedges, this evergreen has upright then arching clumps of fine wiry foliage, tinted gingery-brown. Plant singly to accent low creepers, or in multiples for ground cover with a contemporary look. *Carex testacea* is similar.

H: 1.1m (3½ft); **S**: 90cm (36in)
✽✽✽ ◐ ☼ ☼

Carex oshimensis *'Evergold'*
This bright, gold and green-striped evergreen sedge from Japan makes hummocks of narrow, arching, grassy leaves. Planted in groups it provides colourful ground cover, but it also works well in containers. Remove or trim brown leaves in spring.

H: 30cm (12in); **S**: 35cm (14in)
✽✽✽ ◐ ☼ ☼ ♈

Ceratostigma plumbaginoides
This creeping plant attracts the eye in late summer when the red stems are studded with gentian-blue blooms. In autumn, the carpet of bright green leaves turn red or purple, providing a striking foil for the remaining flowers. Avoid very poor dry soils.

H: 45cm (18in); **S**: 30cm (12in)
✽✽✽ ◐ ◐ ☼ ♈

Cistus x dansereaui *'Decumbens'*
From late spring to midsummer, this rock rose produces a succession of pure white, tissue-paper blooms marked with maroon blotches. The sticky evergreen foliage makes fine ground cover for banks and hot, dry borders. *Cistus x hybridus* is similar.

H: 60cm (24in); **S**: 90cm (36in)
✽✽ ◐ ☼ ♈

Low shrubs, shorter perennials, and ground-cover plants

Cistus x lenis 'Grayswood Pink'

Blooming in summer, this pretty pink-flowered rock rose is one of the hardiest in cultivation. Low growing, it spreads to cover a large area, sometimes rooting where the stems touch the ground. Useful for gravel gardens, walls, and banks.

H: 30cm (12in); **S**: 3m (10ft)
❋❋❋ ◊ ☼ ♛

Convolvulus cneorum

With leaves like strips of silvery metal, this compact, dome-shaped evergreen gleams in sunshine. Starting in spring, flushes of pink buds open to white funnel-shaped blooms. Thrives in shelter on poor, slightly alkaline soils with sharp winter drainage.

H: 60cm (24in); **S**: 90cm (36in)
❋❋ ◊ ☼ ♛

Cotoneaster horizontalis

This tough deciduous shrub produces a herringbone pattern of branches clothed in small, glossy, dark green leaves that turn red in autumn. In late spring, it is smothered in tiny blossoms which ripen to long-lasting red berries. It makes good ground or wall cover.

H: 1.2m (4ft); **S**: 1.5m (5ft)
❋❋❋ ◊ ◑ ☼ ◑ ♛

Cyclamen hederifolium

Carpets of this self-seeding cyclamen steadily build up under established trees and shrubs, thriving in soil rich in leafmould. The delicate pink blooms appear in autumn before the marbled, arrow-shaped leaves, which last throughout winter and spring.

H: 13cm (5in); **S**: 15cm (6in)
❋❋❋ ◑ ☼ ♛

Diascia barberae 'Blackthorn Apricot'

Providing summer-flowering ground cover in well-drained gardens, several diascias are hardy, especially the brick-pink 'Ruby Field' ♛, but need plentiful summer moisture. Clip over in spring. They overwinter best in containers.

H: 25cm (10in); **S**: 50cm (20in)
❋❋ ◑ ☼ ♛

Dicentra 'Stuart Boothman'

This low-growing bleeding heart has feathery blue-grey foliage and, from mid-spring to late summer, arching sprays of deep pink blooms. It prefers fertile, moisture-retentive soil, conditions that prolong both flowering and foliage displays.

H: 30cm (12in); **S**: 40cm (16in)
❋❋❋ ◑ ◑ ☼ ♛

Erica carnea *'Springwood White'*

Between midwinter and mid-spring, the carpet of emerald-green foliage is covered in tiny, white, honey-scented flowers that attract early bees. It has a trailing habit. Another excellent white is *Erica* x *darleyensis* 'Silberschmelze'. Clip after flowering.

H: 15cm (6in); **S**: 45cm (18in)
❋❋❋ ◊ ◗ ☼ ♔

Erigeron karvinskianus

This dainty fleabane self-seeds freely, growing in cracks in walls and paving and forming colonies in gravel. All summer, a profusion of little daisy-like blooms are produced which mature from white through to deep pinky-purple, creating a two-tone effect.

H: 15cm (6in); **S**: 1m (3ft)
❋❋❋ ◊ ☼ ♔

Euonymus fortunei *'Emerald 'n' Gold'*

With copious gold variegation, this evergreen shrub is ideal for a winter border. As temperatures plummet, the foliage becomes pink-tinged. May be clipped to simple shapes. 'Canadale Gold' is similar but stronger growing.

H: 60cm (24in); **S**: 90m (36in)
❋❋❋ ◗ ☼ ◑ ♔

Geranium *'Ann Folkard'*

From midsummer to mid-autumn, this cranesbill's trailing stems produce vivid magenta-purple blooms, each with a prominent black eye. The deeply cut, five-lobed leaves are a bright lime green. Foliage darkens with age and in excessive shade.

H: 60cm (24in); **S**: 1m (3ft)
❋❋❋ ◗ ☼ ◑ ♔

Geranium *'Johnson's Blue'*

A firm favourite with gardeners, this light lavender-blue-flowered cranesbill is easy to please and blooms from late spring well into summer. The dish-shaped flowers are enhanced by prominent pinky-blue centres. *G.* Rozanne is longer in bloom.

H: 45cm (18in); **S**: 75cm (30in)
❋❋❋ ◗ ☼ ◑ ♔

Geranium sanguineum

The bloody cranesbill forms neat hummocks of finely cut leaves and bears small magenta-pink flowers for many weeks in summer. Ideal for gravel gardens and raised beds, it also provides good autumn colour. 'Album' ♔ is white flowered.

H: 20cm (8in); **S**: 30cm (12in)
❋❋❋ ◊ ◗ ☼ ◑ ♔

Low shrubs, shorter perennials, and ground-cover plants

Hakonechloa macra *'Aureola'*
The arching, ribbon-like leaves of this Japanese grass are striped yellow and lime green, developing red tints in full sun, and becoming greener in deep shade. Best on slightly acid soil and excellent in containers. Cut back foliage in spring.

H: 35cm (14in); **S**: 40cm (16in)
❄❄❄ ◊ ☼ ☀ ♆

Hebe cupressoides *'Boughton Dome'*
A remarkably hardy, neat evergreen with grey-green foliage in the form of overlapping scales. The domed shape contrasts well with narrow-leaved ground cover; or plant it in groups to create a repeating pattern.

H: 30cm (12in); **S**: 60cm (24in)
❄❄❄ ◊ ☼

Hebe *'Red Edge'*
The grey-green leaves of this small-leaved, hardy hebe are edged with a fine red line and become red-tinged in winter. Small, lilac-blue flowers appear in summer, unless plants have been clipped over in late spring to enhance the domed form.

H: 45cm (18in); **S**: 60cm (24in)
❄❄❄ ◊ ☼ ♆

Hedera helix *'Parsley Crested'*
Non-variegated ivies are useful for covering the dry ground beneath trees, or for making a lawn substitute surrounded by paving. 'Parsley Crested' has mid-green leaves with an undulating margin. 'Manda's Crested' is similar but copper tinted in winter.

H: 20cm (8in); **S**: 2m (6ft)
❄❄❄ ◊ ◊ ☼ ☀ ♆

Hedera helix *'Little Diamond'*
An aptly named ivy, perfect for the front of a border or edging a container. The small, diamond-shaped leaves are marbled grey-green with a creamy-white edge. A compact, slow-growing plant, it provides dense, bushy cover.

H: 8cm (3in); **S**: 30cm (12in)
❄❄❄❄ ◊ ◊ ☼ ☀

Helleborus x hybridus
This group of mostly evergreen perennials flowers from midwinter to mid-spring in colours from white, through pinks and reds, to dark maroon. Centres are usually speckled. Remove withered foliage. Prefers heavy, fertile, moisture-retentive soil.

H: 45cm (16in); **S**: 45cm (18in)
❄❄❄ ◊ ◑ ☀

Heuchera *'Plum Pudding'*

A compact evergreen perennial with heart-shaped, lobed leaves coloured red-purple with deeper veining. From late spring, dark wiry stems carry tiny white flowers. 'Pewter Moon' has purple leaves overlaid with silver. Susceptible to vine weevil.

H: 40cm (16in); **S**: 30cm (12in)
❄❄❄ ◊ ☼ ◑

Hosta *'Halcyon'*

An elegant hosta with tapered, slug-resistant, grey-blue leaves and soft lavender summer flowers. The blue hostas, 'Krossa Regal' and 'Big Daddy', and the yellow-centred 'Great Expectations', are also slug resistant. For added protection, grow in pots.

H: 40cm (16in); **S**: 70cm (28in)
❄❄❄ ◊ ◗ ◑ ☼ ♆

Juniperus squamata *'Blue Carpet'*

This blue-leaved conifer makes a dense evergreen, weed-suppressing carpet and ultimately needs room to spread. It tolerates thin, chalky soils and requires minimal care, but may be pruned to control its spread by cutting out whole branches.

H: 30cm (12in); **S**: 2m (6ft)
❄❄❄ ◊ ◗ ☼ ♆

Lavandula angustifolia *'Hidcote'*

One of the best dwarf lavenders, 'Hidcote' makes mounds of silvery grey leaves topped in midsummer by dark purple spikes. To keep plants bushy and well clothed in foliage, clip over with shears after flowering. 'Munstead' is similar but paler.

H: 60cm (24in); **S**: 75cm (30in)
❄❄❄ ◊ ☼ ♆

Leucothoe *Scarletta* (syn. *'Zeblid'*)

This member of the heather family has small, glossy, evergreen leaves that turn a rich bronze red in autumn, and it produces equally colourful new foliage. It requires fertile, acid, moisture-retentive soil and shelter from wind. A good container plant.

H: 60cm (24in); **S**: 1.1m (3½ft)
❄❄❄ ◗ ◑

Libertia peregrinans

A slow-spreading grassy evergreen from New Zealand with amber-tinged foliage that brightens in winter, and white, starry spring blooms. The warm brown-leaved 'Taupo Sunset' is an eye-catching newcomer with contrasting white flowers.

H: 50cm (20in); **S**: 50cm (20in)
❄❄ ◊ ◗ ☼ ◑

Low shrubs, shorter perennials, and ground-cover plants

Liriope muscari

Lily turf is a hard-working evergreen perennial that makes a slow-spreading tuft of narrow, leathery, strap-shaped leaves. In late summer, long-lasting spikes of violet-purple flowers emerge. Good as autumn-interest path edging or shady ground cover.

H: 30cm (12in); **S**: 45cm (18in)
❄❄❄ ◊ ◐ ☼ ◑ ☀ ▽

Muscari armeniacum

Grape hyacinth flowers in mid-spring attracting early bees with its honey-scented blooms. The dense spikes of blue flowers emerge through grassy carpets. Unusually this bulb's leaves appear in late summer and last until late spring. 'Blue Spike' is a double.

H: 20cm (8in); **S**: 5cm (2in)
❄❄❄ ◊ ☼ ◑ ▽

Narcissus *'February Gold'*

Dwarf, cyclamineus daffodils are invaluable for creating early spring colour and most naturalize well in informal lawns and under trees. With the narrow foliage dying down gracefully, they are also suitable for borders, even on heavy soils.

H: 30cm (12in); **S**: 8cm (3in)
❄❄❄ ◊ ☼ ◑ ☀ ▽

Ophiopogon planiscapus *'Nigrescens'*

Black mondo grass, actually a member of the lily family, makes a spreading carpet of virtually black, strappy leaves. Tolerating a wide range of conditions, it keeps its colour well even in dry shade.

H: 20cm (8in); **S**: 30cm (12in)
❄❄❄ ◊ ◐ ☼ ☀ ▽

Origanum laevigatum *'Herrenhausen'*

This pretty ornamental oregano is a drought-buster. With purple-tinged leaves and stems, it makes excellent edging. From midsummer, it produces small, rounded heads of pink blooms followed by pretty seedheads.

H: 45cm(18in); **S**: 45cm (18in)
❄❄❄ ◊ ☼ ▽

Osteospermum jucundum

This South African daisy bears long-stemmed flowers, with a darker "eye" and smoky reverse, through summer and into autumn. The evergreen carpeting foliage can be used to flow over the edge of retaining walls or to soften paving on a hot, sunny patio.

H: 50cm (20in); **S**: 90cm (36in)
❄❄❄ ◊ ☼ ▽

Pachysandra terminalis *'Variegata'*

The cream-variegated form of this glossy-leaved, evergreen ground cover is slightly slower growing than the species and useful for lightening areas in dappled shade beneath trees or shrubs. Best given shelter and acidic, moisture-retentive soil.

H: 25cm (10in); **S**: 60cm (24in)
❄❄❄ ◊ ☼ ☀ ♉

Penstemon *'Evelyn'*

Unlike most border penstemons, this evergreen, narrow-leaved perennial is compact and ideal for edging a bed or for planting in pots. The rose-pink tubular blooms continue from midsummer into autumn, especially with frequent deadheading.

H: 60cm (24in); **S**: 30cm (12in)
❄❄❄ ◊ ☼ ♉

Persicaria affinis *'Superba'*

This creeping knotweed produces mini pokers of crimson-opening-to-pink blooms from midsummer to autumn. The neat carpet of foliage turns brown in winter but remains attractive. Good between rocks and for fronting shrub borders.

H: 25cm (10in); **S**: 60cm (24in)
❄❄❄ ◊ ☼ ☼ ♉

Phormium *'Bronze Baby'*

A dwarf New Zealand flax, this cultivar has deep purple, arching, strap-shaped leaves that form bold tufts amongst low-growing plants. It is also excellent for providing height in containers. Protect from sharp frosts with a thick mulch of bark.

H: 80cm (32in); **S**: 80cm (32in)
❄❄ ◊ ◊ ☼

Pieris japonica *'Purity'*

Many varieties of *Pieris japonica* are compact and ideal for urban gardens. 'Purity' produces upright sprays of white, lily-of-the-valley flowers in spring and pale green new leaves in whorls at the shoot tips. Provide acid soil and avoid frosty sites.

H: 90cm (36in); **S**: 90cm (36in)
❄❄❄ ◊ ☼ ☼ ♉

Pinus mugo *'Mops'*

This slow-growing, dwarf mountain pine is almost spherical in habit, with multiple upright stems that are covered in long, evergreen, needle-like leaves. Perfect for gravel-mulched gardens with rocks and pebbles, or as specimens in containers on the patio.

H: 60cm (24in); **S**: 90cm (36in)
❄❄❄ ◊ ☼ ♉

Low shrubs, shorter perennials, and ground-cover plants

Polystichum setiferum
Divisilobum Group
This evergreen soft shield fern has highly dissected, dark green fronds with a felted texture. It makes an attractive sculptural feature in winter shade borders and containers. Remove tired fronds in spring.

H: 70cm (28in); **S**: 70cm (28in)
❄❄❄ ◊ ☼ ☀

Potentilla fruticosa
'Primrose Beauty'
Shrubby cinquefoil does well on clay and soft-coloured cultivars also enjoy partial shade. This compact, grey-green-leaved form flowers from summer to autumn. Prune in spring, removing a third of the oldest stems.

H: 60cm (24in); **S**: 90cm (36in)
❄❄❄ ◊ ☼ ☼ ♔

Rhodanthemum hosmariense
Almost never out of flower, this silver-green, filigree-leaved evergreen produces most of its daisy-like blooms from early to late summer. Use it to soften the edge of a sunny retaining wall, or in gaps in paving, and on poor, stony soils.

H: 30cm (12in); **S**: 30cm (12in)
❄❄❄ ◊ ☼ ♔

Rhododendron *'Vuyk's Scarlet'*
This dwarf evergreen has a low profile making it ideal for the front of a shrub border on acid soil. The scarlet-tinged crimson blooms are single bells with wavy margins and are produced in abundance during mid- or late spring. Tolerates sun.

H: 75cm (30in); **S**: 1.2m (4ft)
❄❄❄ ◊ ☼ ☼ ♔

Rosa *Surrey*
One of the best of the County series, this ground-cover rose bears double pink, lightly fragrant blooms in flushes between midsummer and autumn. Relatively disease free. Cut plants back in spring with a hedge trimmer. Also try the Flower Carpet series.

H: 80cm (32in); **S**: 1.2m (4ft)
❄❄❄ ◊ ☼ ♔

Scabiosa *'Butterfly Blue'*
'Butterfly Blue', and the lilac-pink 'Pink Mist', are dainty mini scabious, flowering over a long period through summer into autumn, especially if deadheaded regularly. Plant at the border edge or in containers. The flowers attract bees and butterflies.

H: 40cm (16in); **S**: 40cm (16in)
❄❄❄ ◊ ☼

Sedum *'Ruby Glow'*

Carpeting stonecrops, like 'Ruby Glow' and 'Vera Jameson', combine dusky purple-tinged succulent leaves with crimson flowerheads that appear from midsummer to autumn. Effective *en masse* in gravel gardens. Drought-resistant and attractive to butterflies.

H: 25cm (10in); **S**: 45cm (18in)
❋❋❋ ◊ ☼ ☀ ♈

Sempervivum tectorum

Common houseleek, also named hen and chicks as the rosettes of leaves are surrounded by offshoots, bears upright, red-purple flower stems in summer; the leaves may also be red tinted. These evergreen succulents are often used for living roof schemes.

H: 15cm (6in); **S**: 50cm (20in)
❋❋❋ ◊ ☼ ♈

Sisyrinchium striatum *'Aunt May'*

This cultivar produces white-striped evergreen leaf fans from which upright stems of creamy flowers arise in summer. Architectural in character, they work well planted in swathes in gravel gardens. Deadhead to prevent seeding.

H: 50cm (20in); **S**: 25cm (10in)
❋❋❋ ◊ ☼

Stipa tenuissima

Although this diaphanous grass makes a good pot specimen, it works best weaving through borders or planted in clumps near paving. It bears pale, biscuit-coloured flower stems through summer and the light green leaves fade but remain attractive all winter.

H: 60cm (24in); **S**: 30cm (12in)
❋❋❋ ◊ ☼

Yucca filamentosa *'Bright Edge'*

This brightly variegated form of Adam's needle is best planted as a single specimen or in small groups mulched with gravel or pebbles. Spires of creamy bells may appear in summer but this is chiefly an evergreen foliage plant. Makes a fine container specimen.

H: 75cm (30in); **S**: 1.4m (4ft)
❋❋❋ ◊ ☼ ♈

Yucca flaccida *'Ivory'*

These architectural evergreens can be temperamental about blooming, but 'Ivory' produces its exotic looking flowers freely. In summer, tall stems bearing a profusion of green-tinted cream bells rise from the basal rosette of blue-green, sword-like leaves.

H: 55cm (22in); **S**: 1.5m (5ft)
❋❋❋ ◊ ☼ ♈

Perennials and ornamental grasses

Acanthus spinosus

This statuesque perennial sends up glossy leaves in early spring which expand to form a mound of deeply-toothed blades armed with spines. In early summer, spires of white-hooded blooms with long-lasting purple bracts appear. A paving or gravel specimen.

H: 1.4m (4½ft); **S**: 90cm (36in)

❄❄❄ ◊ ◐ ☼ ◐ ♛

Agapanthus 'Loch Hope'

This Nile lily has clumps of strap-shaped leaves and tall stems topped with striking round heads of deep blue flowers. Combining well with hot-coloured blooms, they brighten flagging displays in late summer and early autumn. Mulch in winter.

H: 1.2m (4ft); **S**: 60cm (24in)

❄❄❄ ◊ ◐ ☼ ♛

Allium hollandicum 'Purple Sensation'

In early summer, this ornamental onion bears drumstick heads of rich purple above a tuft of grey-green leaves. The sculptural seedheads are long lasting and good for drying, but seedlings will produce paler blooms.

H: 1m (3ft); **S**: 7cm (3in)

❄❄❄ ◊ ☼ ◐ ♛

Anemanthele lessoniana

The pheasant's tail grass, formerly *Stipa arundinacea*, makes a dense clump of narrow, ribbon-like foliage. Arching purple-tinted flower stems reach almost to the ground and, from autumn through winter, the olive leaves are tinted orange and red.

H: 90cm (36in); **S**: 1.2m (4ft)

❄❄❄ ◊ ◐ ☼ ◐ ♛

Anemone hupehensis 'Hadspen Abundance'

An upright, free-flowering perennial that bears unevenly shaped, deep pink blooms with golden stamens from mid- to late summer. The vine-like leaves form substantial clumps. Also try *Anemone* x *hybrida* cultivars.

H: 90cm (36in); **S**: 40cm (16in)

❄❄❄ ◐ ☼ ◐ ♛

Aster x frikartii 'Mönch'

Superior to most Michaelmas daisies, this adaptable lavender-blue aster blooms from midsummer to autumn. It doesn't usually need staking and has good mildew resistance. Working well with most colour schemes, it is also charming with ornamental grasses.

H: 70cm (28in); **S**: 40cm (16in)

❄❄❄ ◐ ☼ ◐ ♛

Astrantia *'Hadspen Blood'*

This easy-care perennial colonizes wilder parts of the garden in dappled shade but is just as valuable in the early- and midsummer border. The dark red blooms are like tiny posies surrounded by papery bracts, and the leaves are attractively lobed.

H: 90cm (36in); **S**: 45cm (18in)
❄❄❄ ◐ ☼ ◑

Calamagrostis *x* acutiflora

A strikingly erect grass with a strong winter presence. Popular cultivars include the arching, cream-striped 'Overdam' ♆ and the taller 'Karl Foerster', which in midsummer bears pinkish-brown plumes. In autumn, both take on bronze or biscuit tones.

H: 1.5m (5ft); **S**: 60cm (24in)
❄❄❄ ◐ ☼ ◑

Centranthus ruber

The red valerian, common in seaside areas, is a drought-tolerant, fleshy-leaved self-seeder that blooms from late spring to late summer. The cone-shaped crimson flower clusters are great butterfly attractors. It benefits from deadheading. 'Albus' is white.

H: 90cm (36in); **S**: 90cm (36in)
❄❄❄ ◊ ☼

Chelone obliqua

This turtlehead is a hardy late summer-flowering perennial that tolerates clay soil and occasional waterlogging. The upright flower stems bear curious pink blooms that open from tightly clustered buds. *Chelone leyonii* is similar but taller. Protect from slugs.

H: 60cm (24in); **S**: 30cm (12in)
❄❄❄ ◐● ☼ ◑

Deschampsia cespitosa

Varieties of the tufted hair grass, such as 'Goldschleier' (syn. 'Golden Veil'), form clumps of narrow, evergreen leaves that produce gracefully arching flower stems in early summer. The airy flowerheads catch the breeze and remain attractive well into autumn.

H: 1.2m (4ft); **S**: 1.2m (4ft)
❄❄❄ ◐ ☼ ◑

Dryopteris affinis *'Cristata'*

Often referred to as the king of British ferns, this handsome cultivar has arching shuttlecocks of semi-evergreen fronds with frilled or crested tips. Surprisingly tolerant, it will withstand some sun and wind exposure. A good container plant.

H: 90cm (36in); **S**: 90cm (36in)
❄❄❄ ◐● ☼ ● ♆

Perennials and ornamental grasses

Echinops ritro *'Veitch's Blue'*

Globe thistles are statuesque plants with coarse, deeply-toothed leaves and spherical, mace-like flowerheads that are a magnet for bees, butterflies and moths. This cultivar produces an abundance of steely blue blooms on upright, silvery stems.

H: 1.2m (4ft); **S**: 45cm (18in)

❄❄❄ ◊ ◑ ☼ ◐

Eryngium *x oliverianum*

One of the most ornamental of the sea hollies, from midsummer this hybrid has branching stems carrying abundant thimble-like heads of metallic blue, each with an elegant spiny "ruff". Although the blooms fade, they persist into autumn.

H: 90cm (36in); **S**: 45cm (18in)

❄❄❄ ◊ ☼ ♛

Euphorbia characias *'Humpty Dumpty'*

This compact, evergreen spurge blooms in spring, its chunky, acid-green flowerheads contrasting well with the grey-green foliage. Remove faded flower stems but avoid touching the sap, which may irritate the skin.

H: 60cm (24in); **S**: 50cm (20in)

❄❄❄ ◊ ☼

Helictotrichon sempervirens

Blue oat grass is evergreen and drought tolerant. In early and mid-summer, the tussocks of narrow, steely blue-grey leaves send up long stems carrying oat-like flowerheads. Use as a specimen in gravel or for massed plantings.

H: 1.2m (4ft); **S**: 60cm (24in)

❄❄❄ ◊ ☼ ♛

Hemerocallis *'Corky'*

A free-flowering daylily that blooms from early to midsummer. Slender stems with dark buds produce a succession of starry yellow blooms with brown stripes on the back of the petals. Clumps of narrow, strap-shaped leaves appear in early spring.

H: 70cm (28in); **S**: 40cm (16in)

❄❄❄ ◊ ☼ ◐ ♛

Iris foetidissima

The stinking iris (its bruised leaves can smell unpleasant) has striking orange berries that burst from large pods in autumn and remain attractive for weeks against the glossy, evergreen foliage. An invaluable plant for dry shade. 'Variegata' ♛ is white striped.

H: 90cm (36in); **S**: 1.2m (4ft)

❄❄❄ ◊ ◑ ☼ ◐ ♛

Iris sibirica *'Perry's Blue'*
Early-summer-flowering Siberian iris cultivars produce blooms in shades of blue, purple, and white and give a strongly vertical accent to the border. Their grassy foliage contrasts nicely with broadleaved plants and they have attractive seed pods.

H: 1.2m (4ft); **S**: 90cm (36in)
❄❄❄ ◐ ● ☼ ◑

Knautia macedonica
Melton pastels
This pincushion-flowered perennial bears blooms in shades of deep crimson through to pinks and purples. The loose tangle of branched stems creates a natural effect suitable for informal gardens. Deadhead regularly.

H: 1.2m (4ft); **S**: 50cm (20in)
❄❄❄ ◊ ☼

Kniphofia *'Little Maid'*
An unusual and dainty red hot poker that forms stiff, grassy clumps from which pale green flower buds appear in late summer and early autumn. These expand to form pokers of pale yellow blooms that fade to cream. Protect flower buds from slugs.

H: 60cm (24in); **S**: 45cm (18in)
❄❄❄ ◊ ☼

Leucanthemum x superbum
The ubiquitous Shasta daisy tolerates a range of situations, including heavy clay, and will even hold its own in light grass cover. The long-stemmed white flowers emerge from a clump of leathery, dark green leaves from early summer to early autumn.

H: 90cm (36in); **S**: 60cm (24in)
❄❄❄ ◐ ☼ ◑

Libertia grandiflora
This architectural New Zealander produces handsome, fan-shaped tufts of olive-green leaves. In late spring and early summer, sprays of white flowers appear followed by brown seed pods, which turn black as they mature. Mulch for winter.

H: 90cm (36in); **S**: 60cm (24in)
❄❄❄ ◐ ☼ ♔

Lilium *'Enchantment'*
An easy, clump-forming lily, this is perfect planted near the front of the border. In early summer, the upright-facing, star-shaped blooms of bold orange open to reveal black-speckled centres. Add compost to sandy soils and watch out for lily beetles.

H: 60cm (24in); **S**: 15cm (6in)
❄❄❄ ◊ ◐ ☼ ◑ ♔

Perennials and ornamental grasses

Miscanthus sinensis *'Kleine Silbespinne'*

This compact ornamental grass with white-ribbed leaves is ideal for small gardens. In late summer, it is crowned with silky tufts of purple-tinged blooms that fade to white in autumn and remain attractive into winter.

H: 1.2m (4ft); **S**: 90cm (36in)
❄❄❄ ◐ ☀ ☼ ♛

Miscanthus sinensis *'Variegatus'*

Variegated with creamy-white stripes, this tall grass adds light and stature to the border. For small gardens choose 'Morning Light' ♛ which reaches 1.2–1.5m (4–5ft) and has narrower blades with a fine white margin. Both bear red-brown flowers in late autumn.

H: 1.8m (6ft); **S**: 1.2m (4ft)
❄❄❄ ◐ ☀ ☼

Panicum virgatum *'Heavy Metal'*

The prairie switch grasses are noted for their autumn foliage tints and airy panicles. 'Heavy Metal' has upright clumps of metallic, blue-grey foliage, which begin turning yellow in autumn. From late summer, plants have a halo of purple-tinged flowers.

H: 90cm (36in); **S**: 75cm (30in)
❄❄❄ ◐ ☀

Penstemon *'Schoenholzeri'*

Narrow-leaved penstemons, like this free-flowering cultivar, are particularly hardy. These evergreen perennials produce a long succession of flowers from midsummer, especially if deadheaded regularly. Cut back to new leaf growth in spring.

H: 75cm (30in); **S**: 60cm (24in)
❄❄❄ ◐ ◐ ☀ ♛

Penstemon *'Stapleford Gem'*

This pretty, two-tone penstemon has broad leaves and an upright habit. The newer Bird Series has produced several excellent taller cultivars, such as 'Osprey', with pink and white blooms, the striking purple 'Raven', and the reddish-purple 'Blackbird'.

H: 60cm (24in); **S**: 45cm (18in)
❄❄❄ ◐ ◐ ☀ ♛

Perovskia *'Blue Spire'*

Russian sage forms a clump of grey-green, toothed leaves. In late summer, wiry, branched, white stems carry tiny clusters of violet-blue flowers. A good dry garden specimen and bee magnet. The frosty-looking stems are attractive in winter.

H: 1.2m (4ft); **S**: 90cm (36in)
❄❄❄ ◐ ◐ ☀ ♛

Phlomis russeliana
This perennial's charm comes from the way the pale yellow flowers are arranged in ball-like clusters along the upright stems. The hooded blooms reach their peak in early summer but carry on until early autumn. Combine with other drought-tolerant plants.

H: 90cm (36in); **S**: 75cm (30in)
❀❀❀ ◊ ☼ ❦

Rudbeckia fulgida *var.* deamii
This black-eyed Susan provides vivid late summer and autumn colour with its golden, daisy-like blooms, each with a dark, raised centre. It is happy on heavy soils and the dried flowers offer winter interest. *R. fulgida* var. *sullivantii* 'Goldsturm' ❦ is similar.

H: 60cm (24in); **S**: 45cm (18in)
❀❀❀ ◕ ☼ ◑ ❦

Salvia x superba
A hybrid sage, used most effectively in large swathes, which produces upright spires of glowing violet-purple flowers between midsummer and early autumn. *S. nemorosa* 'Lubecca' and *S. verticillata* 'Purple Rain' are longer flowering and more compact.

H: 90cm (36in); **S**: 45cm (18in)
❀❀❀ ◊ ◕ ☼ ❦

Sedum 'Matrona'
This fashionably dark-leaved sedum produces domed heads of tight buds that open to pink blooms in late summer and form attractive seed-heads in autumn. Both foliage and stems are a dusky purple. Divide every 3–4 years. Also try 'Herbstfreude' ❦

H: 60cm (24in); **S**: 60cm (24in)
❀❀❀ ◊ ☼ ◑ ❦

Stipa gigantea
Giant feather grass is an evergreen, tussock-forming species that, in summer, produces tall, arching stems with large, oat-like flowers. These are green at first, turning a glistening golden yellow with age. Excellent as a specimen or mingled with flowers.

H: 2.5m (8ft); **S**: 1.2m (4ft)
❀❀❀ ◊ ☼ ❦

Verbena bonariensis
Superb planted *en masse*, this tall-stemmed, elegant, self-seeding plant can be used towards the front of a border or beside paving. The many small, domed heads of violet flowers are produced from midsummer to autumn and attract butterflies.

H: 1.8m (6ft); **S**: 45cm (18in)
❀❀ ◊ ◕ ☼ ❦

EASY PRUNING: PLANT GUIDE

Plant pruning guide (Ab–Ca)

Abelia *x* grandiflora

This *Abelia* is grown for its flowers or attractive variegated or gold foliage. In spring, prune out any stems with leaves that have lost their variegation. Usually requires little pruning except for leggy branches, and dead or damaged stems.

H: 3m (10ft); **S**: 4m (12ft)
❄❄ ◊ ☼ ☼ ♉

Acer davidii

The snake-bark maple is famed for its beautiful bark, which provides wonderful winter interest. It is best grown on a single, clear trunk, which is achieved when the plant is small by removing all the lower branches in summer or winter with secateurs.

H: 15m (50ft); **S**: 15m (50ft)
❄❄❄❄ ◑ ☼ ◐

Acer palmatum

All cultivars are grown for their lovely foliage and autumn colours. Prune leggy branches in midsummer to maintain a good shape. Remove any winter die-back in early spring and dead, diseased, or damaged branches when you see them.

H: 8m (25ft); **S**: 10m (30ft)
❄❄❄ ◑ ☼ ◐

Actinidia deliciosa

Kiwi fruit is a climber grown for its lovely foliage and autumn colours. Prune leggy branches in midsummer to maintain a good shape. Remove any winter die-back in early spring and dead, diseased, or damaged branches when you see them.

H: 10m (30ft)
❄❄ ◊ ☼ ◐

Artemisia '*Powis Castle*'

This feathery shrub has attractive silver foliage that is lightly trimmed in spring to maintain its shape and to encourage growth. Give it a light shear as for lavender, but do not cut it back too hard or the plant will not rejuvenate.

H: 60cm (24in); **S**: 90cm (36in)
❄❄ ◊ ☼ ♉

Aucuba japonica

Grown for its glossy evergreen leaves, female plants can also bear attractive red berries, and many cultivars have decoratively spotted or variegated foliage. Prune plants lightly at any time to keep their shape; they also respond well to hard pruning.

H: 3m (10ft); **S**: 3m (10ft)
❄❄❄ ◊ ◑ ☼ ◐ ☀

Berberis x stenophylla

Grow this prickly gold-flowered plant as a freestanding shrub or hedge. If it gets too big, prune as for a mahonia. To keep compact, after flowering remove one-third of the oldest stems and shorten leggy stems. Wear thick gloves.

H: 3m (10ft); **S**: 5m (15ft)
❄❄❄ ◊ ◐ ☼ ◑ ♈

Berberis thunbergii

Compact, with yellow flowers, bright red berries and great autumn colour, this berberis has many uses. Wearing thick gloves, lightly prune in late summer or early autumn to maintain its shape, or prune like a mahonia if it becomes too big.

H: 1m (3ft); **S**: 2.5m (8ft)
❄❄❄ ◊ ◐ ☼ ◑ ♈

Betula utilis *var.* jacquemontii

Grown for its attractive silvery-white bark, remove the lower branches over several years as it matures. A trunk of 2m (6ft) is ideal for showing off the bark. Also remove any damaged, diseased, or crossing branches from the canopy in midsummer or winter.

H: 18m (60ft); **S**: 10m (30ft)
❄❄❄ ◊ ◐ ☼ ◑

Buddleja davidii

The butterfly bush is a vigorous summer-flowering shrub. Prune it in late winter or early spring. Cut the branches back to two buds from the base of last season's growth. After flowering, also remove spent flowers to prevent them seeding.

H: 3m (10ft); **S**: 5m (15ft)
❄❄❄ ◊ ◐ ☼ ◑

Buxus sempervirens

Often used as a small, formal hedge, this evergreen can also be trained into topiary shapes. When trained in either way, it is advisable to prune at least twice a year: once in late spring, and then again in midsummer.

H: 5m (15ft); **S**: 5m (15ft)
❄❄❄ ◊ ◐ ☼ ◑ ♈

Calluna vulgaris

Common Scottish heather flowers during the summer months, and some cultivars have lovely golden foliage. For best results, it should be trimmed annually with shears in early spring, but don't cut back into old wood as the plant will not rejuvenate.

H: 10–60cm (4–24in); **S**: up to 75cm (30in) ❄❄❄ ◊ ☼

Plant pruning guide (Ca–Ch)

Camellia japonica

This evergreen spring-flowering shrub does not require much pruning. To maintain its shape, branches may need trimming back after flowering. If the plant has grown too large, reduce and rejuvenate it by very hard pruning in summer.

H: 9m (28ft); **S**: 8m (25ft)

❄❄❄ ◗ ☼ ◐

Camellia x williamsii 'Donation'

A spring-flowering evergreen shrub that is grown as a specimen plant or informal hedge. Remove leggy growths after flowering to maintain the plant's health. If it has grown too large, hard prune to rejuvenate after flowering.

H: 5m (15ft); **S**: 2.5m (8ft)

❄❄❄ ◗ ☼ ◐ ♈

Campsis x tagliabuana

Train this vigorous exotic-looking climber, which flowers in the summer, up a wall, fence, or other permanent structure. To keep the plant at a manageable size, spur prune each of the stems back to two pairs of buds in early spring.

H: 10m (30ft)

❄❄ ◌ ◗ ☼ ◐

Carpinus betulus

Hornbeam is a deciduous tree that can be used as either a freestanding ornamental plant or hedging. When grown as a tree, minimal pruning is required, but trim a hedge in late summer, or renovate old hedges in late winter.

H: 25m (80ft); **S**: 20m (70ft)

❄❄❄ ◌ ◗ ☼ ◐ ♈

Caryopteris x clandonensis 'Arthur Simmonds'

This lovely small shrub has beautiful blue flowers in late summer and decorative, aromatic silver foliage. Prune it lightly in early spring, as for *Fuchsia magellanica*.

H: 1m (3ft); **S**: 1.5m (5ft)

❄❄❄ ◌ ☼ ♈

Catalpa bignonioides

When grown as a tree, prune only to remove dead, diseased, and crossing stems. Alternatively, coppice young plants annually, to contain their size and encourage strong growths with extra large, decorative leaves.

H: 15m (50ft); **S**: 15m (50ft)

❄❄❄ ◗ ☼ ♈

Ceanothus 'Blue Mound'

This form of the evergreen California lilac flowers in early summer. A light pruning after flowering helps to maintain the size of the *Ceanothus*, but do not cut hard back into the old wood as plants don't normally regenerate.

H: 1.5m (5ft); **S**: 2m (6ft)
❄❄ ○ ◐ ☼ ◐ ♔

Ceratostigma willmottianum

This wonderful little shrub has lovely blue flowers in the late summer. To prune, cut all the previous year's growths down to just above ground level in early to mid-spring. Mulch with garden compost and the plant will erupt into growth.

H: 1m (3ft); **S**: 1.5m (5ft)
❄❄❄ ○ ◐ ☼ ♔

Cercis canadensis 'Forest Pansy'

A small tree that is grown for its early summer lilac-pink flowers and purple foliage, which turns vibrant red in the autumn. Prune carefully when young to create a good branch structure. Thereafter, prune only if it becomes too large or branches get in the way.

H: 10m (30ft); **S**: 10m (30ft)
❄❄❄ ○ ◐ ☼ ◐ ♔

Chaenomeles cultivars

Grow flowering quinces as free-standing shrubs or train against a wall. Prune after flowering, cutting all new growths back to five or six buds. These will produce spurs covered in flowers the following spring. Also remove long or wayward branches.

H: up to 2.5m (8ft); **S**: up to 3m (10ft)
❄❄❄ ○ ☼ ◐

Chimonanthus praecox

A highly scented, winter-flowering shrub whose flowers are produced from stems that are several years old, so prune just the leggy growths after flowering has finished. If it is too large, hard prune in the winter, but it then will not flower for several years.

H: 4m (12ft); **S**: 3m (10ft)
❄❄❄ ○ ☼

Choisya ternata

The Mexican orange blossom is a flowering evergreen shrub. It requires little pruning, apart from removing in spring growths damaged by winter frosts. If the plant is looking untidy, it responds very well to hard pruning almost to ground level in early spring.

H: 2.5m (8ft); **S**: 2.5m (8ft)
❄❄❄ ○ ◐ ☼ ♔

Plant pruning guide (Cl–Co)

Clematis alpina
Violet-blue flowers appear in spring on last year's growth, followed by attractive fluffy seedheads. To prune, remove dead or damaged growths in early spring. For an overgrown plant, hard prune to 15cm (6in) from the ground in early spring.

H: 2–3m (6–10ft), Group 1
❄❄❄ ◊ ◖ ☼ ◑ ☀ ♈

Clematis armandii
This evergreen clematis has large white, scented flowers. It is not fully hardy and prefers the shelter of a warm, sunny wall or fence. To prune, remove any growths in spring that have died or been damaged by cold winter weather.

H: 3–5m (10–15ft), Group 1
❄❄ ◊ ◖ ☼ ◑

Clematis 'Etoile Violette'
A vigorous clematis that produces masses of purple flowers in late summer on its current year's growth. To prune, cut back all growths to 15–30cm (6–12in) above ground level in early spring.

H: 3–5m (10–15ft), Group 3
❄❄❄ ◊ ◖ ☼ ◑ ☀ ♈

Clematis 'H.F. Young'
This clematis has large blue flowers in early summer. Prune lightly in early spring. Working from the top, prune each stem to the first pair of healthy buds. If the plant becomes too large, hard prune in early spring to 15cm (6in) above ground level.

H: 2.5m (8ft), Group 2
❄❄❄ ◊ ◖ ☼ ◑

Clematis 'Jackmanii'
Producing masses of deep purple-blue flowers in summer on its current year's stems, this old favourite should be pruned in early spring. Cut back all growth to 15–30cm (6–12in) above ground level.

H: 3m (10ft), Group 3
❄❄❄ ◊ ◖ ☼ ◑ ♈

Clematis 'Nelly Moser'
This popular clematis produces large pink flowers in late spring and again in late summer. Prune lightly in early spring, cutting each stem back to the first pair of healthy buds. Hard prune overgrown plants to 15cm (6in) from the ground in early spring.

H: 2–3m (6–10ft), Group 2
❄❄❄ ◊ ◖ ☼ ◑ ♈

Cornus alba

Dogwood is grown for its lovely winter stem colours and, of the many varieties, *C. alba* is a cheerful red. To encourage strong, colourful stems, prune in spring. If left unpruned, the stems start to loose their winter colours with age.

H: 3m (10ft); **S**: 3m (10ft)

❄❄❄ ◌ ◑ ● ☀ ◐

Cornus alternifolia '*Variegata*'

This lovely shrub has white flowers in spring and variegated leaves cover its tiered branches. To prune, remove lower branches of young plants for a more distinct shape, and occasionally thin the canopies of older trees to emphasize their horizontal structure.

H: 3m (10ft); **S**: 2.5m (8ft)

❄❄❄ ◌ ◑ ☀ ◐

Cornus kousa *var.* chinensis

The white bracts in late spring, red summer fruits and autumn leaves make this a valuable garden plant. In summer or winter, remove some lower branches on young plants so you can see the ornamental bark, and cut out crossing stems in the canopy.

H: 7m (22ft); **S**: 5m (15ft)

❄❄❄ ◌ ◑ ☀ ◐ ☼ ♉

Cornus sanguinea '*Winter Beauty*'

To produce wonderful multicoloured stems during the winter, prune this pretty dogwood in late spring to encourage strong growths. When young, it is advisable not to prune it for two years to help it to establish; you can then prune annually.

H: 3m (10ft); **S**: 2.5m (8ft)

❄❄❄ ◌ ◑ ● ☀ ◐

Corylus avellana '*Contorta*'

A slow-growing shrub with contorted stems, this hazel looks its best during the winter. In spring and summer, the branches are hidden under a mass of untidy leaves. Prune it only to remove any damaged, diseased, dead, or crossing branches.

H: 5m (15ft); **S**: 5m (15ft)

❄❄❄ ◌ ◑ ☀ ◐

Cotinus coggygria

The smoke bush is grown for its colourful foliage and plume-like flowers. If left unpruned, it can become very large, so trim annually, but you may lose the flowers. For strong growth with larger leaves, hard prune annually.

H: 5m (15ft); **S**: 5m (15ft)

❄❄❄ ◌ ◑ ☀ ◐ ♉

Plant pruning guide (Co–Eu)

Cotoneaster horizontalis
This low-growing shrub is excellent for covering walls and banks, and it is also suitable as ground cover. *Cotoneaster* has wonderful red berries in the autumn. Prune in early spring to retain its shape and to prevent it from spreading too far.

H: 1m (3ft); **S**: 1.5m (5ft)

Crataegus monogyna
The hawthorn is widely grown as an ornamental tree or as a hedging plant. It has scented flowers in late spring and is covered in red berries in autumn. No pruning is required for a tree but trim a hedge in early spring to reduce any wildlife disturbance.

H: 10m (30ft); **S**: 8m (25ft)

Cytisus *x* praecox
This flowering broom is covered with golden yellow flowers in early summer. It requires minimal pruning, but can be given a light trim immediately after flowering to retain its shape. Do not cut back into the old wood as it will not regenerate.

H: 1.2m (4ft); **S**: 1.5m (5ft)

Daboecia cantabrica *f.* alba
Give summer-flowering members of the heather family a light trim with a pair of shears in early spring. Remove all the old flowers but don't be tempted to cut into the old wood as this plant will not rejuvenate.

H: 25–40cm (10–16in); **S**: 65cm (26in)

Daphne bholua
The sweetly scented flowers of this shrub appear in winter. Pinch out the growing tips of young plants to encourage a bushy habit. This can also be done to older specimens, but do not hard prune as the plant will not respond well.

H: 2–4m (6–12ft); **S**: 1.5m (5ft)

Deutzia *x* hybrida '*Mont Rose*'
This lovely early summer-flowering shrub is easy to grow. Prune after flowering as for *Philadelphus*, and aim to remove about one-third of the old stems to encourage new growths to push through from the base of the plant.

H: 1.2m (4ft); **S**: 1.2m (4ft)

Elaeagnus pungens '*Maculata*'

This evergreen with gold-splashed foliage is grown as a freestanding shrub or a hedge. Prune in winter or spring by cutting back the previous season's growth to two or three leaf buds. To avoid reversion, cut back all-green leaves to golden foliage.

H: 4m (12ft); **S**: 5m (15ft)
❄❄❄ ○ ☼

Erica arborea *var.* alpina

The heather family includes many varieties, and this is one of the larger members. Tree heath produces masses of scented white flowers in the spring. Unlike other heathers, overgrown plants respond very well to hard pruning in mid-spring.

H: 2m (6ft); **S**: 85cm (34in)
❄❄❄ ○ ☼ ♔

Erica carnea

This pretty winter-flowering member of the heather family should be pruned with shears in mid- to late spring. Remove the flowers but do not cut into the old wood, as the plant will not regenerate.

H: 20–25cm (8–10); **S**: 55cm (22in)
❄❄❄ ○ ☼

Erica cinerea *f.* alba

The bell heather flowers from mid- to late summer. Trim in early spring using shears to remove the old flower spikes. Don't cut into old wood as the plant will not regenerate.

H: 30cm (12in); **S**: 55cm (22in)
❄❄❄ ○ ☼

Escallonia '*Apple Blossom*'

Grow this evergreen, early summer-flowering shrub as a hedge or a freestanding plant. From mid- to late summer, cut back flowering shoots by one-half to keep the plant relatively compact. For plants that are too large, hard prune after flowering.

H: 2.5m (8ft); **S**: 2.5m (8ft)
❄❄❄ ○ ◐ ☼ ♔

Eucalyptus gunnii

This beautiful plant has distinctive silver-blue foliage. It can be allowed to grow into a large tree but to keep it as a small bush, hard prune annually in early spring. The resulting vibrantly coloured young foliage also makes an excellent focal point.

H: to 25m (80ft); **S**: to 15m (50ft)
❄❄ ○ ◐ ☼ ♔

Plant pruning guide (Eu–Ha)

Euonymus europaeus

The spindle tree is grown for its autumn colours and interesting fruits. Prune young trees to create a good shape and structure; older trees require little pruning apart from the removal of dead, damaged, or diseased wood, and crossing stems.

H: 3m (10ft); **S**: 2.5m (8ft)

❄❄❄ ◐ ◑ ☼ ◑☼

Euonymus fortunei

Train this evergreen foliage plant up a wall or fence, or grow it as ground cover or a freestanding shrub. Lightly trim in early spring to maintain a good shape. Remove immediately any reversion (stems with all-green foliage) on variegated forms.

H: 60cm (24in); **S**: indefinite

❄❄❄ ◐ ◑ ☼ ◑☼

Exochorda x macrantha 'The Bride'

This late spring-flowering shrub has masses of white flowers that hang from its long branches. To maintain a young, vigorous plant, remove some of the oldest stems each spring. Hard prune an overgrown plant in spring, but you will lose a year's flowering.

H: 2m (6ft); **S**: 3m (10ft)

❄❄❄ ◐ ◑ ☼ ◑☼ ♆

x Fatshedera lizei

This evergreen shrub has large, shiny leaves similar in shape to ivy, and is suitable for shady areas. It is an excellent foliage plant and requires very little pruning apart from removing leggy growths. This is best done in the spring.

H: 1.2–2m (4–6ft); **S**: 3m (10ft)

❄❄ ◐ ◑ ☼ ◑☼

Forsythia x intermedia 'Lynwood Variety'

The vivid yellow spring flowers of this large shrub appear on the previous season's branches. After flowering, remove annually one in three of the oldest branches. Hard prune overgrown plants in early spring.

H: 3m (10ft); **S**: 3m (10ft)

❄❄❄ ◐ ◑ ☼ ◑☼ ♆

Fremontodendron 'California Glory'

This evergreen shrub is normally grown against a sunny wall. Occasionally, very long growths may need to be reduced in length in early summer. Be careful when pruning as the plant can cause skin irritation.

H: 6m (20ft); **S**: 4m (12ft)

❄❄ ◐ ☼ ♆

Fuchsia magellanica

An elegant summer-flowering plant, this fuchsia is grown as a freestanding shrub or a flowering hedge. In early spring, lightly trim the plant just back into green, healthy stems. After a severe winter, however, prune back to ground level.

H: 3m (10ft); **S**: 2–3m (6–10ft)

❄❄ ◊ ◑ ☼ ◐

Garrya elliptica 'James Roof'

A large, slightly tender, evergreen shrub normally grown against a sunny wall for winter protection. It is covered in long, decorative catkins in late winter, which provide an exciting feature. Prune annually in early spring to contain its size.

H: 4m (12ft); **S**: 4m (12ft)

❄❄ ◊ ☼ ◐ ♔

Gaultheria mucronata

A dwarf evergreen, suckering shrub, *Gaultheria* is covered with very showy, wax-like fruits during the autumn. Minimal pruning is required unless the plant is spreading too much and needs to be contained. This is best done in early spring.

H: 1.2m (4ft); **S**: 1.2m (4ft)

❄❄❄ ◑ ☼ ◐

Genista aetnensis

The Mount Etna broom is a large, graceful shrub with scented summer flowers. To keep it in shape and encourage flowering growths, prune lightly immediately after flowering. Do not cut back into old wood as the shrub will not regenerate.

H: 8m (25ft); **S**: 8m (25ft)

❄❄❄ ◊ ☼ ♔

Griselinia littoralis

This is an excellent evergreen that can be grown as a specimen shrub or a hedge. Trim hedges in late summer and freestanding shrubs in early spring if they become too large. Remove growths damaged by cold, frosty weather in early spring.

H: 8m (25ft); **S**: 5m (15ft)

❄❄❄ ◊ ☼ ♔

Hamamelis x intermedia 'Pallida'

Hamamelis is a wonderful, scented late winter- or early spring-flowering shrub. It is suitable for a small garden if it is contained in size. To do this, spur prune all the previous year's growths to two or three buds once flowering has finished.

H: 4m (12ft); **S**: 4m (12ft)

❄❄❄ ◊ ◑ ☼ ◐ ♔

Plant pruning guide (He–Ja)

Hedera helix

Ivies are very versatile, self-clinging climbers. They will cover walls, fences, and trees, and also make good ground cover. When too large, prune back hard in spring to reduce the size. Trim at any time from late spring to midsummer to keep neat.

H: 10m (30ft)

❄❄❄ ◊ ◑ ● ☼ ◐

Hydrangea arborescens 'Grandiflora'

This summer-flowering hydrangea has large, creamy-white flowerheads. It flowers on new growth and can be pruned like a perennial plant, cutting back to 5–10cm (2–4in) above ground level in early spring.

H: 2.5m (8ft); **S**: 2.5m (8ft)

❄❄❄ ◊ ◑ ☼ ◐ ♈

Hydrangea macrophylla

Mophead hydrangea flowerheads are produced on the previous season's growth. Leave them on the plant over winter to give frost protection. In mid-spring, cut back last year's growth to a pair of healthy buds and remove weak or dead shoots.

H: 2m (6ft); **S**: 2.5m (8ft)

❄❄❄ ◊ ◑ ☼ ◐

Hydrangea paniculata

These hydrangeas produce large cone-shaped flowerheads on the current season's growth. To keep them small, prune all the previous season's stems back in early spring to two or three pairs of buds to leave a low structure of stems.

H: 3–7m (10–22ft); **S**: 2.5m (8ft)

❄❄❄ ◊ ◑ ☼ ◐

Hydrangea petiolaris

This self-clinging, climbing hydrangea requires little pruning. Remove growths that are too long in early spring, and old flowerheads after flowering. If the plant is too vigorous, prune hard in early spring, but it may then not flower for up to two years.

H: 15m (50ft)

❄❄❄ ◊ ◑ ☼ ◐

Hypericum 'Hidcote'

To keep this plant compact and producing masses of yellow summer flowers, remove dead or diseased wood in early spring and prune the remaining stems to 5–10cm (2–4in) from the ground. Also cut out one-third of older stems on large shrubs.

H: 1.2m (4ft); **S**: 1.5m (5ft)

❄❄❄ ◊ ◑ ☼ ◐ ♈

Ilex aquifolium 'Pyramidalis Aureomarginata'

This holly makes a bold, freestanding tree. It can also be trained into a formal shape or used as a hedge. Prune in early spring (all hollies tolerate severe pruning) and remove all-green foliage on sight.

H: 6m (20ft); **S**: 5m (15ft)

❄❄❄ ◊ ◗ ☼ ◐

Ilex crenata

Box-leaved holly has small leaves and glossy black berries and makes an excellent clipped hedge or topiary plant. It is a suitable alternative to a box hedge (*Buxus*) and is trimmed in the same way.

H: 5m (15ft); **S**: 4m (12ft)

❄❄❄ ◊ ◗ ☼ ◐

Indigofera heterantha

This flowering shrub is covered with masses of pink, pea-like flowers during the summer. Hard prune large plants in early spring. In severe winters it may suffer from die-back, but if hard pruned, it will produce a mass of shoots from low down.

H: 2–3m (6–10ft); **S**: 2–3m (6–10ft)

❄❄❄ ◊ ◗ ☼ ♉

Itea ilicifolia

This evergreen shrub has masses of finger-like stems of green flowers in the summer. It can be grown as a freestanding shrub or against a wall. When young, prune and pinch the plant to shape it in early spring. When older, just trim long growths .

H: 3–5m (10–15ft); **S**: 3m (10ft)

❄❄ ◊ ◗ ☼ ♉

Jasminum nudiflorum

The winter jasmine produces bright yellow flowers over a long period throughout winter and early spring. It is normally trained against a wall or fence. Prune long, leggy growths immediately after it has finished flowering in early spring.

H: 3m (10ft); **S**: 3m (10ft)

❄❄❄ ◊ ◗ ☼ ◐ ♉

Jasminum officinale

Common jasmine has white, scented flowers in the summer. It is a vigorous climber and can be trained up walls or over other structures. Trim at any time to keep the plant within bounds. Hard prune plants that have grown too large in early spring.

H: 12m (40ft)

❄❄ ◊ ◗ ☼ ◐ ♉

Plant pruning guide (Ke–Lu)

Kerria japonica *'Golden Guinea'*

A clump-forming suckering shrub covered with large, golden flowers in late spring, *Kerria* can soon outgrow its situation. To contain its size, prune it hard or thin out old stems after flowering each year.

H: 2m (6ft); **S**: 2.5m (8ft)
❋❋❋ ◊ ◑ ☼ ◐ ♔

Kolkwitzia amabilis *'Pink Cloud'*

The beauty bush is a large shrub with pendulous branches covered in pink flowers in late spring. Prune it after flowering, removing about one-third of the old flowering stems. Cut back large plants in early spring to 30cm (12in) above the ground.

H: 3m (10ft); **S**: 4m (12ft)
❋❋❋ ◊ ◑ ☼ ♔

Laurus nobilis

Bay laurel is an evergreen shrub that can be trained into many formal shapes and makes an excellent topiary specimen. Prune formal and topiary plants during early summer, but use secateurs rather than shears to shape them.

H: 12m (40ft); **S**: 10m (30ft)
❋❋ ◊ ◑ ☼ ◐ ♔

Lavandula angustifolia

This lavender is a mass of blue-purple aromatic flowers during the summer. It makes an excellent low-growing hedge. For best results, prune twice a year: shear back in early spring and then trim lightly once it has finished flowering.

H: 1m (3ft); **S**: 1.2m (4ft)
❋❋❋ ◊ ☼

Lavatera x clementii *'Barnsley'*

Mallow is a shrubby perennial that produces an abundance of large, pale pink summer flowers. To keep a plant young and healthy, prune in spring to a framework of strong stems about 30cm (12in) high. Also remove any dead, diseased, or weak branches.

H: 2m (6ft); **S**: 2m (6ft)
❋❋❋ ◊ ☼

Lespedeza thunbergii

A lovely late summer-flowering shrubby perennial, bush clover has arching stems covered in deep pink, pea-like flowers. Prune back all the stems in spring to just above ground level and new young shoots will quickly appear.

H: 2m (6ft); **S**: 3m (10ft)
❋❋❋ ◊ ☼ ♔

Leycesteria formosa

This shrub has white flowers surrounded by maroon bracts during the summer, followed by purple berries. It is almost indestructible and can be left unpruned, or it grows just as well if it is hard pruned every year in early spring.

H: 2m (6ft); **S**: 2m (6ft)
❄❄❄ ◊ ◖ ☼ ◐ ♚

Ligustrum lucidum

The panicles of white flowers on this evergreen shrub appear during late summer. It has a lovely, even shape and requires minimal pruning. Occasionally, it may be necessary to trim a few of the branches to maintain its shape.

H: 10m (30ft); **S**: 10m (30ft)
❄❄❄ ◊ ☼ ◐ ♚

Lonicera nitida

This form of evergreen honeysuckle is often used as a hedging plant or a shrub. When grown as a hedge, trim it several times in the summer to maintain its shape. For a free-standing shrub, remove about a third of the older stems in early spring.

H: 3.5m (11ft); **S**: 3m (10ft)
❄❄❄ ◊ ◖ ☼ ◐

Lonicera periclymenum
'Graham Thomas'

If it's a highly scented summer-flowering climber that you are after, this is the plant for you. If it becomes straggly, prune in early spring. Also remove any dead or damaged wood at this time.

H: 7m (22ft)
❄❄❄ ◊ ◖ ☼ ◐ ♚

Lonicera x purpusii

This shrubby honeysuckle is grown for its creamy white, highly scented winter flowers. To keep the plant to a manageable size, remove one-third of the old stems to almost ground level in early spring.

H: 2m (6ft); **S**: 2.5m (8ft)
❄❄❄ ◊ ☼ ◐

Luma apiculata

An evergreen shrub or small tree grown for its attractive peeling bark and small white flowers, which appear in late summer. As it grows, remove some of the lower branches in summer so that you can fully appreciate the wonderful bark.

H: 10–15m (30–50ft); **S**: 10–15m (30–50ft) ❄❄ ◊ ☼ ◐ ♚

Plant pruning guide (Ma–Ph)

Magnolia grandiflora
Grow this lovely evergreen, summer-flowering tree against a south-facing wall, and prune in the spring or summer to maintain its shape. Pruning reduces the chance of die-back and allows the wounds to heal before the cold winter months set in.

H: 6–18m (20–60ft); **S**: 15m (50ft)
❄❄ ◊ ◊ ☼ ◐

Magnolia x loebneri *'Leonard Messel'*
This spring-flowering tree requires minimal pruning. When it is young, you may need to remove a few lower branches in the spring or summer to give it a good shape. As it gets older, cut back any obstructive branches.

H: 8m (25ft); **S**: 6m (20ft)
❄❄❄ ◊ ◊ ☼ ◐ ♈

Mahonia aquifolium
An evergreen suckering shrub that flowers in the winter and makes good ground cover. To keep Oregon grape a reasonable size, cut it down to ground level every three or four years after flowering, or remove one-third of the oldest stems every year.

H: 1m (3ft); **S**: 1m (3ft)
❄❄❄ ◊ ◊ ☼ ◐ ●

Mahonia x media *'Charity'*
If this evergreen, winter-flowering shrub has outgrown its site, hard prune in early spring. To keep it in good shape, shorten leggy growths in early spring and remove flowering shoots to encourage growth from lower down.

H: to 5m (15ft); **S**: to 4m (12ft)
❄❄❄ ◊ ◊ ☼ ◐ ●

Malus *'Golden Hornet'*
When this flowering and fruiting ornamental crab apple is young, remove lower branches in winter to encourage a good shape. On an older tree, remove dead or diseased wood immediately, and cut off any branches causing an obstruction.

H: 10m (30ft); **S**: 8m (25ft)
❄❄❄ ◊ ◊ ☼ ◐

Malus hupehensis
This is an ornamental flowering and fruiting apple tree. When it is young, remove lower branches in winter to encourage a good shape. Remove dead or diseased branches on old plants at any time, and cut off any others that are out of place.

H: 12m (40ft); **S**: 12m (40ft)
❄❄❄ ◊ ◊ ☼ ◐ ♈

Nandina domestica

This evergreen, clump-forming shrub has white flowers during the summer followed by berries in the autumn. It requires minimal pruning to maintain its shape— remove the oldest stems in the summer. Over-pruning reduces the number of flowers produced.

H: 2m (6ft); **S**: 1.5m (5ft)
❊❊ ◊ ◑ ☼ ♟

Olearia stellulata

The daisy bush is a compact, free-flowering evergreen shrub that is covered in white flowers in late spring. Hard prune leggy, untidy specimens immediately after flowering has finished.

H: 2m (6ft); **S**: 2m (6ft)
❊❊ ◊ ☼

Osmanthus heterophyllus '*Variegatus*'

An evergreen compact shrub with small, fragrant white flowers and holly-like leaves, used for hedging or topiary. Prune hedges in late spring or early summer, and clip topiary in the summer.

H: 5m (15ft); **S**: 5m (15ft)
❊❊ ◊ ☼ ◑

Parthenocissus tricuspidata

Boston ivy is a vigorous self-clinging climber that is grown for its attractive autumn foliage colours, which range from brilliant red to purple. Prune in spring before it comes into leaf or autumn after leaf fall to maintain its shape and keep it in check.

H: 20m (70ft)
❊❊❊ ◊ ◑ ☼ ◑ ♟

Perovskia '*Blue Spire*'

This is an attractive compact shrub with blue flowers in the late summer and attractive silvery foliage. Prune annually in spring, cutting back the stems to 15cm (6in) to encourage strong growths, which will flower during the forthcoming summer.

H: 1.2m (4ft); **S**: 1m (3ft)
❊❊❊ ◊ ☼ ♟

Philadelphus

Mock orange is grown for its white, highly scented flowers, which appear in early summer. Hard prune the shrub to 15cm (6in) in early spring every three or four years, or remove one-third of the oldest stems annually after flowering.

H: to 3m (10ft); **S**: to 2.5m (8ft)
❊❊❊ ◊ ◑ ☼ ◑ ♟

Plant pruning guide (Ph–Rh)

Photinia *x fraseri* '*Red Robin*'

An evergreen shrub that has attractive bright red new growths and can be grown as a freestanding shrub or decorative hedge. If grown as a hedge, trim in late summer; a freestanding plant should be shaped in early spring.

H: 5m (15ft); **S**: 5m (15ft)

❄❄❄ ◊ ◖ ☼ ◑ ♈

Phygelius *x rectus* '*African Queen*'

This plant has long tubular orange flowers during the summer. To prevent the plant becoming leggy, treat it like a perennial, cutting back all the stems to almost ground level in the spring.

H: 1.5m (5ft); **S**: 1.5m (5ft)

❄❄ ◊ ◖ ☼ ♈

Physocarpus opulifolius '*Dart's Gold*'

An attractive clump-forming shrub with bright yellow new foliage, it produces white flowers in early summer. Little pruning is required, except to remove any of the outer stems that are spoiling its shape.

H: 2m (6ft); **S**: 2.5m (8ft)

❄❄❄ ◊ ◖ ☼ ◑ ♈

Pittosporum tenuifolium

Many of the forms of this evergreen shrub have variegated foliage and it makes an attractive formal focal point. The only pruning required is to retain the plant's symmetry by lightly trimming it in late spring.

H: 4–10m (12–30ft); **S**: 2–5m (6–15ft)

❄❄ ◊ ◖ ☼ ◑ ♈

Potentilla fruticosa '*Goldfinger*'

An attractive small shrub with golden flowers during the summer, this pretty shrubby potentilla requires just a light trim in early spring to maintain its rounded shape.

H: 1m (3ft); **S**: 1.5m (5ft)

❄❄❄ ◊ ☼

Prunus avium '*Plena*'

This ornamental cherry has large white flowers in mid-spring. Prune in early summer to reduce the risk of infection. Remove dead, diseased, or crossing branches. Young trees should be pruned at the same time.

H: 12m (40ft); **S**: 12m (40ft)

❄❄❄ ◊ ◖ ☼ ♈

Prunus laurocerasus

Cherry laurel is an evergreen with glossy green leaves. Prune freestanding shrubs in early spring to reduce their size, and a hedge in early autumn. Use secateurs, as shearing shreds the leaves. Prune overgrown plants to just above the ground in spring.

H: 8m (25ft); **S**: 10m (30ft)
❄❄❄ ◊ ◑ ☼ ◐ ☀ ♚

Prunus mume

This attractive, early flowering ornamental cherry blossoms on last year's shoots. In early summer, reduce the length of all main branches by 30cm (12in) to encourage new growths, which will be covered in flowers the following spring.

H: 9m (28ft); **S**: 9m (28ft)
❄❄❄ ◊ ◑ ☼

Prunus serrula

The attractive mahogany-red bark on this ornamental cherry makes an eye-catching feature in winter. In early summer, remove the lower branches of a young tree to give at least 1.8m (6ft) of clear trunk. Remove dead and diseased branches as seen.

H: 10m (30ft); **S**: 10m (30ft)
❄❄❄ ◊ ◑ ☼ ♚

Pyracantha 'Orange Glow'

Firethorn is an evergreen shrub or small tree grown for its orange autumn and winter fruits. It can be grown against a wall, as a hedge, or as a freestanding shrub. Prune in spring to maintain its shape, taking care not to remove flower buds.

H: 3m (10ft); **S**: 3m (10ft)
❄❄❄ ◊ ☼ ◑ ☀ ♚

Pyrus salicifolia *var.* orientalis 'Pendula'

This attractive silver-leaved weeping pear has creamy-white flowers and small brown, inedible fruits. Remove the lower branches of a young tree in winter to create a clear stem for the weeping branches to cascade down.

H: 5m (15ft); **S**: 4m (12ft)
❄❄❄ ◊ ☼ ♚

Rhamnus alaternus 'Argenteovariegata'

Prune this fast-growing evergreen shrub in early spring to remove any leggy growths and to maintain the shape of the bush. If any stems with all-green leaves appear, remove them without delay.

H: 5m (15ft); **S**: 4m (12ft)
❄❄ ◊ ☼ ♚

Plant pruning guide (Rh–Ro)

Rhamnus frangula (*syn.* Frangula alnus *'Aspleniifolia'*)

In the autumn, alder buckthorn has attractive yellow foliage and ornamental berries. The shrub responds well to being hard pruned to almost ground level every three or four years.

H: 3–4m (10–12ft); **S**: 2–3m (6–10ft)

❄❄❄ ◊ ☼ ☼

Rhododendron luteum

This deciduous, clump-forming azalea is grown for its attractive yellow, scented flowers in early summer and its autumn foliage colour. It normally requires very little pruning, but you can hard prune overgrown plants to almost ground level in early spring.

H: 4m (12ft); **S**: 4m (12ft)

❄❄❄ ◊ ◊ ☼ ☼ ♚

Rhododendron *Nobleanum Group*

Most hybrid rhododendrons require little or no pruning, although plants that have rough bark, such as those in the Nobleanum Group, can be pruned in early spring if they are too large. They will regenerate.

H: 5m (15ft); **S**: 5m (15ft)

❄❄❄ ◊ ◊ ☼ ☼

Rhododendron *'Rose Bud'*

This attractive evergreen azalea normally requires very little pruning. However, it can be trained into formal shapes and also makes an attractive, low-growing hedge. In early summer, after flowering has finished, lightly trim with shears.

H: to 90cm (36in); **S**: to 90cm (36in)

❄❄❄ ◊ ◊ ☼

Rhus typhina

A deciduous shrub or small tree, the stag's horn sumach has attractive divided foliage, which turns a brilliant orange-red in the autumn. Hard prune it in early spring to keep compact: cut the stems back to between 30–60cm (12–24in) from the ground.

H: 5m (15ft) or more; **S**: 6m (20ft)

❄❄❄ ◊ ◊ ☼ ♚

Ribes sanguineum *'Pulborough Scarlet'*

The stems of this ornamental currant bear masses of dark red, white-centred flowers in spring. To contain the plant's size and vigour, remove one-third of the oldest stems annually immediately after flowering.

H: 3m (10ft); **S**: 2.5m (8ft)

❄❄❄ ◊ ◊ ☼ ☼ ♚

Ribes speciosum

This currant is normally grown and trained against a wall or fence, and has beautiful red flowers from mid- to late spring. Remove one-third of the older stems immediately after flowering and tie the remaining stems to the wall or support.

H: 2m (6ft); **S**: 2m (6ft)
❄❄❄ ◊ ◗ ☼ ◐ ♚ ♡

Robinia pseudoacacia '*Frisia*'

The main feature of this deciduous tree is its golden foliage. To produce a small golden shrub, coppice young plants every spring. Do not prune large trees except to remove dead or diseased wood as the wounds heal slowly.

H: 15m (50ft); **S**: 8m (25ft)
❄❄❄ ◊ ◗ ☼ ♚

Rosa *Baby Love*

This patio rose is grown for its single, clear yellow summer flowers. Prune in early spring, cutting the stems back by one-half to encourage flowering growths. Also remove any dead or diseased stems and crossing growths.

H: 1.2m (3½ft); **S**: 75cm (30in)
❄❄❄ ◊ ◗ ☼ ♡

Rosa '*Climbing Iceberg*'

Prune climbing roses in autumn or early spring. Remove the oldest stems and spur prune the previous season's flowering growths to two or three buds to encourage more flowers in early summer. Tie in any strong new stems.

H: 3m (10ft)
❄❄❄ ◊ ◗ ☼ ♡

Rosa '*Crimson Shower*'

Grow this rambling rose for its rich red flowers. If trained on a support, remove some of the oldest canes in early spring and spur prune. When trained through a tree, you only need to cut out dead or diseased growth.

H: 2.5m (8ft); **S**: 2.2m (7ft)
❄❄❄ ◊ ◗ ☼ ♡

Rosa '*Félicité Parmentier*'

This is a lovely scented, old-fashioned shrub rose. Prune in early spring, reducing the height of the plant by cutting back the main stems by one-quarter, and lightly trimming the side-shoots. Remove any dead, diseased, and crossing stems.

H: 1.3m (4½ft); **S**: 1.2m (4ft)
❄❄❄ ◊ ◗ ☼ ♡

Plant pruning guide (Ro–Sa)

Rosa glauca
This rose is mainly grown for its attractive blue-green foliage. To keep it tidy and to encourage strong young growths, prune in early spring by removing one-third of the older stems. Hard prune overgrown plants to about 15cm (6in) from ground level.

H: 2m (6ft); **S**: 1.5m (5ft)
✳✳✳ ◊ ◊ ☼ ♈

Rosa *Lovely Lady*
A hybrid tea rose with salmon-pink scented flowers, Lovely Lady is pruned in early spring like other hybrid tea roses. Remove all but three or four older growths, and cut these back to about 15cm (6in), ideally to an outward facing bud.

H: 75cm (30in); **S**: 60cm (24in)
✳✳✳ ◊ ◊ ☼ ♈

Rosa mulliganii
Covered with white, scented flowers in the summer and red hips in the autumn, this rose will climb up supports or into trees. Remove the oldest canes in early spring and spur prune lateral growths to three buds to encourage flowers.

H: 6m (20ft)
✳✳✳ ◊ ◊ ☼ ♈

Rosa *Paul Shirville*
The dark reddish-green foliage of this hybrid tea rose contrasts beautifully with its fragrant rose-pink flowers, which appear from summer to autumn. Prune as for Lovely Lady (*above*).

H: 1m (3ft); **S**: 75cm (30in)
✳✳✳ ◊ ◊ ☼ ♈

Rosa *Queen Elizabeth*
Queen Elizabeth is a pink-flowered floribunda rose that blooms from summer to autumn. Prune in early spring, leaving 6 or 8 strong stems. Cut these back to about 20-30cm (8-12in) from the ground, to an outward facing bud if possible.

H: 2.2m (7ft); **S**: 1m (3ft)
✳✳✳ ◊ ◊ ☼

Rosa *Queen Mother*
Prune this floriferous, pale pink-flowered patio rose in early spring. Prune all the stems back by about one-half to encourage lots of flowering growths. Also remove any dead or diseased stems, and any crossing growths.

H: 40cm (16in); **S**: 60cm (24in)
✳✳✳ ◊ ◊ ☼ ♈

Rosa rugosa

This species rose has thorny stems and red, richly perfumed flowers from summer to autumn. It makes an effective hedging plant and requires minimal pruning apart from removing one or two of the oldest stems each year in late winter or early spring.

H: 1–2.5m (3–8ft); **S**: 1–2.5m (3–8ft)
❄❄❄ ◌ ◗ ☀

Rosa *'Sally Holmes'*

'Sally Holmes' is a modern shrub rose that flowers from summer to autumn and needs to be pruned in early spring. Reduce its height by one-quarter and remove any dead, diseased, or crossing stems and any weak twiggy growths.

H: 2m (6ft); **S**: 1m (3ft)
❄❄❄ ◌ ◗ ☀ ♔

Rosa *Trumpeter*

Like Queen Elizabeth (*facing page*), this rose is a floribunda. It is appreciated for its clusters of vivid orange-red flowers that brighten up beds and borders from summer to autumn. Prune as for Queen Elizabeth.

H: 60cm (24in); **S**: 50cm (20in)
❄❄❄ ◌ ◗ ☀ ♔

Rosmarinus officinalis

This aromatic herb has small, silvery evergreen leaves and blue flowers in late spring. Old plants do not respond well to hard pruning and are best replaced. Shear young plants in early summer after the flowers have faded to maintain an even shape.

H: 1.5m (5ft); **S**: 1.5m (5ft)
❄❄ ◌ ◗ ☀

Rubus cockburnianus

Grow this thorny decorative bramble for its winter interest when the stems are covered in brilliant white bloom. Prune to almost ground level annually in early spring to encourage strong growths. Take care when cutting this shrub because the thorns are vicious.

H: 2.5m (8ft); **S**: 2.5m (8ft)
❄❄❄ ◌ ☀

Salix alba *var.* vitellina *'Britzensis'*

The attractive orange-yellow stems make this form of white willow a must for winter interest. Coppice or pollard all shoots, first removing weak, dead, or diseased growth, to two or three pairs of healthy buds.

H: 25m (80ft) if unpruned; **S**: 10m (30ft) ❄❄❄ ◌ ◗ ● ☀ ♔

Plant pruning guide (Sa–Sy)

Salix daphnoides
Violet willow is grown for winter interest when the stems are covered in white bloom. Grey catkins follow. Prune hard in spring, cutting strong branches back to two or three pairs of buds from the ground. Remove all weak, dead, or diseased stems.

H: 8m (25ft); **S**: 6m (20ft)
❄❄❄ ◊ ◑ ☼

Sambucus nigra '*Aurea*'
This ornamental elder is grown for its white flowers, ornamental fruit, and golden yellow leaves. Prune annually in early spring – cut back all its stems to two or three buds of the previous year's growth, to leave a structure similar to *Cotinus*.

H: 6m (20ft); **S**: 6m (20ft)
❄❄❄ ◊ ◑ ☼ ◐ ♔

Santolina chaemaecyparissus
Aromatic grey foliage and bright yellow pompom flowers in the summer define this shrub. It can be grown as a low hedge or edging plant and also on its own. Trim over in spring using shears in a similar fashion to lavender.

H: 50cm (20in); **S**: 1m (3ft)
❄❄ ◊ ☼ ♔

Schizophragma hydrangeoides
This vigorous, self-clinging climber produces fragrant, creamy-white, flat-topped flowerheads in midsummer, which are set off by the dark green leaves. Its pruning requirements are the same as for *Hydrangea petiolaris*.

H: 12m (40ft)
❄❄❄ ◊ ◑ ☼ ◐

Skimmia japonica '*Nymans*'
A useful evergreen shrub with scented flowers that appear in mid- to late spring followed by red berries. It requires minimal pruning apart from occasionally shortening some shoots to maintain its shape.

H: 6m (20ft); **S**: 6m (20ft)
❄❄❄ ◊ ◑ ◐ ◑ ♔

Solanum crispum '*Glasnevin*'
The Chilean potato tree is a vigorous, slightly tender climber grown for its scented, purple-blue summer flowers. It requires minimal pruning, but can be cut back in spring if it has outgrown its situation.

H: 6m (20ft)
❄❄ ◊ ◑ ☼ ♔

Sorbus commixta

A small, upright tree grown for its autumn foliage colour and red berries. Sorbus trees require little pruning apart from shaping young specimens in early summer. Remove any dead or diseased branches as soon as you see them.

H: 10m (30ft); **S**: 7m (22ft)

❄❄❄ ◊ ◑ ☼ ◔

Spiraea japonica

This is a small, deciduous clump-forming shrub with pink or white flowers which appear from mid- to late summer. It flowers on the current year's growth, so hard prune in early spring if required.

H: 2m (6ft); **S**: 1.5m (5ft)

❄❄❄ ◊ ◑ ☼

Spiraea nipponica '*Snowmound*'

A fast-growing shrub, with white midsummer flowers that appear on shoots formed the previous year. To encourage these shoots, cut back one-third of the older stems to the base of the plant immediately after flowering.

H: to 2.5m (8ft); **S**: to 2.5m (8ft)

❄❄❄ ◊ ◑ ☼ ♈

Stachyurus '*Magpie*'

A variegated shrub that produces pendulous stems of creamy yellow flowers in spring. It can be grown on its own or against a wall. Freestanding plants require no pruning, while those grown as wall shrubs can be pruned to shape after flowering.

H: 1–4m (3–12ft); **S**: 3m (10ft)

❄❄❄ ◊ ◑ ☼ ◔

Stewartia pseudocamellia

White flowers in summer and good autumn foliage colour distinguish this tree. It also has ornamental bark, which can be enjoyed by removing young lower branches in early spring to achieve a clear stem of up to 1.8m (6ft). No other pruning is required.

H: 20m (70ft); **S**: 8m (25ft)

❄❄❄❄ ◊ ☼ ◔ ♈

Syringa vulgaris

Lilac trees offer richly scented flowers from late spring to early summer. They grow without pruning, but if plants need containing, they tolerate being cut back hard every year after flowering, when some of the oldest growths can be removed.

H: 7m (22ft); **S**: 7m (22ft)

❄❄❄ ◊ ◑ ☼

Plant pruning guide (Ta–Wi)

Tamarix parviflora

Tamarisk is a delightful small tree with fine green foliage and masses of small pink flowers in late spring. As the plant ages it becomes untidy and needs pruning to maintain its shape. It flowers on the previous year's growth so prune after flowering.

H: 5m (15ft); **S**: 6m (20ft)
❄❄❄ ◊ ◖ ☼

Tamarix ramosissima '*Pink Cascade*'

This form of tamarisk has fine green foliage and masses of rich pink airy flowers, which form on new shoots from late summer to early autumn. Prune in early spring, cutting back stems to maintain its shape.

H: 5m (15ft); **S**: 5m (15ft)
❄❄❄ ◊ ◖ ☼

Taxus baccata

Yew is an evergreen conifer that can be used as a hedging plant or topiary specimen, or trained into formal shapes. Prune hedges in late summer, and trim topiary and formal-shaped specimens in the summer.

H: to 20m (70ft); **S**: to 10m (30ft)
❄❄❄ ◊ ☼ ◑ ☀ ♈

Tilia cordata '*Winter Orange*'

This lime tree has bright yellow foliage in the autumn. It can ultimately become a large tree, but with careful training it is ideal for pleaching. Prune to shape in the winter.

H: 25m (90ft); **S**: 15m (50ft)
❄❄❄ ◊ ◖ ☼ ◑

Toona sinensis '*Flamingo*'

A clump-forming tree grown for its bright pink new foliage, *Toona* also has white flowers in late summer and attractive autumn tints. Remove any frost-damaged growths in late spring, and hard prune large plants in spring, cutting back to almost ground level.

H: 15m (50ft); **S**: 10m (30ft)
❄❄❄ ◊ ☼

Trachelospermum jasminoides

An evergreen climber with sweetly scented white flowers during the summer, star jasmine prefers to grow against a sheltered wall. No routine annual pruning is required, but you can reduce its height by pruning in late spring.

H: 9m (28ft)
❄❄ ◊ ☼ ◑ ♈

Viburnum x bodnantense 'Dawn'

Grown for it scented pink flowers that are produced during the autumn and early winter, this shrub can be left unpruned to become a large plant or kept small in size by removing one-fifth of the oldest stems to ground level in early spring.

H: 3m (10ft); **S**: 2m (6ft)
❄❄❄ ◊ ◐ ☼ ◑ ♛

Viburnum tinus 'Eve Price'

This evergreen shrub is grown for its white flowers, which are produced from autumn to early spring. It does not require routine annual pruning, but remove damaged or diseased growths when seen. Hard prune overgrown plants in early spring.

H: 3m (10ft); **S**: 3m (10ft)
❄❄❄ ◊ ◐ ☼ ◑ ♛

Vitex agnus-castus var. latifolia

The chaste tree is a deciduous shrub with attractively divided foliage that sets off the spikes of lilac- to dark blue late summer flowers. Prune the previous year's growths back to two or three buds in early spring.

H: 2–8m (6–25ft); **S**: 2–8m (6–25ft)
❄❄ ◊ ☼

Vitis vinifera 'Purpurea'

In autumn or early winter cut back this vigorous climbing grape. Spur prune all side stems to two buds from the previous season's growth to leave short, stubby growths either side of the main stem. Shorten overly long stems in summer.

H: 7m (22ft)
❄❄❄ ◊ ◐ ☼ ♛

Weigela florida

A deciduous shrub grown for its tubular dark pink flowers that appear mainly from late spring to early summer. To prune, thin out and remove one-third of the oldest growths immediately after flowering in summer.

H: 2.5m (8ft); **S**: 2.5m (8ft)
❄❄❄ ◊ ☼ ◑

Wisteria sinensis

Wisteria is a vigorous climber that produces long, scented chains of flowers in late spring. In the winter, spur prune all the summer's growth back to two buds. During the summer, shorten long, leggy stems by up to two-thirds.

H: 9m (28ft) or more
❄❄❄ ◊ ◐ ☼ ◑ ♛

Pruning calendar: spring

Trees to prune

Evergreens, such as *Magnolia grandiflora* and holly (*Ilex*), prefer to be pruned at this time of year, but most other trees are best pruned in summer or winter. In particular, avoid pruning trees that bleed sap profusely, such as birch (*Betula*) and walnut (*Juglans*), from mid-spring onwards.

Shrubs to prune

Prune winter-flowering shrubby honeysuckles, such as *Lonicera fragrantissima* and *Lonicera standishii*. In mid-spring, cut back heather (*Erica*), *Buddleja davidii*, early-flowering *Camellia*, witch hazel (*Hamamelis*), *Mahonia*, winter-flowering viburnum (*Viburnum* x *burkwoodii*), dogwood (*Cornus*), willow (*Salix*), and *Rubus*. In late spring, prune hydrangeas and, after flowering, forsythia.

Prune mahonias after flowering.

Climbers to prune

Prune clematis in Groups 2 and 3 in in the spring, plus any long, wayward stems of climbing hydrangeas (*Hydrangea petiolaris*), and any climbing or rambling roses you missed in autumn. Also trim climbing honeysuckles (*Lonicera*), *Jasminum nudiflorum* and overgrown ivy (*Hedera*).

Hedge care

In late winter or early spring, renovate hornbeam (*Carpinus*), beech (*Fagus*), yew (*Taxus*) and holly (*Ilex*) hedges, and prune wildlife hedges before birds begin to nest. Pruning the latter also ensures that plants develop plenty of flowering shoots and, later, autumn berries for wildlife. Prune lavender (*Lavandula*) in mid-spring.

Renovate hornbeam and beech hedges in early spring.

Main pruning tasks

Spring is a busy time for pruning jobs. The sap is rising and buds are swelling, which means that plants are more likely to recover from a haircut.

The main pruning tasks in the spring are cutting back shrubs with winter stem interest, such as dogwood (*Cornus*), willow (*Salix*), and decorative bramble (*Rubus*).

Follow this by pruning floribunda, hybrid tea and shrub roses. You can also still prune climbing and rambler roses now if you didn't have time in the autumn.

As there are no leaves on most deciduous trees and shrubs at this time of year, you can clearly see and cut out wood damaged in winter by the cold and windy weather.

Other jobs to do now

In spring, tie in the new, flexible stems of climbers. When pruning, you will have removed a lot of the old twining growths that helped the plants hold on to their supports, so they will now need extra help until the new stems have become more established.

Climbing and rambling roses, in particular, don't have a natural twining habit so they definitely need to be tied in. Likewise, clematis has lots of soft growth that is easily damaged by the wind if it is not secured.

Use garden twine to tie plants to their supports. If you are tying in large climbers with thicker stems, such as roses, you could use sturdy, flexible tube ties.

Pruning calendar: summer

Trees to prune

Summer is a good time to prune all trees, especially the stone fruits, such as cherries, flowering cherries, and plums (*Prunus*), and members of the rowan (*Sorbus*) family. These trees are prone to bacterial cankers and silver leaf, and pruning now helps to avoid these diseases. In late summer, prune espalier apple and pear trees.

Shrubs to prune

In early summer, prune *Garrya*. Shorten leggy growths on late-flowering *Camellias* after flowering has finished; if they have outgrown their situation, they can be hard pruned now. Prune spring- and early summer-flowering shrubs like *Deutzia*, *Philadelphus*, shrubby *Lonicera*, *Kolkwitzia*, and *Weigela* so they grow plenty of new stems for next year's flowers. In late summer, prune *Escallonia*.

Climbers to prune

In early summer, trim *Clematis macropetala* and *C. alpina*, and trim overgrown *C. montana*. Prune leggy growth of wisterias to help flower bud production, and ivy (*Hedera*) if you didn't prune it in spring. After flowering, cut back climbing honeysuckles (*Lonicera*) and the old flowerheads of climbing hydrangeas (*Hydrangea petiolaris*).

Hedge care

Prune all types in late summer once nests are abandoned; berrying hedges can be left until spring to provide food for wildlife. Prune formal hedges at least twice in summer. Trim lavender (*Lavandula*) hedges lightly after flowering.

Prune all stone fruits, such as *Prunus serrula*.

You can prune ivy from spring to autumn to keep it neat.

Main pruning tasks

Summer is the time to enjoy the results of your winter and spring pruning, but there are still important pruning jobs to do to keep your garden looking its best.

Formal hedges need to be trimmed several times during the summer to keep their clean, sharp edges. Topiary should also be trimmed a few times to maintain its shape. Do not prune boundary hedges until late summer.

Deadhead roses to encourage repeat flowering, and prune late spring- and early summer-flowering shrubs immediately after they have bloomed, since next year's flowers will be on stems made this year. Also prune back any shrubs, trees, or climbers that are putting on too much growth or causing an obstruction.

Other jobs to do now

Continue to train and tie in climbers during the summer. Climbing and rambling roses must be tied in regularly to protect long growths from wind damage, since they hold next year's flowering display. Also tie in Group 3 clematis to hold plants together, and wisteria to fill any gaps in coverage and to protect stems from wind damage.

Remove any diseased or dead growth on trees at any time. Dispose of diseased material by burning responsibly or taking it to a waste disposal site – don't compost it.

Trees can look quite different when clothed with leaves so compare them in summer and winter before deciding what to prune. Leaves weigh down branches and can block paths or views, so some stems may need removing.

Pruning calendar: autumn

Trees to prune

Autumn is not a good time to prune trees as fungal spores can land on pruning cuts, increasing the risk of infection.

Shrubs to prune

Although most pruning jobs are best left until late winter or early spring, you should reduce the height of hybrid tea and floribunda roses by one-third to prevent their stems from rocking in winter winds and damaging the main stem and roots. Also remove *Buddleja* flowerheads and the top one-third of the shoots to prevent the plant self-seeding. Do not remove spent hydrangea flowerheads as they help to protect developing flower shoots from frost, and also provide attractive architectural structure in winter. Seedheads, fruits and berries that are left on shrubs now have both wildlife and decorative value.

Climbers to prune

Autumn is the ideal time to prune climbing and rambling roses. These plants still have sap in their stems, which makes them pliable and easy to train onto their supports. If the job is left until winter, the stems lose their flexibility and are more likely to snap. You can also prune Virginia creeper and Boston ivy (*Parthenocissus*) after leaf fall.

Hedge care

Any hedges not pruned in summer can be cut back now, but do not prune wildlife hedges, which are best left until spring, as their fruit and berries provide food for birds and other wildlife through the colder months.

Trees are prone to infections in autumn so do not prune them.

Prune the climber *Parthenocissus* after leaf drop.

Main pruning tasks

Don't prune trees and shrubs in the autumn unless it is absolutely necessary. There are many fungal spores around at this time of the year and a high risk of diseases penetrating the cut surfaces.

It is, however, a good time to prune and train climbing and rambling roses as their stems are quite flexible and easily trained now. Reduce the height of hybrid tea and floribunda roses by one-third to prevent wind rock. Catch up with any pruning that you missed or didn't have time for in the summer, such as pruning back leggy growths on wisterias. It is also an ideal time to clean and sharpen pruning tools. Then sit back and admire the foliage and fruiting displays around you.

Other jobs to do now

The autumn is tidying-up time. Cover trees or shrubs that need frost protection, such as palms, tree ferns, and fruits like apricots. Leave the fronds on tree ferns and palms as they protect plants from frost. For further protection, tie them together over the crown.

As the leaves fall, the basic structure of plants becomes more visible, and you will be able to see more clearly what needs to be pruned in spring. Rake up fallen leaves and fruit, such as apples, and use to make compost and leaf mould, which you can later spread under pruned plants to feed and mulch them.

If you have any logs left from pruning in the summer, you could construct a log pile, which benefits wildlife.

Pruning calendar: winter

Trees to prune

This is a good time to prune a wide range of trees and shrubs (with the exception of stone fruits) as you can clearly identify crossing branches and diseased wood. Prune trees with ornamental bark, such as *Acer davidii* and *Acer griseum* and birches. Apple and pear trees should also be pruned in winter.

Shrubs to prune

Prune any large or overgrown shrubs, such as *Mahonia* or *Philadelphus*, which can be cut back hard now or in early spring. You may lose the coming year's flowers by hard pruning, but the plant will recover the following year.

Climbers to prune

Spur prune wisteria in the winter, as the buds are not swelling and so less likely to be damaged. Also tackle *Actinidia* and Virginia creeper (*Parthenocissus*), and renovate overgrown ivies (*Hedera*). Remove long growths from around doors and window frames, and also where they have invaded gutters and grown under roof tiles. Shorten the main stems of all overly tall climbers, such as *Hydrangea petiolaris*.

Hedge care

Winter is the time for renovation work, reducing the height and width of overgrown hedges. Brush off snow from flat-topped hedges as its weight can damage their structure. Leave the crisp, bronzed foliage on hornbeam and beech hedges in the winter months because it adds ornamental value and also makes an excellent windbreak.

Prune apple trees in winter when their structure is more visible.

Brush snow off the top of hedges to prevent structural damage.

Main pruning tasks

Late winter or early spring is a good time to hard prune overgrown shrubs, which are dormant at this time of the year. You can also see clearly the structure and naked silhouettes of trees, making them easier to prune. Summer is the ideal time to prune many trees, but winter is sometimes better because you may have more time to do the job properly. However, do not prune cherries and plums (*Prunus*), or members of the rowan (*Sorbus*) family.

You can also now admire the results of your earlier pruning efforts, with the attractive trunks and stems of trees and shrubs like the snake-bark maple (*Acer davidii*), birch (*Betula*), cherry (*Prunus serrula*), and dogwood (*Cornus*) creating stunning winter features.

Other jobs to do now

Tie in anything that needs to be supported. At the same time, check that ties and supports have not been damaged during storms, or become too tight around stems and trunks. Bring berries and evergreen branches into the house for festive winter decorations.

You can dispose of pruning material (and old Christmas trees) in a variety of ways. Shred the woody bits to make a valuable mulching material, and compost soft growth. Burning material is an alternative method, but can be antisocial if you live near other houses. Alternatively, take all your off-cuts to your local waste disposal site, along with any diseased material, if you do not plan to burn it.

VEGETABLES IN A SMALL GARDEN: PLANT GUIDE

Root vegetables: potatoes

Potato 'Red Duke of York'
A vigorous first early, producing abundant, good-sized, red-skinned tubers with delicious pale yellow flesh. Perfect in salads when small, and boiled or baked when larger. Young shoots need protection from frost.

Plant: early spring
Harvest: early to midsummer
◌ ◑ ☀ ⚱

Potato 'Foremost'
Harvest this useful early variety from early summer or lift as required throughout the summer. The white-skinned, white-fleshed crop has a firm texture, ideal for salads and boiling. Protect young shoots from frost.

Plant: early spring
Harvest: early to late summer
◌ ◑ ☀ ⚱

Potato 'Arran Pilot'
A popular first early, excellent for gardeners keen to enjoy large yields of new potatoes with creamy, waxy flesh. Good scab resistance and tolerance of dry spells. Young shoots need protection from frost.

Plant: early spring
Harvest: early to midsummer
◌ ◑ ☀

Potato 'Mimi'
The ideal first early for containers, producing masses of small red tubers with incredibly tasty, waxy, cream-coloured flesh. An excellent salad potato with good scab resistance. Protect new shoots from frost.

Plant: early spring
Harvest: early summer
◌ ◑ ☀ ⚱

Potato 'Charlotte'
A supermarket favourite because of its long, smooth, yellow tubers, with fabulously flavoured, waxy flesh. This second early is easy to grow in the garden, and one of the best salad potatoes.

Plant: mid-spring
Harvest: mid- to late summer
◌ ◑ ☀ ⚱

Potato 'Saxon'
For baking, boiling and chipping, try this floury textured second early. The large, white tubers have a mild, creamy flavour, and the plants display a useful resistance to both blackleg and eelworm.

Plant: mid-spring
Harvest: mid- to late summer
◌ ◑ ☀

Potato *'Royal Kidney'*
An old maincrop salad variety, 'Royal Kidney' produces delicious, yellow-fleshed salad potatoes from late summer. It is also tempting to dig up the plants earlier for crops of tender baby potatoes.

Plant: mid-spring
Harvest: late summer
◌ ◍ ☼

Potato *'Ratte'*
The long, slightly knobbly tubers harvested from this maincrop variety are a real treat. Their dense, waxy, yellow flesh has a strong nutty flavour, making them perfect for salads.

Plant: mid-spring
Harvest: late summer
◌ ◍ ☼ 🏆

Potato *'Pink Fir Apple'*
A curious old maincrop variety, producing long, irregular tubers with pink-tinged skin that is best left on during cooking. The waxy flesh, with its earthy flavour, is popular in salads, and the tubers store well.

Plant: mid-spring
Harvest: from early autumn
◌ ◍ ☼ 🏆

Potato *'Kerrs Pink'*
This versatile and high-yielding maincrop variety is reliable in most soils. The blush-pink tubers have delicious floury cream flesh that is perfect for mashing, chipping, roasting, and baking. Stores well.

Plant: mid-spring
Harvest: from early autumn
◌ ◍ ☼

Potato *'Sante'*
An excellent choice for organic gardeners because of its excellent pest and disease resistance, this maincrop variety yields large cream tubers that are great for baking, boiling, and roasting. Stores well.

Plant: mid-spring
Harvest: from late summer
◌ ◍ ☼

Potato *'Nicola'*
Resistance to eelworm and blight makes this variety a good option for maincrop salad potatoes. Large crops of long, yellow, waxy tubers are reliably produced and store well over winter.

Plant: mid-spring
Harvest: from late summer
◌ ◍ ☼

Root vegetables: carrots, beetroot, parsnips

Carrot *'Parmex'*

Dumpy, spherical roots make this one of the best carrots for sowing into patio pots or shallow soils. Despite their shape they have a fine sweet flavour. The earliest crops can be sown under glass or protected with cloches.

Sow: early to late spring
Harvest: late spring to early autumn
○ ☼ ♈

Carrot *'Infinity'* F1

This late maincrop carrot has an elegant, slender root that is delicious raw or cooked. The sweet carrots are deep orange right to their core and keep well in the soil into autumn or can be lifted and stored successfully.

Sow: early spring to midsummer
Harvest: late summer to late autumn
○ ☼ ♈

Carrot *'Flyaway'* F1

Specially bred to be less prone to attack by carrot fly, this maincrop carrot produces good crops where the pest would render others inedible. The stout, cylindrical roots are smooth-skinned and sugary.

Sow: early spring to midsummer
Harvest: late spring to mid-autumn
○ ☼ ♈

Carrot *'Purple Haze'* F1

As its name suggests, this variety has unconventional dark purple roots, which reveal contrasting orange cores when they are sliced. Flavour is not sacrificed and is particularly good when raw.

Sow: early spring to early summer
Harvest: early summer to late autumn
○ ☼

Carrot *'Bangor'* F1

Long, stocky roots are produced in large quantities, especially in moist soils, by this excellent maincrop variety. Crops can be harvested from late summer and throughout autumn, and store well once lifted.

Sow: mid-spring to early summer
Harvest: midsummer to late autumn
○ ☼ ♈

Carrot *'Carson'* F1

Autumn and winter bring good crops of this medium-sized, tapering variety. The rich orange colour, combined with the delicious crunchy texture and sweetness, makes them irresistible when eaten raw.

Sow: mid-spring to midsummer
Harvest: late summer to early winter
○ ☼ ♈

Beetroot '*Boltardy*'
A reliable variety yielding traditional deep red globe-shaped roots with a fine sweet flavour. Perfect for sowing under cloches in early spring because of its excellent resistance to bolting.

Sow: early spring to midsummer
Harvest: early summer to mid-autumn

Beetroot '*Chioggia Pink*'
A beautiful curiosity; the rich red skin of this spherical root conceals flesh marked with concentric rings of blush pink and white. Its sweet mild flavour is delightful raw or cooked.

Sow: mid-spring to midsummer.
Harvest: early summer to mid-autumn

Beetroot '*Forono*'
Elongated, burgundy-coloured roots make this variety ideal for slicing. Tender young roots have a particularly intense flavour, so sow successionally for a continuous supply. Prone to bolting if sown too early.

Sow: mid-spring to early summer
Harvest: midsummer to late autumn

Beetroot '*Pablo*' F1
One of the best varieties for growing in patio containers and perfect to harvest as baby beets. The smooth, deep red, spherical roots taste exceptionally sweet; they also stand well in the soil without bolting or becoming woody.

Sow: mid-spring to early summer
Harvest: midsummer to mid-autumn

Parsnip '*Gladiator*' F1
A popular hybrid parsnip that matures quickly, producing consistently reliable, early maturing crops of white-skinned roots. 'Gladiator' also benefits from good canker resistance.

Sow: late winter to mid-spring
Harvest: mid-autumn to early spring

Parsnip '*Tender and True*'
On deep soils this variety forms exceptionally long roots, which are often considered to have one of the finest parsnip flavours. It is also resistant to canker and is a firm favourite with exhibition growers.

Sow: late winter to mid-spring
Harvest: late autumn to early spring

Root vegetables: turnips, swedes, radishes

Turnip 'Snowball'

For a quick crop, this fast-maturing variety is one of the best. The pure white globes are best harvested while young, when their deliciously crisp, firm, white flesh can be enjoyed raw or cooked.

Sow: early spring to midsummer
Harvest: late spring onwards

◊ ◗ ☼ ◐

Turnip 'Purple Top Milan'

A good choice for early sowings under cloches, this turnip crops reliably and matures quickly. The flat-topped roots are a vivid shade of purple above the soil and pure white beneath it, making them attractive as well as delicious.

Sow: early spring to midsummer
Harvest: mid-spring onwards

◊ ◗ ☼ ◐

Swede 'Brora'

This gem among swedes has the classic purple top and cream base, but has been bred to produce the finest smooth flesh without any bitterness. Best harvested in early winter to avoid woodiness.

Sow: late spring to midsummer
Harvest: mid-autumn to midwinter

◊ ☼ ♈

Radish 'French Breakfast'

A torpedo-shaped variety with rosy red skin and a bright white tip. Its shape makes it great for slicing, and the crunchy flesh has a mild flavour with just a hint of peppery heat. Easy and quick to grow.

Sow: early spring to early summer
Harvest: late spring to mid-autumn

◊ ◗ ☼ ◐ ♈

Radish 'Cherry Belle'

Probably one of the best vegetables for the absolute beginner, these small, round, brilliant red radishes tolerate poor quality soils. They grow rapidly, are slow to become woody, and have tasty, mild-flavoured flesh.

Sow: early spring to early summer
Harvest: late spring to mid-autumn

◊ ◗ ☼ ◐ ♈

Chinese radish 'Mantanghong' F1

For a taste of the exotic, try these easy-to-grow, tennis ball-sized radishes. Their plain, pale green skin hides vivid magenta flesh with a white outer layer, which has a nutty flavour and a touch of heat.

Sow: early summer to midsummer
Harvest: late summer to early winter

◊ ◗ ☼ ◐

Brassicas: cabbages

Cabbage *'Pixie'*
One of the earliest pointed cabbages, which can be picked young as spring greens or allowed to mature into a firm-hearted cabbage. A reliable crop that can be harvested in time to leave soil clear for spring sowings.

Sow: midsummer
Harvest: midwinter to late spring
◌ ◉ ☼ ◑ ♔

Cabbage *'Derby Day'*
A traditional, pale green ballhead cabbage for early summer harvest. Its resistance to bolting has long made it popular with gardeners, and the mature cabbages can stand even summer heat.

Sow: late winter to early spring
Harvest: early to late summer
◌ ◉ ☼ ◑ ♔

Cabbage *'Hispi'* **F1**
Another favourite, this pointed cabbage reliably produces compact, tasty, dark green heads. The cabbages mature rapidly, and successional sowings provide a harvest from late spring into autumn.

Sow: late winter to late summer
Harvest: late spring to late autumn
◌ ◉ ☼ ◑

Cabbage *'Marner Early Red'* (syn. *'Marner Fruerot'*)
This dense-hearted cabbage is one of the first reds to reach maturity. The outer leaves are tinged with grey; the head is an intense red and has a peppery flavour best appreciated raw.

Sow: midwinter to early spring
Harvest: midsummer to late summer
◌ ◉ ☼ ◑

Cabbage *'Minicole'* **F1**
Ideal for small gardens, this white ballhead cabbage produces small, uniform heads on compact plants. Plant closely for a bumper harvest of autumn cabbages, which will stand in the ground for up to three months.

Sow: early to late spring
Harvest: early autumn to early winter
◌ ◉ ☼ ◑

Cabbage *'Red Jewel'* **F1**
The claret-coloured leaves dusted with silver make this one of the best cabbages for ornamental plantings. The tight round heads also taste delicious and will stand in the ground well or store indoors.

Sow: early spring to early summer
Harvest: midsummer to early autumn
◌ ◉ ☼ ◑

Brassicas: cabbages, calabrese, broccoli, cauliflower

Cabbage 'January King 3'
This traditional winter cabbage has good frost resistance and appetizing sweet crunchy leaves. The frilly-edged leaves are tinged with pink and also look beautiful in the winter garden.

Sow: mid-spring to early summer
Harvest: late autumn to late winter

◌ ◐ ☼ ☀

Cabbage 'Tundra' F1
A cross between a savoy and a white cabbage, this extremely hardy variety produces solid round heads of tasty crisp leaves. The long cropping season makes this a really useful addition to the vegetable patch.

Sow: early spring to early summer
Harvest: mid-autumn to early spring

◌ ◐ ☼ ☀ ♔

Cabbage 'Savoy Siberia' F1
A truly tough vegetable, this savoy withstands hard winters, so is ideal for exposed or cold gardens. The blue-green, blistered leaves taste sweet, and the cabbages stand well in the ground for long periods.

Sow: early spring to early summer
Harvest: early autumn to midwinter

◌ ◐ ☼ ☀

Calabrese 'Corvet' F1
A reliable variety of autumn vegetable, producing robust plants and a bumper crop of dense, green heads. Cut the central head while its flowers are still tightly closed for a second harvest of smaller shoots a few weeks later.

Sow: mid- to late spring
Harvest: late summer to early autumn

◌ ◐ ☼

Broccoli 'Bordeaux'
This purple sprouting variety is very useful for those who can't wait until spring for broccoli. It is not winter-hardy and does not require the usual exposure to cold to produce its tasty spears.

Sow: late winter to mid-spring
Harvest: midsummer to mid-autumn

◌ ☼ ♔

Broccoli 'White Star'
Creamy-white rather than purple flowers make the spears of this spring variety reminiscent of cauliflower; many consider the taste similar, too. Reliably high yields produced over a long period make it a popular choice.

Sow: mid- to late spring
Harvest: early to mid-spring

◌ ☼ ♔

Broccoli 'Claret' F1

A large, vigorous plant that may need staking in windy gardens, this variety produces huge yields of chunky, succulent spears in spring. The purple flowerheads are tightly packed and uniform, and taste delicious.

Sow: mid- to late spring
Harvest: early to mid-spring
○ ☼ ♆

Broccoli 'Late Purple Sprouting'

To extend your broccoli crop into late spring, try this slightly later-flowering variety. It is slow to run to seed, and the delicious purple-budded spears can be cut over a long period.

Sow: mid- to late spring
Harvest: early to late spring
○ ☼ ♆

Cauliflower 'Walcheran Winter Armado April'

An extremely hardy winter variety that tolerates heavy frosts and produces large, solid, pure white heads. It ties up a bed for 12 months, so may not be suitable for very small gardens.

Sow: mid- to late spring
Harvest: early to late spring
○ ◐ ☼

Cauliflower 'Mayflower' F1

High quality, dense, white curds are consistently produced by this vigorous early summer variety. Unlike many others, it does not require high nitrogen levels and is harvested early enough to avoid midsummer droughts.

Sow: mid- to late winter and mid-autumn **Harvest:** late spring to midsummer ○ ◐ ☼ ♆

Cauliflower 'Romanesco'

If you fancy something different, try this strange summer/autumn variety, with pyramid-shaped heads in a vibrant shade of acid green. Grow over a long season for large heads or sow successionally for frequent small crops.

Sow: early to late spring
Harvest: late summer to early winter
○ ◐ ☼

Cauliflower 'Violet Queen' F1

The vivid purple curds formed by this variety will brighten up any vegetable plot, although they turn green when cooked. Plenty of nitrogen and water are required to sustain strong growth.

Sow: late spring to early summer
Harvest: late summer to early autumn
○ ◐ ☼ ♆

Brassicas: Brussels sprouts, kale, kohlrabi, oriental greens

Brussels sprouts 'Red Delicious'
This magnificent variety is a striking shade of red-tinged-purple from its crowning leaves to the base of its stem. Unlike many other red varieties, the sprouts retain their colour after cooking and have a fine flavour.

Sow: early to mid-spring
Harvest: early winter

◊ ◊ ☼

Brussels sprouts 'Trafalgar' F1
If your aim is sweet sprouts for Christmas, then this variety will not disappoint. Dense crops of firm, uniformly-sized sprouts grow on tall, sturdy plants and can be harvested throughout the winter.

Sow: early to mid-spring
Harvest: late autumn to midwinter

◊ ◊ ☼

Brussels sprouts 'Bosworth' F1
Dark green, dense, sweet sprouts are produced in abundance by this tough hybrid variety, which will stand well through cold winter weather. Some tolerance to downy mildew helps ensure a healthy crop.

Sow: early to mid-spring
Harvest: late autumn to early winter

◊ ◊ ☼ ♆

Kale 'Redbor' F1
All kales are useful hardy winter crops, but the tall leaves of this variety resemble large clumps of burgundy, curly-leaved parsley, so add some welcome colour to dull days. Great steamed or stir-fried.

Sow: early to late spring
Harvest: early autumn to early spring

◊ ◊ ☼ ☀ ♆

Kale 'Starbor' F1
More compact than most kales, this variety is well suited to the small or windswept garden. The tightly curled green leaves stand up well to winter cold. Try successional sowings for a year-round crop of tasty baby leaves.

Sow: early spring to early summer
Harvest: early autumn to early spring

◊ ◊ ☼ ☀

Kale 'Nero di Toscana'
Also known as Black Tuscany or Cavolo Nero, this is the favoured kale in Italian kitchens. Its upright leaves are almost black and blistered like those of savoy cabbages. Use mature leaves in soups and stews; baby ones in salads.

Sow: early spring to early summer
Harvest: early autumn to early spring

◊ ◊ ☼ ☀

Kohlrabi 'Olivia' F1

Harvest the swollen stem that sits just above soil level when it is about the size of a tennis ball, and enjoy the crisp, white flesh grated raw in salads or lightly steamed. Reliable, with little woodiness, this variety is slow to bolt.

Sow: early spring to early summer
Harvest: late spring to mid-autumn
◌ ◑ ☼ ☀

Mizuna

Often found in supermarket salad mixes, these jagged-edged, slightly mustard-flavoured leaves are simple to cultivate over summer. Harvest baby leaves for salads or allow plants to mature and use leaves for stir-frying.

Sow: early spring to early autumn
Harvest: late spring to late autumn
◌ ☼

Kohlrabi 'Purple Danube' F1

The vibrant purple skin and stems of this variety cut a dash in the garden and its sweet nutty flavour is one of the best. Purple varieties take longer to mature than white, so this makes a good late summer and autumn crop.

Sow: mid-spring to early summer
Harvest: midsummer to late autumn
◌ ◑ ☼ ☀

Mibuna

A similar flavour to mizuna, but with a stronger peppery tang and long, smooth-edged foliage. Like mizuna, this is an ideal cut-and-come-again crop that can be sown successionally from spring to autumn.

Sow: early spring to early autumn
Harvest: late spring to late autumn
◌ ☼

Pak choi 'Joi Choi'

Summer stir-fries will be fresher and tastier with the addition of these succulent, crispy, home-grown leaves. This variety has attractive bright white stems that carry deep green, rounded leaves, and it is easy to grow.

Sow: mid-spring to early autumn
Harvest: early summer to mid-autumn ◌ ◑ ☼ ☀

Mustard 'Red Giant'

Another beautiful, strongly flavoured leaf, this ruby-tinged mustard is best harvested while the leaves are small, otherwise the peppery flavour can be overpowering. Hardy enough to stand over winter from an autumn sowing.

Sow: early spring to early autumn
Harvest: late spring to midwinter
◌ ☼

Salad and leafy vegetables: lettuce, spinach, rocket

Lettuce '*Sangria*'

This butterhead type matures to form a loose heart with soft leaves, and a pretty red flush that will brighten up a salad. Easy to grow and quick to mature, it does well on poorer soils and has some resistance to mildew.

Sow: early spring to late summer
Harvest: late spring to mid-autumn
◊ ◊ ☼ ◐ ◑ ♈

Lettuce '*Tom Thumb*'

A gardeners' favourite, this compact, green, butterhead lettuce rapidly forms dense, sweet-tasting hearts. Ideal for small gardens because it can be planted at high densities and is ready for harvest quickly.

Sow: early spring to midsummer
Harvest: late spring to early autumn
◊ ◊ ☼ ◐

Lettuce '*Little Gem*'

This cos lettuce is familiar from the supermarket shelves, but is even crisper and sweeter if you grow it yourself. Its diminutive size makes it perfect for small gardens and it is one of the fastest cropping cos types.

Sow: early spring to midsummer
Harvest: late spring to early autumn
◊ ◊ ☼ ◐ ◑ ♈

Lettuce '*Freckles*'

This semi-cos variety forms an open head with green leaves that are spectacularly splattered with red. A good choice for flower borders, where it matures quickly. Plants are slow to bolt, even in warm weather.

Sow: early spring to late summer
Harvest: late spring to mid-autumn
◊ ◊ ☼ ◐

Lettuce '*Delicato*'

Loose leaf lettuces are the quickest and easiest to grow, either as cut-and-come-again baby leaves or for harvesting whole when mature. This deep red, oak leaf variety has a pleasant flavour.

Sow: early spring to midsummer
Harvest: mid-spring to mid-autumn
◊ ◊ ☼ ◐ ♈

Lettuce '*Catalogna*'

A tasty, green, oak leaf lettuce that you will not want to forget to sow successionally right through summer. The tender leaves have a fine flavour and the non-hearting plants are slow to bolt, should they get the chance.

Sow: early spring to midsummer
Harvest: mid-spring to mid-autumn
◊ ◊ ☼ ◐ ♈

Lettuce *'Lollo Rossa-Nika'*

The red leaves of this frilled lettuce are so dark as to be almost purple and are incredibly ornamental as well as appetizing. Young leaves taste sweet, and, although they turn bitter as they grow, the curled heads look fabulous.

Sow: early spring to midsummer
Harvest: late spring to mid-autumn
◌ ◑ ☼ ◐

Lettuce *'Challenge'*

Crisphead lettuces are similar to the iceberg types. This reliable variety forms large, solid hearts of crunchy leaves and performs well when sown early and late under cloches. Good resistance to mildew and bolting.

Sow: early spring to midsummer
Harvest: late spring to mid-autumn
◌ ◑ ☼ ◐ ♔

Lettuce *'Sioux'*

A pretty red-tinged iceberg variety, with leaves that intensify in colour in warmer weather, giving the plants good ornamental qualities that are so valuable in small gardens. Perfect colour and crunch for salads.

Sow: early spring to midsummer
Harvest: early summer to mid-autumn ◌ ◑ ☼ ◐ ♔

Spinach *'Perpetual Spinach'*

Not a true spinach, but spinach beet, with a taste similar to Swiss chard. It is easy to grow because it rarely runs to seed, even in dry conditions. Succulent green leaves are produced prolifically and crops can be gathered all winter.

Sow: mid-spring to midsummer
Harvest: any time
◌ ◑ ☼ ♔

Spinach *'Tetona'* F1

A high yielding spinach producing a profusion of rounded dark green leaves. This is the perfect variety for sowing as a cut-and-come-again crop to produce baby leaves for salads, but it can also be left to mature.

Sow: early spring to late summer
Harvest: late spring to late autumn
◌ ◑ ☼ ◐ ♔

Rocket *'Apollo'*

This cultivated variety has large, rounded, green leaves and a strong peppery flavour without any bitterness. The plant is easy to grow as a cut-and-come-again crop in pots or in the ground. Water well in hot weather.

Sow: early spring to midsummer
Harvest: mid-spring to mid-autumn
◌ ◑ ☼ ◐

Leafy vegetables: rocket, chicory, Swiss chard

Rocket *'Rocket Wild'*

A popular salad leaf with slim, divided leaves and a pungent peppery taste. Easy to grow in pots or beds, it does not bolt as quickly as cultivated forms, but pick the leaves frequently for a longer cropping period.

Sow: early spring to early autumn
Harvest: from mid-spring (through winter under cover) ◖ ◌ ☼ ☀

Chicory *'Italiko Rosso'*

Red-stemmed asparagus, or catalogna chicory, grows well on poor soils and is ideal for harvesting as baby leaves to add a slightly bitter tang to salads. Alternatively, allow the foliage to mature and eat lightly steamed.

Sow: late spring to early autumn
Harvest: midsummer to late autumn
◌ ☼ ☀

Chicory *'Sugar Loaf'*

Treat in the same way as lettuce to produce tall, pale heads of crisp, bitter leaves or cut-and-come-again baby leaves. Chicory grows well on poorer soils, although watering may be required in dry spells.

Sow: mid-spring to late summer
Harvest: midsummer to mid-autumn
◌ ☼ ☀

Swiss chard *'Bright Lights'*

Multi-coloured stems ranging from white and yellow to pink and purple make this a vibrant addition to the vegetable plot and flower border. Easy to grow, it re-emerges in early spring if given winter protection.

Sow: mid-spring to midsummer
Harvest: early spring to mid-autumn
◖ ◌ ☼ ♕

Swiss chard *'Charlotte'*

One of the most attractive ruby chards, with bright red stems and contrasting green leaves veined a striking red. It looks fabulous in a pot or flower border, and the baby leaves liven up salads. A must for every garden.

Sow: mid-spring to midsummer
Harvest: at any time
◖ ◌ ☼ ♕

Swiss chard *'Lucullus'*

Decorative and delicious, this chard rapidly produces generous crops of large green leaves on sturdy, pure white stems. Leaves and stems may be boiled, steamed, or stir-fried; their mild flavour is similar to beetroot.

Sow: mid-spring to midsummer
Harvest: early spring to mid-autumn
◖ ◌ ☼ ♕

Cucurbits: courgettes, marrows

Courgette 'Zucchini'
A reliable variety that forms a bushy plant, well suited to growing in a container. Courgettes with dark green skins and tasty pale flesh are produced in profusion from midsummer. Like all courgettes they are best picked young.

Sow: mid-spring to early summer
Harvest: midsummer to early autumn
◌ ◑ ☼

Courgette 'Defender' F1
A phenomenally productive early variety. If harvested small, fruits will keep coming until mid-autumn, and they are delicious. Plants are resistant to cucumber mosaic virus, which can cause other varieties to fail.

Sow: mid-spring to early summer
Harvest: midsummer to mid-autumn
◌ ◑ ☼ ♔

Courgette 'Burpee's Golden'
Another prolific courgette variety that bears numerous decorative and delicious bright yellow fruits. The courgettes have a particularly fine flavour, especially when harvested small.

Sow: mid-spring to early summer
Harvest: midsummer to early autumn
◑ ◌ ☼

Courgette 'Tromboncino'
This vigorous Italian variety is best trained up a sunny wall to afford everyone a good view of its long, curved, bulbous-ended fruits. The pale green fruits can reach more than 30cm (12in) long.

Sow: mid-spring to early summer
Harvest: midsummer to early autumn
◑ ◌ ☼

Courgette 'Venus' F1
Unusually compact, these plants are great for containers or small gardens, and still produce ample crops of delicious, mid-green courgettes. In good conditions, fruits are ready to harvest 60 days after planting.

Sow: mid-spring to early summer
Harvest: early summer to
mid-autumn ◑ ◌ ☼ ♔

Marrow 'Long Green Bush'
Despite its name, this variety forms quite a compact, bushy plant, making it suitable for the smaller garden. Long, deep green fruits, with pale green marrow stripes, swell rapidly, but can be picked as courgettes when small.

Sow: mid-spring to early summer
Harvest: midsummer to mid-autumn
◑ ◌ ☼

Cucurbits: squashes, cucumbers

Squash 'Sunburst' F1
A yellow 'Patty Pan' variety, this squash has vibrant butter-coloured fruits, shaped like flying saucers. Large crops of flavoursome fruits are produced by this easily grown variety if regular harvesting is carried out.

Sow: mid-spring to early summer
Harvest: midsummer to mid-autumn
◊ ◊ ☀

Squash 'Uchiki Kuri'
Also known as 'Red Kuri', this squash produces several medium-sized, bright orange fruits, with delicious, nutty, golden flesh. It performs particularly well in temperate climates. Fruits store well once cured.

Sow: mid- to late spring
Harvest: late summer to mid-autumn
◊ ◊ ☀

Squash 'Pilgrim Butternut' F1
A less vigorous and so more manageable butternut squash for the smaller garden. The semi-bush habit of the vine does not prevent a good crop of beige-skinned, orange-fleshed squashes, which store well.

Sow: mid- to late spring
Harvest: late summer to mid-autumn
◊ ◊ ☀

Squash 'Crown Prince' F1
This trailing squash is a favourite because of its exceptionally good nutty-flavoured flesh. The steely grey skin of the fruits contrasts dramatically with the orange flesh and looks attractive on the vine.

Sow: mid-spring to late spring
Harvest: late summer to mid-autumn
◊ ◊ ☀

Squash 'Turk's Turban'
Not an exceptional culinary squash, with pale yellow flesh and a turnip-like flavour, but often grown for its ornamental qualities. The rich orange skin folds and forms a bulge splashed with green and cream.

Sow: mid- to late spring
Harvest: late summer to mid-autumn
◊ ◊ ☀

Squash 'Festival' F1
Ornamental and delicious, this trailing vine produces high yields of small, squat, orange and cream striped squashes, with sweet, nutty-tasting, cream flesh. The squashes are perfect for stuffing or baking, and store well.

Sow: mid- to late spring
Harvest: late summer to mid-autumn
◊ ◊ ☀

Cucumber 'Bush Champion' F1

Grow this ridge cucumber outdoors – its compact plants are ideal for small gardens and pots, and have good tolerance to cucumber mosaic virus. The slightly knobbly, dark green, sweet fruits reach about 10cm (4in) long.

Sow: mid-spring to early summer
Harvest: late summer to mid-autumn

Cucumber 'Marketmore'

An excellent, high-yielding cucumber, producing sturdy, deep green fruit up to 20cm (8in) long, with no bitterness. This variety does well outdoors up a wigwam or trellis. Resistance to cucumber mosaic virus is a bonus.

Sow: mid-spring to early summer
Harvest: late summer to mid-autumn

Cucumber 'Masterpiece'

Crisp, juicy, white flesh under a deep green, slightly spiny skin, makes this ridge cucumber a good choice for outdoor cultivation. This variety crops reliably, but performs best when allowed to climb.

Sow: mid-spring to early summer
Harvest: late summer to mid-autumn

Cucumber 'Zeina' F1

An all-female variety that can be grown in the greenhouse or outdoors. Small, succulent, smooth-skinned cucumbers can be harvested over a long season and are a handy size to eat at one meal.

Sow: early spring to early summer
Harvest: midsummer to mid-autumn

Cucumber 'Petita' F1

For an abundance of juicy, miniature cucumbers from the greenhouse, this is the variety to choose. It is easy to grow, even in difficult conditions, and has all female flowers so bitter fruits are not produced.

Sow: early spring to early summer
Harvest: midsummer to mid-autumn

Cucumber 'Carmen' F1

Resistance to powdery mildew, scab, and leaf spot makes this all-female variety a good choice for greenhouse cultivation. Impressive harvests of straight, smooth, green fruits are simple to produce.

Sow: early spring to early summer
Harvest: midsummer to mid-autumn

Allium family: onions, shallots, spring onions

Onion '*Ailsa Craig*'

An old favourite, this reliable variety yields heavy crops of large, sweet onions, with smooth, yellow-brown skin. Best sown as seed in spring to produce a good autumn crop that stores well if allowed to dry.

Sow: late winter to early spring
Harvest: late summer to early autumn

○ ☼

Onion '*Sturon*'

Traditionally grown from sets, this variety produces large, round, yellow-brown coloured bulbs that have a strong skin, which makes them an excellent choice for winter storing. Seed is occasionally available.

Plant sets: late winter to early spring
Harvest: late summer to early autumn

○ ☼ ♈

Onion '*Red Baron*'

Widely available as both seeds and sets, this variety has a rich red skin, with pronounced pink stripes between the bulb's layers. It will store for only a limited time.

Sow: late winter to mid-spring **Plant sets:** early spring
Harvest: early to mid-autumn

○ ☼

Onion '*Senshyu*'

Sets of this useful winter Japanese variety should be planted in autumn and seeds sown a little before for an early summer harvest. The semi-flat, straw-coloured bulbs grow to a good size and have a strong flavour.

Sow: late summer **Plant sets:** early to mid-autumn.
Harvest: early to midsummer ○ ☼

Onion '*Shakespeare*'

For an early summer crop of globe-shaped onions with rich brown skins, try this British overwintering variety. The dense white flesh and sturdy skin mean that they store well, and they have an excellent flavour.

Sow: early to mid-autumn
Harvest: early to midsummer

○ ☼

Shallot '*Longor*'

An attractive, elongated variety of shallot, with a pink flush to the skin and inner layers. The strongly flavoured bulbs store well through autumn and winter if carefully dried. Quicker to crop than traditional bulb onions.

Plant sets: late winter to mid-spring
Harvest: mid- to late summer

○ ☼ ♈

Shallot 'Red Sun'

One of the most reliable red shallots, this variety has wonderful burgundy skin and white flesh with layers divided by pink rings. Appetizing chopped raw in salads, it is also well suited to cooking and pickling.

Plant sets: early to mid-spring
Harvest: mid- to late summer

○ ☼

Shallot 'Golden Gourmet'

Large and yellow-skinned, this high-yielding variety produces bumper crops of good quality bulbs from sets and is easy to store right through the winter. It is less prone to bolting in dry conditions than many shallots.

Plant sets: late winter to mid-spring
Harvest: mid- to late summer

○ ☼ ♔

Spring onion 'Paris Silverskin'

A dual-purpose small white onion that can be harvested young as a salad onion or left in the ground to bulb up for pickling. Easy to grow and compact, it makes an ideal crop for small gardens.

Sow: early to mid-spring
Harvest: mid- to late summer

○ ☼

Spring onion 'Guardsman'

This trusted, white-stemmed variety is extremely easy to grow. It is a good choice to sow successively from spring to autumn because it is hardy enough to overwinter and give an early spring crop. Resistant to white rot.

Sow: early spring to mid-autumn
Harvest: late spring to mid-autumn; late winter to early spring ○ ☼

Spring onion 'North Holland Blood Red'

An attractive variety with bold red bases and a mild flavour. Use thinnings from early sowings as spring onions, leaving wider-spaced plants to develop into red-skinned maincrop onions.

Sow: early spring to early summer
Harvest: late spring to late summer

○ ☼

Spring onion 'White Lisbon'

A trusted old favourite, this variety produces white bulbs and bright green tops with a good, strong flavour. It is easy to grow but prone to downy mildew, so keep rows well spaced to avoid the spread of disease.

Sow: early spring to midsummer
Harvest: late spring to early autumn

○ ☼ ♔

Allium family: leeks, garlic

Leek 'Musselburgh'

An extremely hardy sturdy leek, with a broad white stem topped by impressive green leaves, known as flags. This old variety can withstand the coldest winter, and can be harvested from late autumn until late winter.

Sow: early to mid-spring
Harvest: late autumn to late winter
◊ ☼

Leek 'Hannibal'

This handsome leek has deep green leaves and a long, white, straight stem. Suited to autumn and early winter cropping, it also produces impressive mini leeks when planted close together.

Sow: early to mid-spring
Harvest: early autumn to early winter
◊ ☼

Leek 'Swiss Giant, Zermatt'

An elegant variety with a long, slender stem, which despite its name forms excellent mini leeks when planted at high densities. It is ready for harvest by late summer – an advantage for those with limited space in the garden.

Sow: early to mid-spring
Harvest: midsummer to late autumn
◊ ☼

Garlic 'Solent Light'

One of the best garlics for cool climates that is best planted in autumn but also does well planted in spring. It matures in late summer and because it is a non-flowering, softneck type, stores extremely well.

Plant cloves: mid-autumn to early spring **Harvest:** midsummer to early autumn ◊ ☼

Garlic 'Early Light'

This flowering, hardneck, purple-skinned variety is best used fresh but will store for about three months. The harvest will be eagerly anticipated, as this is one of the earliest varieties to crop in cool climates.

Plant cloves: mid-autumn to midwinter **Harvest:** late spring to early summer ◊ ☼

Garlic 'Elephant Garlic'

Closely related to the leek, this giant produces bulbs up to 10cm (4in) in diameter. Use the large, juicy cloves fresh from the soil to enjoy their mild, sweet flavour, which makes them particularly suitable for roasting.

Plant cloves: mid-autumn to midwinter. **Harvest:** midsummer to early autumn ◊ ☼

Legumes: peas

Pea *'Feltham First'*

Early and dwarf, this is a useful, high-yielding pea variety for small gardens. Better results are often achieved from autumn sowings in containers, where plants are given some protection.

Sow: mid- to late autumn; midwinter to early spring
Harvest: late spring to midsummer

💧 ⬦ ☀️

Pea *'Twinkle'*

An excellent early variety, the first sowings of which perform best if protected under cloches when young. Dwarf plants give good crops of full pods and have resistance to pea wilt and tolerance to downy mildew.

Sow: late winter to mid-spring
Harvest: late spring to midsummer

💧 ⬦ ☀️

Pea *'Hurst Greenshaft'*

Pairs of long pods develop high on these plants, making harvesting of this traditional variety's consistently large crops somewhat easier. The peas are large and sweet, and plants have good disease resistance.

Sow: early spring to early summer
Harvest: late spring to early autumn

💧 ⬦ ☀️ 🏆

Pea *'Rondo'*

One of the tastiest and heaviest cropping peas, this double-podded variety has dark green, straight pods up to 10cm (4in) long. Plants need supports, but the succulent peas should be ample reward.

Sow: early spring to early summer
Harvest: late spring to early autumn

💧 ⬦ ☀️ 🏆

Pea *'Sugar Snap'*

A really versatile sugar snap variety that can be picked young and eaten whole, raw or stir-fried, or harvested when mature and podded for fresh peas. Plants grow up to 1.8m (6ft) tall, so need support from trellis or canes.

Sow: early spring to early summer
Harvest: late spring to late summer

💧 ⬦ ☀️

Pea *'Oregon Sugar Pod'*

An excellent mangetout variety that produces wide, flat pods best eaten whole, either raw, steamed or stir-fried. Expect large yields of these crisp, sweet pods from plants that grow to 90cm (36in).

Sow: early spring to early summer
Harvest: late spring to late summer

💧 ⬦ ☀️ 🏆

Legumes: beans

Runner bean 'Butler'

This attractive, red-flowered runner bean grows vigorously and forms many long, stringless pods filled with pretty purple beans. They can be picked over a long season and, being stringless, are still palatable when a little larger.

Sow: mid-spring to early summer
Harvest: midsummer to mid-autumn
◗ ◌ ☼ ☼

Runner bean 'Liberty'

A favourite with exhibitors, this runner bean has glorious scarlet flowers followed by extremely long (up to 45cm/18in) pods. The heavy crops of smooth-skinned pods are prized for their tasty, thick flesh.

Sow: mid-spring to early summer
Harvest: midsummer to mid-autumn
◗ ◌ ☼ ◐ ♆

Runner bean 'White Lady'

The pure white flowers of this runner bean are thought to be less attractive to birds. Hot weather can prevent pods setting on other varieties, but 'White Lady' still performs well, making it suited to later sowings.

Sow: mid-spring to early summer
Harvest: midsummer to mid-autumn
◗ ◌ ☼ ◐ ♆

Runner bean 'Wisley Magic'

A runner bean with bright red flowers that develop into slim pods up to 35cm (14in) long, with a delicious fresh flavour. The plants grow rapidly and produce good yields but pods are not stringless so are best harvested young.

Sow: mid-spring to early summer
Harvest: midsummer to mid-autumn
◗ ◌ ☼ ◐ ♆

French bean 'Purple Queen'

Perfect for a container or border, this compact dwarf French bean grows without supports and develops heavy crops of glossy, rich purple pods. The stringless pods have a fine flavour and turn green when cooked.

Sow: mid-spring to midsummer
Harvest: early summer to late autumn
◗ ◌ ☼ ◐

French bean 'Delinel'

A dwarf bean for a bumper crop. In containers or beds it produces large yields of rounded, long green beans with a firm texture and good flavour. Plants are resistant to common bean mosaic virus and anthracnose.

Sow: mid-spring to midsummer
Harvest: early summer to late autumn
◗ ◌ ☼ ◐ ♆

French bean 'The Prince'
This dwarf variety has long, flat, green pods, best harvested young when they are stringless. The flavour is excellent, and crops can be reliably harvested by early summer. They are also produced over a long period.

Sow: mid-spring to midsummer
Harvest: early summer to late autumn
⬤◯☼◐☼🏆

French bean 'Ferrari'
A fine dwarf French bean – slim, succulent, bursting with flavour, and stringless. The plants do well sown in mid-spring if protected from frosts and thrive in containers. The connoisseur's choice, as well as easy to grow.

Sow: mid-spring to midsummer
Harvest: early summer to late autumn
⬤◯☼◐☼🏆

French bean 'Cobra'
Train up wigwams or trellis to achieve large crops of stringless, tender green beans, up to 20cm (8in) long. The flowers are an unusual shade of violet, which make the plants ornamental as well as productive.

Sow: mid-spring to midsummer
Harvest: early summer to late autumn
⬤◯☼◐☼🏆

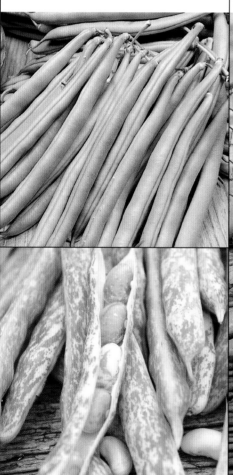

Borlotto 'Lingua di Fuoco'
Grown in the same way as a climbing French bean, this Italian borlotto bean has long, flattish, pale green pods marked with red. Eat whole when young or remove the purple-blotched seeds from mature pods and dry them.

Sow: mid-spring to midsummer
Harvest: early summer to late autumn
◐◯☼

Broad bean 'Aquadulce Claudia'
An old favourite, this hardy broad bean can overwinter outdoors. Plants grow to 90cm (3ft) and yield a good crop of tender white beans in "cotton wool" lined pods. Black bean aphid is often a pest on shoots.

Sow: mid- to late autumn; mid- to late winter **Harvest:** late spring to early summer ◯☼🏆

Broad bean 'The Sutton'
Compact and bushy, this broad bean reaches only 45cm (18in), so is ideal for small gardens and for sowing under cloches in late winter and on windy sites. It produces abundant small pods packed with juicy white beans.

Sow: midwinter to early spring
Harvest: early to late summer
◯☼🏆

Fruiting vegetables: tomatoes

Tomato *'Totem'* F1

A dwarf upright bush variety that is the perfect size for patio containers and large windowboxes. It crops well outdoors: by midsummer, its trusses are heavy with small tasty red fruits.

Sow: (indoors) midwinter to mid-spring; (outdoors) early spring to mid-spring **Harvest:** midsummer to mid-autumn ◌ ◑ ☼

Tomato *'Tumbler'* F1

Ideal outdoors in hanging baskets or large containers, this bush tomato has stems that trail attractively over the side of a pot. It provides a prolific crop of sweet, red cherry tomatoes.

Sow: (indoors) midwinter to mid-spring; (outdoors) early spring to mid-spring **Harvest:** midsummer to mid-autumn ◌ ◑ ☼

Tomato *'Early Bush Cherry'*

Easy to grow and quick to ripen, this bush variety does well outdoors in containers, or in the greenhouse. Its huge numbers of small, round, cherry-like fruits have a sweet flavour.

Sow: (indoors) midwinter to mid-spring; (outdoors) early spring to mid-spring **Harvest:** midsummer to mid-autumn ◌ ◑ ☼

Tomato *'Sungold'* F1

Masses of incredibly sweet, orange cherry tomatoes make this a popular variety. It is a cordon tomato, so needs staking and side-shooting. It grows well under glass or outdoors.

Sow: (indoors) midwinter to mid-spring; (outdoors) early spring to mid-spring **Harvest:** midsummer to mid-autumn ◌ ◑ ☼

Tomato *'Sweet Olive'* F1

For baby plum tomatoes that grow outdoors, try this reliable cordon variety. The clusters of scarlet fruits have an excellent, intense flavour, and the skins do not split readily. Plants may require some staking.

Sow: early to mid-spring
Harvest: midsummer to mid-autumn
◌ ◑ ☼ ♛

Tomato *'Shirley'* F1

This dependable greenhouse variety yields heavy crops of large, rounded, scarlet fruits, even in poor weather conditions. A cordon variety, it requires staking and side-shooting, but has some disease resistance.

Sow: midwinter to early spring
Harvest: early summer to early autumn ◌ ◑ ☼ ♛

Tomato *'Tigerella'* F1

Unusual red fruits striped with yellow make this variety stand out, but they also taste delicious and mature early. A cordon tomato that crops well indoors and outside.

Sow: (indoors) midwinter to mid-spring; (outdoors) early spring to mid-spring **Harvest:** midsummer to mid-autumn ◌ ◑ ☼ ♈

Tomato *'Gardener's Delight'*

Perfect for a sheltered spot outside or a greenhouse, this is an extremely popular cordon tomato variety because of its bumper crops of fine-flavoured, large cherry tomatoes.

Sow: (indoors) midwinter to mid-spring; (outdoors) early to mid-spring **Harvest:** midsummer to mid-autumn ◌ ◑ ☼ ♈

Tomato *'Ferline'* F1

An excellent cordon tomato producing large, rounded, red fruits, with increased blight tolerance. Plants grow well inside or out, and the fruits have a rich flavour.

Sow: (indoors) midwinter to mid-spring; (outdoors) early to mid-spring **Harvest:** midsummer to mid-autumn ◌ ◑ ☼

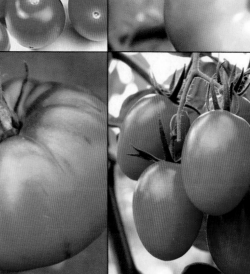

Tomato *'Supersweet 100'* F1

For long trusses of juicy, sugary, scarlet fruits, this is a great variety to try under glass. With good resistance to verticillium wilt, these vigorous cordon plants are easy to grow and yield reliably generous crops.

Sow: midwinter to mid-spring **Harvest:** midsummer to mid-autumn ◌ ◑ ☼

Tomato *'Super Marmande'*

This variety has a bushy habit, but benefits from some support. The large fleshy, puckered fruits are bursting with flavour and are a favourite in France. Plants thrive outdoors in warm areas.

Sow: midwinter to mid-spring **Harvest:** midsummer to mid-autumn ◌ ◑ ☼

Tomato *'Summer Sweet'* F1

An early plum tomato for a sunny spot outdoors or in a greenhouse, this cordon variety yields plenty of small, tasty, red fruits over a long season. Plants have resistance to Fusarium to help ensure a good crop.

Sow: midwinter to mid-spring **Harvest:** midsummer to mid-autumn ◌ ◑ ☼ ♈

Fruiting vegetables: aubergines, peppers, sweetcorn

Aubergine *'Moneymaker'* F1
This is one of the most dependable aubergines in cool climates. The upright plants look good in containers and while the best long dark purple fruits are achieved under glass, plants also do well in a sunny outdoor spot.

Sow: early to mid-spring
Harvest: midsummer to early autumn
⬦ ⬥ ☼

Aubergine *'Black Beauty'*
A prolific variety, producing many glossy, deep purple, oval-shaped fruits. The highest yields are achieved with the protection of a greenhouse. Plants are best tied to supports to help bear the weight of the fruits.

Sow: early to mid-spring
Harvest: midsummer to early autumn
⬦ ⬥ ☼

Aubergine *'Mohican'*
With its compact bushy habit and immaculate white fruits, this aubergine makes a striking pot plant for a sunny patio or greenhouse. Plants reach only 60cm (24in). Pick the fruits small to increase the yield.

Sow: early to mid-spring
Harvest: midsummer to early autumn
⬥ ⬦ ☼ 🏆

Pepper *'Gypsy'* F1
Good, early crops are reliably produced by this sweet pepper, which performs well under glass. Tapering fruits ripen to bright red from yellow-green and have thick, succulent flesh. Plants are resistant to tobacco mosaic virus.

Sow: early to mid-spring
Harvest: midsummer to mid-autumn
⬦ ☼ 🏆

Pepper *'Marconi Rosso'*
The elongated fruits of this pepper are best eaten when red, because at this stage they are extremely sweet and ideal for roasting. Plants are high yielding indoors or in a warm, sunny spot outside.

Sow: early to mid-spring
Harvest: midsummer to mid-autumn
⬦ ☼

Pepper *'Corno di Torro Rosso'*
Delicious, long, thin-walled peppers are sweet once they have turned to purple and red. This early variety appreciates the extra heat in a greenhouse, but crops outdoors in warm areas.

Sow: early to mid-spring
Harvest: midsummer to mid-autumn
⬦ ☼

Pepper *'Hungarian Hot Wax'*

An attractive, compact chilli pepper bearing tapering fruits that are sweet and yellow when young, but hot and bright red when mature. The best crops are achieved with the protection of a greenhouse or large cloches.

Sow: early to mid-spring
Harvest: midsummer to mid-autumn
◊ ☼

Pepper *'Prairie Fire'*

These tiny, bullet-shaped chillies are extremely fiery and look decorative pointing up from the bushy plants, which reach no more than 20cm (8in) tall. Ideal for windowsills or against a sunny wall. Plants crop heavily.

Sow: early to mid-spring
Harvest: midsummer to mid-autumn
◊ ☼

Pepper *'Friar's Hat'*

Best grown in the greenhouse, these tall plants produce heavy yields of bizarre chillies shaped like floppy sun hats. Plants need staking, while fruits need a long, hot growing season to ripen and build up a hot chilli flavour.

Sow: early to mid-spring
Harvest: midsummer to mid-autumn
◊ ☼

Sweetcorn *'Butterscotch'* **F1**

A super sweet mid-season variety, forming large cobs up to 20cm (8in) long that are filled with tender, sugary, butter-yellow kernels. Grows vigorously and crops well even in cool weather conditions.

Sow: mid- to late spring
Harvest: late summer to early autumn
◊ ☼

Sweetcorn *'Indian Summer'*

These spectacular multi-coloured cobs have sweet-tasting kernels in shades of yellow, cream, red, and purple. Keep the plants separate from other sweetcorn varieties to prevent cross-pollination and maintain the colours.

Sow: mid- to late spring
Harvest: late summer to mid-autumn
◊ ☼

Sweetcorn *'Lark'* **F1**

This variety consistently produces a high proportion of healthy seedlings from each sowing, and is ideal for beginners. The sweet, tender cobs are delicious when boiled quickly and topped with melted butter.

Sow: mid- to late spring
Harvest: late summer to mid-autumn
◊ ☼ ♆

Perennial/stem vegetables: asparagus, artichokes, celeriac, celery

Asparagus 'Connover's Colossal'
A traditional variety that yields a heavy crop of thick green spears early in the season. Buy young crowns and try not to harvest in their first year – just cut a few spears in the second and reap the reward in the third.

Plant: late winter to early spring
Harvest: late spring
◊ ☼ ♔

Jerusalem artichoke 'Fuseau'
This relative of the sunflower produces long, smooth tubers, with a flavour similar to globe artichokes, which are usually eaten cooked. Plants may reach 3m (10ft) in height, each yielding about 10 tubers.

Plant: late winter to late spring
Harvest: early to late winter
◊ ◐ ☼ ☀

Globe artichoke 'Green Globe'
Often difficult to find in the shops, but easy to grow, this reliable globe variety has large flowerheads with delicious, tender hearts. Grow from offsets where available.

Sow: late winter to early spring
Plant offsets: late spring to early summer **Harvest:** late spring to early summer ◊ ◐ ☼ ☀

Celeriac 'Monarch'
Easier to grow than celery, with a milder flavour, celeriac is delicious raw, steamed, or roasted. This cultivar has unusually smooth skin, making it easier to clean than most, and has fine-textured, creamy flesh.

Sow: early to mid-spring
Harvest: mid- to late autumn
◊ ◐ ☼ ☀ ♔

Celery 'Victoria' F1
The attractive pale green stems of this variety have a particularly good flavour and crispness. There is no need to earth up the stalks to blanch them and the plants are slow to bolt.

Sow: late winter to mid-spring
Harvest: late summer to mid-autumn
◊ ◐ ☼ ♔

Celery 'Celebrity' F1
An excellent self-blanching variety that grows equally well outdoors or in a greenhouse. The light green stems have a delicious strong flavour, and plants resist bolting well.

Sow: late winter to mid-spring.
Harvest: late summer to mid-autumn
◊ ◐ ☼ ♔

Herbs

Parsley 'Plain Leaved 2'
A fine French parsley, with soft, flat, rich green leaves that have a good strong flavour. Easily grown as an annual indoors or outside, although parsley is biennial and hardy enough to persist in most gardens.

Sow: early spring to late summer
Harvest: year-round

◌ ◑ ☀ ◐

Parsley 'Envy'
Handsome and vigorous, this variety produces a mass of tightly curled, bright green, full-flavoured leaves. Parsley seeds may be slow to germinate, but be sure that the soil is soaked after sowing.

Sow: early spring to late summer
Harvest: year-round

◌ ◑ ☀ ◐ ♟

Basil 'Sweet Genovase'
Large-leaved and intensely aromatic, this is the basil to use in Italian dishes. The tender plants will grow in a sunny spot outdoors, but often do best on a bright windowsill or in a greenhouse. Pinch out young leaves regularly.

Sow: early spring to midsummer
Harvest: year-round

◌ ☀

Basil 'Magic Mountain'
With its glossy, purple-tinted foliage and tall spikes of lilac flowers, this tender herb makes a pretty garden plant in its own right. The leaves have a delicate aniseed scent, which makes them suitable for Thai cooking.

Sow: early spring to midsummer
Harvest: year round

◌ ☀

Thyme 'Silver Posie'
The tiny grey and cream leaves of this compact and low-growing thyme are intensely fragrant, complementing the flavours of chicken and fish. An evergreen hardy perennial, it has clusters of pink flowers in summer.

Sow: early to late spring
Harvest: year round

◌ ☀

Thyme 'Doone Valley'
The vibrant yellow variegation of this thyme's evergreen foliage, combined with a flush of purple summer flowers, makes it a beautiful plant for a pot or herb garden. The lemon-scented leaves taste good with fish or in stews.

Sow: early to late spring
Harvest: year round

◌ ☀

Herbs and sprouting seeds

Oregano (*Origanum vulgare*)
A pungent Mediterranean herb often used in Italian cuisine and reliably perennial in freely draining soils. Its rounded, yellow-green leaves and low-growing habit make it an attractive garden plant, useful for edging paths.

Sow: early to late spring
Harvest: year round
◊ ☼

Rosemary (*Rosmarinus officinalis*)
This shrub bears the tough, narrow, strongly scented leaves that combine so well with lamb. As an evergreen, rosemary provides useful structure in the herb or vegetable garden, and can be pruned to maintain its shape.

Sow: early to late spring
Harvest: year round
◊ ☼

Fennel (*Foeniculum vulgare*)
Elegant and airy, fennel comes in green and bronze forms and may reach 1.8m (6ft) tall. It is a good looking perennial in ornamental borders, where its aniseed-flavoured leaves, and later its seeds, can be harvested as required.

Sow: early to late spring
Harvest: late spring to early autumn
◊ ☼

Apple mint (*Mentha suaveolens*)
Delicious, but invasive, this mint is best confined to a pot in small gardens. It is perennial and sends up new shoots clothed with soft, furry, sweetly minty leaves each spring, which are perfect for cooking with new potatoes.

Sow: early to late spring
Harvest: late spring to late summer
◊ ◖ ☼

Spearmint (*Mentha spicata*)
Spearmint's clean, crisp flavour is ideal for adding to salads, desserts and drinks. The pointed, deep green leaves are glossy and appealing, but this is also an invasive perennial, so keep its spreading shoots in check.

Sow: early to late spring
Harvest: late spring to early autumn
◊ ◖ ☼

Chives (*Allium schoenoprasum*)
The clumps of these easy-to-grow perennials have spiky leaves topped with purple pompon flowers, making them excellent path edging. The delicate onion flavour of chives suits soups, salads, and quiches.

Sow: early to late spring
Harvest: at any time
◊ ☼ ☼

Coriander 'Cilantro for Leaf'

A lush, leafy annual, bred to yield several cuts of spicy leaves, rather than seeds. Sow successively every six weeks to ensure a constant supply and keep plants well watered to prevent them rapidly running to seed.

Sow: mid-spring to early autumn
Harvest: early spring to early autumn
💧 ☀

Common sage (*Salvia officinalis*)

Ornamental, with many culinary uses, this aromatic shrub has pale green leaves covered in an attractive grey down. Encourage bushy growth by pinching out growing tips, but replace old plants every five years.

Sow: mid to late spring
Harvest: at any time
💧 ☀

Lemon grass (*Cymbopogon citratus*)

Tropical and tender, this grass needs to be kept above 7°C (45°F) in winter. The stout, citrus-scented stems can be slow to bulk up in cool climates, but form clumps from which stems can be separated and used in Thai dishes.

Sow: mid to late spring
Harvest: late spring to early autumn
💧 ☀

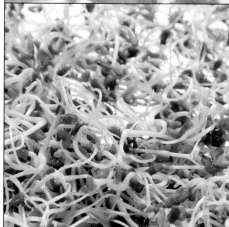
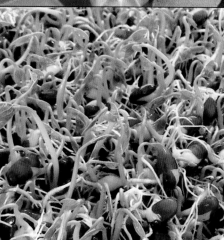

Alfalfa

A nutritious, crisp sprout, with a slightly nutty flavour, alfalfa is delicious in salads and sandwiches. Soaking the seeds for eight hours before sprouting helps speed up the process. Sprouts should be ready from trays or jars in 4–5 days.

Sow: at any time
Harvest: at any time

Mung beans

These tiny green beans burst rapidly into life to become the well-known white Chinese beansprouts, so often included in stir-fries. Soak the beans for 8–12 hours, before sprouting in a jar, tray, or sprouting bag for 2–5 days.

Sow: at any time
Harvest: at any time

Chickpeas

Sprouted chickpeas are a tasty snack or addition to a salad and require only 2–3 days in a jar, tray, or sprouting bag before they are ready to eat. Soak them in water for 8–12 hours before sprouting, to ensure that the seed coat is softened.

Sow: at any time
Harvest: at any time

Index

Index

Index

Index

W

Walls
    borders by 37
    climbers for 22
    growing near 216
wall shrubs 106, 117, 194–5, 304, 307, 308, 309, 314
    tying in 115
walls 100, 116, 117, 120, 148, 149, 318, 322
    brick 118, 119
    painted 100, 101, 105, 108, 109, 114, 118, 149
    rendered 100, 101, 105, 118
wand flower 280
water butts 221
water features 16, 99, 100, 102, 105, 106

water supply 216, 221
watering 112, 220, 221, 270
    containers 115, 144, 146
water-retaining crystals 91
weed-suppressing membrane 49, 123
    planting through 98, 99, 113, 142
weeding 113, 115
    perennials 266
weedkillers 113
weeds
    annuals/biennials 267
    perennials 266
    suppressing 110, 126
Weigela 359
    W. 'Eve Rathke' 285
    W. florida 357
    W. florida 'Foliis Purpureis' 315
    W. 'Praecox Variegata' 176
    W. Wine and Roses 176

whitefly 229, 268
wildlife 106–107, 117, 122, 140, 314, 325, 331
    encouraging 33, 268
windy sites 37
winter colour 132–3
winter planting 20, 28–9, 86–7
    for perfume 96–7
wildlife
windowboxes 254–5
windowsills 217
wintersweet 279
wisteria 22, 204–5
    alternate buds 169
    spur pruning 173
    tiny-tree pruning 155
    W. sinensis 156, 157, 357
witch hazel 28
wood edging 48

wooden containers 89
woodland planting 37
woodstone 122
yellow planting 13, 74–5
yew *19*
Yucca
    Y. filamentosa 'Bright Edge' 136, 137, 325
    Y. flaccida 'Ivory' 325

Z

Zauschneria californica 299
Zen gardens 105, 125

Acknowledgements

The publisher would like to thank the following for their kind permission to reproduce their photographs:

(Key: a-above; b-below/bottom; c-centre; l-left; r-right; t-top)

10: Harpur Garden Library: Marcus Harpur/ Design: Dr Mary Giblin, Essex (t). Andrew Lawson: Designer: Anthony Noel (b). **11:** The Garden Collection: Liz Eddison (b). John Glover: Ladywood, Hampshire (t). **12:** The Garden Collection: Liz Eddison/Tatton Park Flower Show 2002/Designer: Andrew Walker. **13:** Marianne Majerus Photography: RHS Rosemoor (t), S & O Mathews Photography: The Lawrences' Garden, Hunterville, NZ (c), Leigh Clapp: (b). **14:** DK Images: Sarah Cuttle/RHS Chelsea Flower Show 2005/4Head Garden/Designer: Marney Hall (tr), Mark Winwood/Hampton Court Flower Show 2005/Designer: Susan Slater (br). **16:** Marianne Majerus Photography/ Designer: Pat Wallace (t), Designer: Ann Frith (b). **17:** Marianne Majerus Photography/ Designer: George Carter (t), The Garden Collection: Jonathan Buckley/Designer: Helen Yemm (b). **18:** Derek St Romaine/ RHS Chelsea Flower Show 2000/Designer: Lindsay Knight (t), The Garden Collection: Liz Eddison/ Hampton Court Flower Show 2005/ Designer: Daryl Gannon (b). **19:** The Garden Collection: Liz Eddison/

Whichford Pottery (l); Liz Eddison/ Hampton Court Flower Show 2002/ Designer Maureen Busby (r). **20:** Andrew Lawson: (t) (c) (b). **21:** The Garden Collection: Jonathan Buckley/ Designer: Helen Yemm. **22:** The Garden Collection: Derek Harris. **23:** Leigh Clapp: St Michael's House (t). Andrew Lawson: (b). **24:** The Garden Collection: Liz Eddison/Hampton Court Flower Show 2001/Designer: Cherry Burton (t). **25:** Leigh Clapp: Green Lane Farm. **26:** Andrew Lawson. **27:** The Garden Collection: Jonathan Buckley/ Designer: Mark Brown (t); Jonathan Buckley (b). **28:** Marianne Majerus Photography: Designer: Kathleen Beddington (t). **29:** The Garden Collection: Liz Eddison (tl), Andrew Lawson (r): Waterperry Gardens, Oxon (bl). **30:** John Glover: Ladywood, Hants (t). **32:** Derek St Romaine/ Mr & Mrs Bates, Surrey (t). Nicola Stocken Tomkins: Berrylands Road, Surrey (b). **33:** Marianne Majerus Photography/ Designer: Julie Toll (t), Leigh Clapp (b). **34:** Leigh Clapp: Copse Lodge (l). Nicola Stocken Tomkins: Longer End Cottage, Normandy, Surrey (c), Nicola Browne/ Designer: Jinny Blom (r). **35:** Leigh Clapp: Merriments Nursery (l). Andrew Lawson: RHS Chelsea Flower Show 1999/Selsdon & District Horticultural Society (c). Nicola Stocken Tomkins: Hampton Court Flower Show 2004/Designer: S Eberle (r). **37:** Marianne Majerus Photography:

Manor Farm, Keisby, Lincs. (br). **42:** crocus.co.uk (bl). **44:** Andrew Lawson. **48:** Forest Garden (br). **67:** DK Images: Mark Winwood/Capel Manor College/ Designer: Irma Ansell: The Mediterranean Garden. **68–9:** Thompson & Morgan. **71:** DK Images: Mark Winwood/Capel Manor College/Designer: Elizabeth Ramsden: Modern Front Garden. **73:** DK Images: Mark Winwood/Hampton Court Flower Show 2005/Designer: Susan Slater: 'Pushing the Edge of the Square'. **74:** Marianne Majerus/ Designers: Nori and Sandra Pope, Hadspen (bl). **75:** Marianne Majerus Photography/ Designers: Nori and Sandra Pope, Hadspen. **77:** DK Images: Mark Winwood/Hampton Court Flower Show 2005: Designed by Guildford College: 'Journey of the Senses'. **79:** DK Images: Mark Winwood/Capel Manor College/ Designer: Sascha Dutton-Forshaw: 'Victorian Front Garden. **80–1:** DK Images: Mark Winwood/Capel Manor College/ Designer: Irma Ansell: The Mediterranean Garden. **83:** Modeste Herwig. **84:** Leigh Clapp/ Designers: Acres Wild (bl). **85:** Leigh Clapp/ Designers: Acres Wild. **86:** S & O Mathews Photography: RHS Rosemoor (bl) (br). **87:** S & O Mathews Photography: RHS Rosemoor. **98:** Steven Wooster, Designers: Sarah Brodie & Faith Pewhustel/'Where For Art Thou?'/Chelsea Flower Show 2002.

99: The Garden Collection: Torie Chugg, Designer: Jill Anderson/ Hampton Court 2005 (t), Marianne Majerus Photography: Designer: Lynne Marcus (b). **100:** The Garden Collection: Liz Eddison, Designer: Bob Purnell (t), The Garden Collection: Liz Eddison (br), DK Images: Peter Anderson, Designer: Kati Crome/Tufa Tea/Chelsea Flower Show 2007 (bl). **101:** The Garden Collection: Marie O'Hara, Designer: Marney Hall/ Chelsea Flower Show 2005. **102:** Garden Picture Library: Botanica (t), GAP Photos Ltd: Clive Nichols, Designer: Stephen Woodhams (b). **103:** The Garden Collection: Jonathan Buckley, Designer: Anthony Goff (t), Garden Picture Library: Ron Sutherland, Designer: Anthony Paul (b). **104:** DK Images: Steven Wooster, Kelly's Creek/Chelsea Flower Show 2000. **105:** Clive Nichols: Designer: Liz Robertson/Hampton Court 2003 (tl), The Garden Collection: Jonathan Buckley, Designer: Paul Kelly (br), DK Images: Brian North, Designers: Marcus Barnett & Philip Nixon/The Savills Garden/Chelsea Flower Show 2007 (c). **106:** DK Images: Peter Anderson, Designer: Heidi Harvey & Fern Alder/Full Frontal/Hampton Court Palace Flower Show 2007 (t). **107:** The Garden Collection: Jonathan Buckley, Designer: Christopher Lloyd/Great Dixter (l), DK

Acknowledgements

Images: Brian North, Designer: Mark Browning/The Fleming's & Trailfinders Australian Garden/Chelsea Flower Show 2007 (br). **108:** DK Images: Peter Anderson, Designer: Geoff Whiten/The Pavestone Garden/ Chelsea Flower Show 2006 (b). **109:** The Garden Collection: Liz Eddison, Designer: Reaseheath College (t), DK Images: Peter Anderson, Designers: Louise Cummins & Caroline De Lane Lea/The Suber Garden/Chelsea Flower Show 2007 (b). **110:** The Garden Collection: Nicola Stocken Tomkins (b), DK Images: Peter Anderson, Designer: Jinny Blom/ Laurent-Perrier Garden/Chelsea Flower Show 2007 (t). **111:** The Garden Collection: Liz Eddison, Design: Butler Landscapes (t). **112:** DK Images: Brian North, Designer: Harpak Design/A City Haven/Chelsea Flower Show 2007 (t). **114:** Designer: Chris Parsons/Hallam Garden Design (t), DK Images: Brian North, Designer: Teresa Davies, Steve Putnam & Samantha Hawkins/Moving Spaces, Moving On/Chelsea Flower Show 2007 (bc), Designer: Jinny Blom/ Laurent-Perrier Garden/Chelsea Flower Show 2007 (br). **115:** DK Images: Steve Wooster, Designers: Xa Tollemache & Jon Kellett/The Merrill Lynch Garden, Chelsea Flower Show. **118:** DK Images: Peter Anderson, Designers: Chloe Salt, Roger Bullock & Jeremy Salt/Reflective Height/ Chelsea Flower Show 2006 (br). **119:** DK Images: Peter Anderson, Designer: Mike Harvey/The Unwind Garden/Hampton Court Palace Flower Show 2007. **120:** DK Images: Peter Anderson, Designer: Gabriella Pape & Isabelle Van Groeningen/The Daily Telegraph Garden/Chelsea Flower Show 2007 (br). **121:** DK Images: Peter Anderson, Designer: Chris Beardshaw/The Chris Beardshaw Garden/Chelsea Flower Show 2007 (t). **122:** Stonemarket **123:** Stonemarket (bl) (br), DK Images: Peter Anderson, Designers: James Mason & Chloe Gazzard/The Path Not Taken/Hampton Court Palace Flower Show 2007 (bc). **124:** The Garden Collection: Liz Eddison, Designer: Thomas Hoblyn. **125:** Stonemarket (bl), Garden Picture Library: Mark Bolton (br), DK Images: Peter Anderson, Designer: Ulf Nordfjell/A Tribute to Linnaeus/ Chelsea Flower Show 2007 (tr). **127:** Marianne Majerus Photography. **128–9:** DK Images: Peter Anderson, Designer: Linda Bush/ The Hasmead

Sand & Ice Garden/Chelsea Flower Show 2007. **130–1:** Marianne Majerus Photography: Designers: Brita von Schoenaich & Tim Rees/Ryton Organic Garden (t). **133:** Clive Nichols: Woodpeckers, Warwickshire. **137:** Garden Picture Library: Ron Evans. **138–9:** DK Images: Peter Anderson, Designers: Laurie Chetwood & Patrick Collins/Chetwoods Urban Oasis/ Chelsea Flower Show 2007. **140:** Alamy Images: CuboImages srl (cr). **142–3:** DK Images: Peter Anderson, Designer: Scenic Blue/The Marshalls Sustainability Garden/Chelsea Flower Show 2007. **148:** Alamy Images: The Photolibrary Wales (bl). **149:** Ronseal (br), DK Images: Brian North, Designers: Harry Levy & Geoff Carter/ The Water Garden/Tatton Park 2007 (tr). **150** Alamy Images: Ian Fraser, Cothay Manor, Somerset. **153** DK Images Steve Wooster, Designer: Tom Stuart-Smith/ Homage to Le Nôtre/ Chelsea Flower Show 2000 (t), Peter Anderson, designer: Tom Stuart-Smith/ Chelsea Flower Show 2006. **155** DK Images: Peter Anderson, designers: Marcus Barnett and Philip Nixon/Savills Garden, Chelsea Flower Show 2006. **165** www.henchman.co.uk; Tel: 01635 299847. **210** Sarah Cuttle (tr) (br); Jacqui Dracup (bl). **216** Airedale: Sarah Cuttle (l). DK Images: Peter Anderson (r). **217** Airedale: David Murphy (l); Amanda Jensen: Designer: Paul Stone, Mayor of London's Office, The Sunshine Garden, Hampton Court 2006 (r). **218** DK Images: Peter Anderson. **219** Airedale: Sarah Cuttle (tl) (bl) (br). DK Images: Peter Anderson (tr). **220** Airedale: David Murphy. **221** Airedale: Amanda Jensen (t). **222** DK Images: Peter Anderson. **223** DK Images: Peter Anderson (tl) (b). **225** Airedale: Sarah Cuttle (tl). Thompson & Morgan (fbr). **226** Airedale: Sarah Cuttle. **227** Airedale: Sarah Cuttle (tr) (fbr). Chase Organics Ltd (fbl). **229** Airedale: David Murphy (tl); Sarah Cuttle (br) (fbr). DK Images: Peter Anderson (tr). **230** Airedale: Sarah Cuttle. **231** Airedale: Sarah Cuttle (tl) (br). **232** Airedale: Sarah Cuttle. **233** Airedale: Sarah Cuttle (br). Chase Organics Ltd (fbr). **234** Airedale: Sarah Cuttle. **235** Airedale: Sarah Cuttle (fbl) (bl). **236** Airedale: Sarah Cuttle. **240** Airedale: Sarah Cuttle. **250** Airedale: Sarah Cuttle (cr). DK Images: Peter Anderson (tr). Thompson & Morgan (tl). **251** RHS *The Garden*: Tim Sandall. **252** Airedale: Sarah Cuttle (tl). Suttons Seeds (cr). DT Brown (bl). **253** Airedale: David Murphy. **254** Malcolm Dodds (tl).

255 Airedale: Sarah Cuttle (br). DK Images: Peter Anderson (bl). Derek St Romaine (tl). **257** Derek St Romaine: RHS Garden Rosemoor. **258–9** Airedale: Sarah Cuttle. **260** Airedale: Sarah Cuttle (tl) (bl). **261** Airedale: Sarah Cuttle. **262** Airedale: Sarah Cuttle (br). Thompson & Morgan (cl). **263** DK Images: Steve Wooster. **264** Airedale: Sarah Cuttle. **265** Airedale: David Murphy (tl); Sarah Cuttle (ca). DK Images: Peter Anderson (cb). **266** DK Images: Deni Bown (c); Peter Anderson (ca) (tr) (cr) (bc). Airedale: David Murphy (cl). **267** Airedale: Sarah Cuttle (bc) (br). DK Images: Deni Bown (tr) (c) (bl). Malcolm Dodds (tl). **268** Airedale: Sarah Cuttle (bl) (bc). DK Images: Peter Anderson (br). **269** DK Images: Peter Anderson (c) (cr) (bc). Photoshot/ NHPA: N A Callow (bl). **270** DK Images: Peter Anderson (tr) (br). Airedale: David Murphy (bl). **271** Airedale: David Murphy (tl). DK Images: Peter Anderson (cl) (bl). **362** Thompson & Morgan (bl). **363** Airedale: Sarah Cuttle (tc) (br). Thompson & Morgan (tl). DT Brown (tr). **364** Thompson & Morgan (tr). Fothergills (tl) (bl). **365** Airedale: Sarah Cuttle (tr). Suttons Seeds (br). Thompson & Morgan (bc). Fothergills (bl). **366** Airedale: Sarah Cuttle (bc). Suttons Seeds (tl) (tr). Fothergills (tc). **367** Airedale: Sarah Cuttle (bl). Chase Organics Ltd (tl) (tc). Thompson & Morgan (bc) (br). Fothergills (tr). **368** Airedale: Sarah Cuttle (tr). Thompson & Morgan (tl) (bl). DT Brown (tc) (br). Fothergills (bc). **369** Airedale: Sarah Cuttle (tc). Suttons Seeds (tl). Thompson & Morgan (tr) (br). Fothergills (bl). **272:** crocus.co.uk (bl), **273:** crocus.co.uk (bc). **275:** crocus.co.uk (bc). **281:** crocus.co.uk (tr). **284:** Garden World Images: (bl). **296:** Garden World Images: (bl) (br). **304:** Caroline Reed (tr). **309:** Caroline Reed (bc). **310:** Caroline Reed (tr). **311:** Jenny Hendy (bl). **312:** Caroline Reed (tl), Jenny Hendy (br) **314:** Caroline Reed (bc). **323:** Clive Nichols: (bc). **323:** GAP Photos Ltd: S & O (br). **326:** Alamy Images: Niall McDiarmid (br). **370** Suttons Seeds (br). DT Brown (bc). **371** Chase Organics Ltd (tl). Thompson & Morgan (tc). DT Brown (tr). **372** Airedale: Sarah Cuttle (tl); David Murphy (bl); Mike Newton (tr). Fothergills (tc) (bc) (br). **373** Airedale: Sarah Cuttle (tl) (tr) (bl). Thompson & Morgan (bc). DT Brown (br). Fothergills (tc). **374** (bl). DT Brown (tr) (bc). **375** Airedale: Sarah Cuttle (tr) (bc). Marshalls Seeds (tl). Thompson & Morgan (tc). **376** Marshalls Seeds (bl)

(br). Joy Michaud/Sea Spring Photos (tc). W. Robinson & Son Ltd. (bc). DT Brown (tl). Fothergills (tr). **377** Airedale: Sarah Cuttle (tr) (br). Joy Michaud/Sea Spring Photos (tc). DT Brown (tl) (bc). **378** Airedale: Sarah Cuttle (tc). Thompson & Morgan (bl) (bc) (br). Fothergills (tl). **379** Airedale: Sarah Cuttle (tc). Chase Organics (tl). Thompson & Morgan (br). DT Brown (tr) (bl) (bc). **380** Airedale: Sarah Cuttle (tc) (tr) (bl). Joy Michaud/Sea Spring Photos (tl). **381** Airedale: Sarah Cuttle (tc). Marshalls Seeds (tr). DT Brown (bc). Fothergills (tl) (bl) (br). **382** Suttons Seeds (bc). Thompson & Morgan (tr). Fothergills (tl). **383** Marshalls Seeds (bc) (br). Thompson & Morgan (tl) (tr). **384** DT Brown (br). **385** Airedale: Sarah Cuttle (tr) (bc). Chase Organics (bl). DT Brown (tl) (tc). **386** Airedale: Sarah Cuttle (tl) (bl). Thompson & Morgan (tr). DT Brown (tc). Fothergills (bc). **387** Airedale: Sarah Cuttle (br). Thompson & Morgan (bl). Fothergills (tl) (tc) (bc). **388** Airedale: Sarah Cuttle (tl) (tr). DT Brown (tc). **389** DT Brown (tl). **390** Airedale: Sarah Cuttle (tl) (bl) (bc). DT Brown (br). **391** Airedale: Sarah Cuttle (tc).

All other images © Dorling Kindersley
For further information see:
www.dkimages.com